T0014078

"From the psychology of toddlers comes a surprisingly intuitive blueprint for a better life. This is one of the most original advice books I've read in a long time!"

—**Cal Newport,** *New York Times* bestselling author of
Digital Minimalism and *Deep Work*

"*Sleep Well, Take Risks, Squish the Peas* is one of those books that you find yourself thinking about well after you've finished it. It turns out we already know how to live a fulfilling life. We just forgot the lessons. Hasan Merali provides a much-needed fresh perspective, showing us with plenty of evidence to back it up, why we need to be a little more like a toddler. A must-read for anyone looking to have a healthier, happier, more productive life."

—**Steve Magness,** author of *Do Hard Things* and
coauthor of *Peak Performance*

Sleep Well, Take Risks, Squish the Peas

Secrets from the
Science of Toddlers
for a Happier, More
Successful Way of Life

Hasan Merali, MD

Health Communications, Inc.
Boca Raton, Florida

www.hcibooks.com

Library of Congress Cataloging-in-Publication Data
is available through the Library of Congress

©2024 MERALI INNOVATIONS INC.

ISBN-13: 978-07573-2471-0 (Paperback)
ISBN-10: 07573-2471-1 (Paperback)
ISBN-13: 978-07573- 2472-7 (ePub)
ISBN-10: 07573-2472-X (ePub)

Publisher: Health Communications, Inc.
          301 Crawford Boulevard, Suite 200
          Boca Raton, FL 33432–3762

Cover, interior design, and typesetting by Larissa Hise Henoch

*For Arya,
my source of daily toddler
inspiration*

Contents

Part II: A Gold Star at Work   121

Introduction:

Toddlerhood

*Who is that little person, and why did they
put a bead up their nose?*

Imagine, if you will, a different type of world. You arrive at work one morning on your bright red tricycle and just as you are pulling into a parking space, someone in a Power Wheels SUV cuts you off and takes the spot. It turns out it's Frankie. He's new to the company, and you don't know him well yet. Without even a bit of frustration, you wave a happy "Good morning!" to him and find your own space much farther away from the office building. You prefer the extra exercise anyway. After you dismount from your tricycle, Lucy, who you just met a week ago, sees you in the parking lot. She runs as fast as she can toward you to greet you with a big hug. Your hair is completely messed up; your shirt is on backward for some reason; and there is chocolate smeared on your cheek from the chocolate chip pancakes you ate for breakfast. Lucy does not care. In fact she doesn't even notice (and for that matter, neither do you). All she sees is a person with a good heart. She holds your hand and the two of you walk into work together.

Later that morning, you sit in on the quarterly finance meeting full of excitement and with a big smile on your face the entire time. Any opportunity you get, you try to make jokes, and your colleagues make even more jokes as they know you will laugh. *This meeting is actually fun,* you think to yourself. Questions fill your brain, and without a worry of how stupid they will make you look, you ask each one. Your objective is purely to understand things better, which, by the end of the meeting, you do. You have absolutely no fears about speaking your mind, and every idea you have is acknowledged by your coworkers. Over the last year, several of your ideas have propelled the company forward, but you feel you have not had an equitable raise. Without hesitation, you set up a meeting with your boss to discuss this. Your series of honest questions and remarkable confidence help her better understand your contribution, and she agrees to an even higher raise than what you had in mind. She also notes during the meeting that you are regarded by everyone in your company as the most generous and empathetic person they know. Great, now you can buy some toys for your siblings!

As you sit at your desk after the meeting, you get back to working on an important proposal that is due next week. One section deals with a particularly challenging problem that you are not sure how to solve and feel slightly frustrated. No worries, you immediately start talking to yourself from a third-person perspective to help you think through how you will complete it. It works. You successfully finish the section and are able to calm your frustration using the same technique.

Because you love exercise so much, it's difficult to be at your desk for too long, and the meeting you have at the end of your morning becomes a walking meeting. You take your lunch break later than most people today, not because you have too much to do but because you simply do not feel hungry. You eat only when you are hungry and stop when you are full, without snacking unnecessarily. You don't even feel tired in the afternoon because you didn't overeat, and you are well rested. Last night you got eleven hours of sleep and always take your scheduled nap in the late afternoon. Later in your workday, as you are walking to the supply room, you notice that Frankie is on the phone with tech support because he can't get a document from the company shared drive. You overhear him saying, "I already tried that," clearly frustrated. Now you, being the helpful person you are, disregard how he took your parking space that morning. Instead, you politely ask him to hang up the phone and then spend fifteen minutes with him fixing the shared drive issue. Whenever you see someone who needs you, you help them, no matter what.

This, my friends, is an insight into the beautiful world of the toddler mind. It is a world filled with wonder, excitement, and true happiness. A place where there is complete honesty, unflappable empathy, little judgment based on your appearance, a drive to be active and eat appropriately, and where your ideas and what you are willing to try are endless. There are, of course, things I left out of that story, such as the five minutes you spent crying and yelling when you lost your pen, the multiple injuries your coworkers sustained from coffee tables and other furniture as they jumped around believing they could fly, and how everyone in the meeting that morning pooped their pants. But focusing on the upside is the purpose of this book: to highlight how these smart tykes can teach you how to improve your work and personal life and to generally be a better person.

How would you like to get to a point where you are generous and kind to everyone, including those who have been selfish in the past? Would you like to eat better and get your weight under control? How would you like to have no fears at work to the point where you feel comfortable asking any question? How would you like to have the ability and confidence to take more risks in your personal and professional life? I'm sure we all would, but the decades since we were toddlers have taken most of us in a different direction. It's time to go back, at least partly, to that wonderful time. You can think of this book as a reminder of a period in your life you likely don't remember well; however, it was a time when you had all those things figured out. In this book, I hope to show you why it is so important to act like a toddler.

Let's take a step back for a minute to discuss the magical time known as toddlerhood. It's a time when children take their first steps, start speaking, learn to sing, and develop their own unique dance moves. Toddlerhood starts at age one, and while the definition of when it ends varies, it is generally thought to extend to sometime when the child is three years old. This period of discovery and learning new skills blends into the next phase: the preschool phase. Preschoolers are between the ages of three and five, and it is during this time that they start to ask questions, draw beautiful pictures (at least in the eyes of their parents), and become toilet trained. It is during these two phases, when children are constantly challenged with new tasks as they learn about the world, that they demonstrate some of the best qualities we have as humans. This book focuses on those two age ranges, and the majority of the research that will be discussed centers on children one to five years old. I mention this because, in this book, I often use the word *toddler* to encompass this age range more generally, which follows infancy (up to one year) and precedes middle childhood (after five years).

So why is it that toddlers demonstrate remarkable openness, dedication to their tasks, and unmatched curiosity? The answer is simple: Their brains are different. Early childhood is a period of rapid brain growth and development, and toddlers' brains have been evolutionarily tuned to learning, often better than adults. Neurons, or brain cells, have synapses, which are communication pathways between neurons. At birth, each neuron has about 2,500 synapses, and by age two there are 15,000. The ability of the brain to create and reorganize pathways is referred to as neuroplasticity, and it is this malleability that allows toddlers to think differently and learn remarkably quickly. Over time, however, the brain naturally undergoes a process to eliminate synapses, called pruning, and by adulthood only about half these synapses remain.[1,2] So while you may be able to see patterns based on your experience and reach conclusions much faster than a toddler, they remain open to more possibilities, learning whatever they can in every situation.

A second major reason why the toddler brain is different than that of an adult, and hence why they behave so differently, is that they have a less developed prefrontal cortex. This area of the brain is responsible for executive control, which is what allows us to perform goal-directed behavior. Important functions such as planning and utilizing working memory to hold information in our minds while using it are examples of executive control.[3] While toddlers are obviously less skilled than older children and adults in these areas, an underdeveloped prefrontal cortex provides several advantages. For example, adults have much more selective attention, focusing only on the most relevant information. Their prefrontal cortex filters out what the brain perceives as irrelevant. Toddlers, on the other hand, distribute their attention more generally, allowing them to notice more details.

I see this best whenever I am walking with my toddler daughter, Arya. Our morning walk to day care would only take five minutes if I were alone, but with her, it is closer to fifteen minutes. This is not only due to her having small legs; it's because she notices things I don't and must stop to consider them carefully. Even though she has now done this walk hundreds of times, there is always something new she asks about. A bird call she has not heard before, the smell of wet grass after it has rained, or a cloud that perhaps looks like a bunny. This toddler-level attention to detail makes them better than adults at gathering information, which in turn makes them more adaptable to different situations.[4]

Another result of having a less mature prefrontal cortex is creativity. Unlike adults, children are much more flexible in their thinking: For example, they can see alternate uses of objects. When adults see an object, they automatically associate it with certain functions based on past experience thanks to their fully developed prefrontal cortex.[5] Young children do not have this problem, which is why, for example, kindergarteners perform so well in the Marshmallow Challenge. In this activity, the goal is to build the tallest freestanding structure using twenty sticks of spaghetti, one yard of tape, one yard of string, and one marshmallow. When different groups have been tested, kindergartners have been shown to outperform business school students, lawyers, and most other adults. There were only two groups that beat kindergartners. The first were architects and engineers, and the second were CEOs, but only if they had an executive administrator. CEOs alone were still beaten by the kindergarteners. One of the major differences observed in how the various groups carry out the test is that adults plan the best course of action and then execute while children build multiple successive prototypes improving their design in an iterative process.[6] The less mature prefrontal cortex can be advantageous when faced with novel scenarios. As we age and the prefrontal cortex matures, we gain executive function but lose some of the natural abilities we had to explore, learn, and be creative.[7]

Finally, young children are right-brain dominant. Rather than focusing on logic as the left hemisphere of the brain does, the right hemisphere is more emotional, nonverbal, and experiential.[8] Toddlers show their right hemisphere dominance in many ways; they live in the moment and take risks. They will jump off tall structures, chase wild animals, and stop everything they are doing to help a stranger. They are impulsive but often in a way we can admire. They don't need to think things over for a day, discuss with colleagues, and weigh the pros and cons. They make quick decisions, and given their strong sense of empathy, they are often the best decisions. Sometimes they get injured, but their ability to steadily push beyond their physical and cognitive limits expands their range and confidence in tackling new tasks.

As toddlers get older and their brains mature, the left hemisphere engages more, and they are then driven to understand the world better. They start to ask "Why?" consistently. Since the left hemisphere has not yet balanced the right at this point, they have no fear or anxiety in asking any and every question that comes to mind, unlike an adult who may feel the question is socially awkward or inappropriate. Learning, understanding, and engaging with people and their environment are a toddler's goals.

The adult brain, with narrowly focused synaptic pathways, a mature prefrontal cortex, and a better balance between hemispheres, has many advantages. As adults, we can plan complex tasks for the future, apply reasoning skills, and make decisions that follow a logical pattern. With this maturation, however, there are drawbacks. We lose creativity, spontaneity, curiosity, fearlessness, and an intense drive to learn and test new hypotheses.[9] Luckily for us, neuroplasticity continues throughout adulthood. We have the ability to constantly reshape our brains so that we can improve and learn from others.[10] In this book, we will explore many of the ways that toddlers are the best teachers for self-improvement.

This is a book I have wanted to write for some time. As a researcher and pediatrician who specializes in pediatric emergency medicine, I have the unique privilege of interacting with children regularly. I see them in perfect health, with overly worried new parents who bring in their baby for spit-up, and when they are just hanging on to life, like the six-year-old who was hit by a car while biking. I am also the proud father of a toddler. Some of you may also be fortunate enough to work with children or maybe you have children or grandchildren of your own. Even if you don't interact with young children regularly, or don't like children, there is a lot we can learn from them. Don't believe the images on television and in popular culture of a toddler alternately having a temper tantrum and then throwing food throughout the day. The more informal definitions of toddlers, such as "a cross between a sociopath, a rabid animal, a cocker spaniel, a demon, and an angel,"[11] are also incorrect. There are many misconceptions about toddlers, and those of you who either work with them or have raised them will know better. Despite popular culture, there is no such thing as the "terrible twos" if viewed from a developmentally appropriate lens. There is no such thing as a "sugar high" or that they are all picky eaters. They are in fact incredibly gentle, loving souls and are far more advanced in their thinking and actions on many issues when compared to adults.

This is a different type of book than the excellent books about how to parent, teach, and raise your child to be happy and healthy. It is also not a book of funny quotes from children (which I love!). Instead, in this book, the roles are reversed in that I will outline many of the ways these intelligent and curious little people can teach you how to improve your work and personal lives. I will highlight a variety of interesting research studies along the way that have helped us understand how toddlers react in certain situations, and I will argue that our lives as adults would be better if we could adopt some or all of these traits.

Here, I must acknowledge the researchers whose studies I discuss in this book. Everything from the way the studies were set up to the researchers' objective analyses was brilliant, and I enjoyed selecting the most relevant ones. And I will say the researchers had their own challenges that come with toddlers. In research, some people, or *subjects* as they are referred to, are often excluded because they didn't meet some criteria for a study. For example, they were too young or old for a certain medication or vaccine. I found it interesting to note reasons why some toddlers were excluded from studies. These included impulse control failures, lack of cooperation, what they said didn't make any sense, and that they tried to trick the experimenter.[12,13] Note that this book is not meant to be a comprehensive overview of all the literature on child psychology and development. Rather, it is a collection of some of the most important and interesting studies that highlight what we can learn from our toddler teachers. I will not go into the technical details or analyses, and I try to present the facts simply as they are in the study, with some author interpretations. Some issues may be a bit controversial, and I have noted those as well.

So let's dive in and explore the wonderful ways in which these little people think and function. In the ten chapters that follow, we will cover a wide range of topics, such as sleep, teamwork, and risk-taking. At the end of each chapter, you will also see key toddler teachings. These are actionable items you can start implementing in your personal and professional life. To summarize the entire book, I have included a sample toddler schedule at the end so you can see how this could map your schedule. Try to make use of this in your daily life as you integrate the toddler teachings.

The only other suggestion I have, if at all possible, is to observe and interact with toddlers. Many of the themes presented in this book will jump right out and you will likely discover even more ways of how thinking and acting like a toddler will help you in your life. Remember, at one time, you personified all the characteristics presented in this book. So try to go back to that and make yourself the happier, healthier version of you that you once were.

Part I:

A Gold Star in Life

Chapter 1:

The Basics

Eat what you want, take naps,
and run around.

A good night's rest, healthy eating habits, and exercise all have
extraordinary benefits for our bodies and minds. These benefits include, but are not limited to, improved mood, a decreased risk
of several diseases, a healthy weight, and improved memory. Ensuring the basics are taken care of can help you with concentration
and working more efficiently at your job. For most of us, at least one
of these areas is something we can improve upon. Without an initial
focus on these three elements, it will be challenging to implement
the ideas that come later in the book or even to pay attention while
you are reading this. Therefore, this chapter comes at the beginning
of the toddler lessons. So let us take some time and see how remarkable toddlers are at ensuring that the basics are taken care of.

One Last Bite

Jack Danger loves raw vegetables. In a series of videos posted when he was four years old, Jack is seen walking around his garden in Alaska picking vegetables and crunching on them. In one scene he uproots a turnip and after taking a bite realizes something is off, "Got some . . . dirt." But that's not a problem; he shakes it off and continues munching and then makes his way over to the kale. When asked about the kale by his mom—"What's it good for?"—Jack responds in between bites, "It's a plant with fiber" and understands that fiber "can help me poop."[1,2] And while Jack is certainly a model for healthy eating that not all toddlers are, toddlers do have better eating habits than most adults, and we can learn some valuable lessons from them.

Unlike Jack, many of us do not eat enough whole foods. While most of us are fortunate to live in countries where food is readily available, much of this food is highly processed and calorie dense. Eating this type of food, combined with the problem many of us have of overeating, shows at our waistlines. Three out of ten Canadians and four out of ten Americans are obese, and there is an increasing trend toward obesity. In the United States, it is projected that nearly half of all adults will be obese by 2030.[3] The key factor for weight loss is not exercise but consuming fewer calories.[4] Exercise is incredibly beneficial, but more so for keeping the weight off once you lose it.[5] If we limit how many calories we consume, we could avoid being overweight and obese. This is something you may know, but very few of us pay attention to the calories we consume, let alone track them. If you do, that is fantastic, but for most of us, the answer is no.

Compared to calorie counting, there is a much simpler way to limit the calories we consume. Think back to your toddler days, a time when you were perfectly able to stop yourself from eating when you felt full. You even fought back if someone tried to give you more and threw the food at them! These little people are smart and more in tune with their bodies than we adults are. As a pediatrician, I cannot tell you how many children I have seen (yes, even in the emergency room) because "My child won't eat," yet the toddler is gaining weight appropriately. Is it that the child is undereating? Or perhaps it is the parent who overestimates the proper portion size and expects the child to overeat. Toddlers can simply better detect what it means to be full, and what the next step should be: stop eating.

Unlike adults, who eat due to varying emotions such as boredom, or because others around them are eating, toddlers have the amazing ability to eat mainly for hunger, and a bit of play, of course. Abnormal eating patterns develop throughout a child's life as a result of caregiver approaches to try to feed them when they are not hungry.[6] Even when presented with foods that are high in sugar, children can regulate themselves and resist. In one experiment, researchers at the Pennsylvania State University examined thirty-one (originally thirty-two, but one child "refused to participate") three- to five-year-old children at day care. Over a period of three months, the children were offered either wheat crackers or cookies during their afternoon snack time. Initially, children were given equal access to the crackers or the cookies each day for three weeks. They could eat as much of each one as they wanted during that phase of the experiment. Then, there was a restriction phase that lasted five weeks. During the restriction phase, each child received a large portion of crackers while the cookies were kept in a transparent jar on the table where they were sitting. They could see the cookies but were not allowed to eat them. After ten minutes of eating crackers and staring at the cookies, they were allowed two minutes to access the cookies and eat them before they were sealed up again. After five weeks of this, children were again monitored for another three weeks when they had equal access to crackers or cookies, just as in the initial phase.

Amazingly, when the data was analyzed, researchers showed that before and after the restriction phase there was no difference in the children choosing cookies or crackers, as well as no difference in how much they ate of each. However, during the restriction phase they clearly chose the cookies more often, asked for them more, and made more attempts to get them.[7] So this image we have of toddlers always trying to get cookies is simply because they have been told they are special treats and are kept away from them. The true nature of the toddler is not to overindulge.

While adults cannot be trusted like toddlers not to overindulge, there are other strategies we can use. The easiest is to simply not keep junk food in the house. When you do feel like snacking, you are more likely to reach for something healthier if you have no other choice. If you do decide to keep some of your favorite high-calorie snacks at home, it is best to keep them out of sight and not readily accessible. Adult data has shown that obese individuals are more likely to have visible food kept in more locations around the house compared to nonobese individuals.[8]

Not only can toddlers avoid high-calorie food and eat for hunger rather than pleasure, they also have the remarkable ability to adjust their calorie needs based on portion size and the number of times they eat in a day. In one national study, a research team led by Mathematica Policy Research used a random sample of more than three thousand American infants and toddlers to assess meal size and frequency of eating. Using a database of twenty-four-hour recall data that parents gave on what their children had eaten, the researchers found that toddlers (one- and two-year-olds) would eat smaller meals if they were eating more often and larger meals if they were eating less often.[9] They would do this without even thinking. Unfortunately, the ability to do this diminishes as children get older.[10] However, it still remains an excellent strategy: Whenever you are sitting down for your next meal, think for a moment about your previous meal and whether it was large or small and how long ago you ate. Perhaps you can adjust your current meal based on this by either changing your portion size or how often you eat to help balance your total calories for the day. Portion size has been shown to be linked to calorie consumption in adults[11] as well as children.[12] Although we might not easily be able to eat less since we have been trained to eat everything on our plates, we can try to serve smaller portions.

On the topic of food self-regulation, let us take a step backward for a moment to infancy. Not only can children less than one year of age vary the amount they eat based on the frequency they are eating, like toddlers, but they can also regulate how much they eat based on the energy density of their food. Energy density is a measure of how many calories per unit of weight are in a certain food. An entire cabbage, for example, has a low energy density as it is heavy but has very few calories. Nuts, on the other hand, are highly energy dense as they contain a lot of calories and weigh very little. Let us say for a minute that an infant, who mostly eats purees and milk or formula, suddenly had a full mouth of teeth and was able to eat the same foods older children and adults can. If, for example, an infant ate fast food for lunch, they would automatically adjust their calorie needs and eat a salad for dinner because they have internal calorie counters. This ability, unfortunately, is lost after twelve months of age,[13] but we always have the option of doing it manually. The difficulty in calorie counting is that it is time-consuming and can feel overwhelming at first. However, if it is done properly, it can be effective for weight loss and, over a few months, it will take less time to do it each day.[14] There is a large body of research indicating that adults consistently underestimate calories, so if you have tried everything else, it may be worthwhile to start using a calorie counter.

The next time you are eating, listen to your internal cues of whether you are hungry or not. Just because it is a certain time of day, or other people are eating, or you are bored does not mean you have to eat. After you have started eating, as soon as you feel full, stop. And taking this a step further, it is even better if you can practice *Hara Hachi Bu*. This is practiced by some of the healthiest people in the world who live in Okinawa, Japan, and it means: Stop eating when you're 80 percent full.[15] You are an adult and do not have to "finish that last bite" as you have probably been trained to do (to your detriment). This idea of "just three more bites" is a form of socializing children to eat past their internal hunger cues,[16] and it is time we all stop this, for our children and for ourselves. Toddlers know how to control their eating, and if it were not for parents pressuring kids to eat, restricting certain foods, modeling excessive eating, and offering large portions, we likely would all have a better relationship with food.[17] Adjusting your portion sizes and frequency of eating the way toddlers do may be helpful. And if all else fails, give calorie counting a try with one of the many great apps that are now available.

Fast Asleep

As we have all experienced (sometimes daily), sleeping is critical for optimal functioning, concentration, and mood. Unfortunately, many of us do not prioritize sleep and get much less than we need.

Current recommendations are that adults should be getting a minimum of seven hours per night regularly. Less than this is associated with a multitude of health problems including high blood pressure, heart disease, stroke, depression, dementia, and obesity. There is also clear evidence that less than seven hours decreases performance and increases errors.[18] Some of us also accept a sleep deficit during the week and promise ourselves that we will make up for it on the weekend by sleeping more. Sadly, weekend recovery sleep does not reduce many of the negative effects of decreased sleep, such as weight gain.[19]

For children, sleep is even more important as they need it for growth and development. Current World Health Organization (WHO) guidelines are that children between one and two years of age should get eleven to fourteen hours of good quality sleep while those three to four years of age should get ten to thirteen hours. This recommendation is for a twenty-four-hour period and includes naps.[20] Over time, however, we as a society are headed in the wrong direction when it comes to sleep. Researchers from the University of South Australia examined sleep data of nearly 700,000 children and adolescents from twenty countries from 1905 to 2008. Looking at the data in aggregate, there were consistent declines in the length of time youth are sleeping, and over that 103-year period, there has been a decrease of more than one hour per night in sleep overall.[21]

While there are many factors that contribute to poor and inadequate sleep, I will point to three things that help toddlers sleep better, and hopefully they can help you. The first is having an established bedtime routine that specifically includes reading, the second is decreasing screen time before bed, and the third is napping during the day.

The Importance of Routine

Toddlers thrive on having a routine. It gives them a sense of order and security, and nowhere else in their lives is it more important, or more helpful, than at bedtime. One of the most important things that allows toddlers to get a good night's sleep is sticking to a scheduled time to be in bed each night and having a consistent set of activities that precede this. Many adults do not have a regular bedtime and as a result often feel tired or have a low mood the next day, both of which are counterproductive. A bedtime routine for toddlers has many benefits, including an earlier bedtime, an easier time falling asleep, reduced nighttime awakenings, and most importantly, increased sleep duration. There are also many benefits to having a consistent bedtime routine beyond sleep quality. It has been associated with improved emotional regulation, behavioral regulation, and even literacy.[22]

A bedtime routine does not have to be complicated, and in fact it is better if it includes only a few activities. Popular activities for toddlers are bathing, getting a massage, reading, and cuddling. Any of these I am sure could work for you as well.[23] And one of the most important things, as any child caregiver knows, is consistency. The better children are about sticking to the routine, the better their sleep is.[24] You must also stay consistent with yourself around your own routine and the time you go to sleep.

What is great about improving your sleep with a routine is that results can come rather quickly. To test how well a bedtime routine works, researchers at the Children's Hospital of Philadelphia did a study where two hundred one- to three-year-olds were randomized to two different groups. What this means is that once the families agreed to participate in the study, a computer decided indiscriminately whether they went into the intervention group or the control group. The intervention group is the group that has the new idea tested on them, and the control group is the group that does things as they normally would. Having a computer decide this is a method researchers use to decrease bias and get closer to the truth.

For this study, in the intervention group, caregivers spent one week doing their usual routine and baseline data was collected. Then, for two weeks, the caregivers were told to do three simple things before bed: bathe the child, apply lotion, and do a quiet activity like cuddling or singing a lullaby. The entire routine was to last half an hour after the end of the bath. The mothers in the control group did not have any instructions and continued to put their child to bed as they normally would. Some may already have been doing elements of a bedtime routine, but they did not have specific instructions on what to do and how many things to do. After the three-week study period, several benefits were seen in the intervention group when compared to the control group including falling asleep faster, decreased night awakenings, and longer periods of sleep.[25] Since these results were seen over the duration of a two-week intervention period, the researchers later dug a little deeper using the same procedure in one- to two-year-olds (and some infants as well). What they found was even better news: the children who had the set bedtime routine showed benefits after just three nights.[26]

When thinking more about what you can do for your bedtime routine, it is helpful to examine the specific activities that toddlers do to help them sleep. Adapting a consistent toddler-like nighttime routine can help you, as well, get a better night's sleep.[27] So far, we have discussed the importance of a consistent bedtime, and taking a bath, but what should we do just before falling asleep? The answer comes from an incredible child development study where over four thousand children from twenty American cities were followed from birth to five years of age. This study included home visits so researchers could see exactly what toddlers were doing at bedtime. A remarkable number of factors were examined as part of a larger study, but if we focus on sleep, the researchers found that language-based bedtime routines were associated with longer nighttime sleep duration. Language-based routines are things such as reading, story-telling, and even singing.[28] It turns out the perfect way to end your bedtime routine is with a good book.

Turn Off the Screens

Any toddler will tell you, no matter how good their bedtime routine is, the last few minutes must be devoted to tucking them in. Being under a cozy blanket is calming and provides them with a sense of security they need to be able to sleep in their own beds. Although media mogul Arianna Huffington has adult daughters who do not need tucking in, she has adapted this for something completely different: her cell phone. As an advocate for better sleep and author of the book *The Sleep Revolution,* Huffington understands the importance of not having screen time before bed.[29] In fact, she has even designed a cell phone bed, complete with satin sheets, where she tucks in her phone, outside her bedroom, and charges it each night.[30]

If you have read anything about better sleep, it is very likely that you have come across the advice to decrease screen time before going to bed. This is challenging to implement since smartphones and streaming television have become increasingly addictive for a variety of reasons. It is critical, however, that you disengage from these at night for better sleep. Screen time before bed affects everyone, including toddlers. In a study led by researchers at East Michigan

University, nearly five hundred two-year-olds had two home visits where a researcher recorded everything that was happening around the child's bedtime. The parents were even given microphones so researchers could listen in when the parent and child were alone. Observations were made in the hour prior to the bedtime routine (the pre-bedtime period), as well as during the actual bedtime routine. To get an accurate measure of the child's sleep, the children all wore an actigraph. This is a watch-like device that can objectively measure rest. As expected, screen time in the pre-bedtime period or during the bedtime routine was associated with more sleep problems, including going to sleep later and less consolidated sleep.[31]

There are several reasons why screen time prior to bed is harmful. First, it interferes with melatonin production. Melatonin is a hormone produced by the pineal gland in your brain and is released into your bloodstream at night. It regulates our circadian rhythm (internal clock) and facilitates falling asleep.[32,33] Light, particularly short-wave blue light emitted by your cell phone, suppresses melatonin in humans.[34] Lowered levels of melatonin can thus lead to insomnia, and it is why taking melatonin can help with sleep, particularly if your circadian rhythm is off balance. Importantly, natural levels of melatonin decrease with age, so the older you are, the more important it is to maintain the levels of melatonin needed for your natural sleep-wake cycle and not suppress it.

The second reason why screen time prior to sleeping is counterproductive is that the light emitted from our devices leads to a wakeful and more alert state. Part of this is due to the suppression of melatonin, but even during the daytime when melatonin is practically undetectable in the bloodstream, light produces a more wakeful state. Studies using positron-emission tomography (PET) scans, which can measure increased activity in the brain, show that light exposure at night activates multiple areas of the brain involved with attention.[35]

Finally, there is the simple issue of time displacement. The more time you spend watching TV, texting, or are trapped in a YouTube cycle, the less time you are devoting to sleep.[36] The problem is, sleep seems like the least exciting option. However, once you begin to build a sleep routine and start to realize the benefits of improved sleep, you will likely choose to sleep much more often.

Given that the effects of screen time are largely physiologic, adults are affected as much as toddlers, if not more, given the age-related decline in melatonin. Researchers in Belgium who studied 844 Flemish adults ages eighteen to ninety-four demonstrated that using a cell phone at bedtime predicted higher self-reporting of insomnia, fatigue, and longer sleep latency.[37] Perhaps the best way to guard against the urge to binge-watch, or scroll, is to ensure all electronic devices, except a basic alarm clock, are kept outside the bedroom. In an aptly titled study, "Sleeping with the Frenemy," researchers at the University of East London demonstrated that subjective wellness increased in three out of four measures for adults who did not have their phone in the bedroom for a week compared to those that did.[38] Like the subjects in this study and Ms. Huffington, it may be worthwhile for you to try this experiment and keep your cell phone outside your bedroom.

Power Naps

Toddlers are an extremely happy bunch of people. As we will see in Chapters 3 and 5 when we discuss laughter and play, they know how to enjoy their lives. Fun and giggles are how they go about most of their day, and there are generally only two things that can regularly spoil their mood. The first is being hungry, as with everyone else, and the second is sleep deprivation. They are incredibly sensitive to being well rested, and skipping a nap is a guaranteed way to make a toddler cranky. In the hospital, even with fever, toddlers will bounce back to their normal, pleasant state after a single dose of fever medication, but a skipped nap is something that cannot be fixed.

To ensure that they are getting adequate amounts of sleep, one thing that toddlers always incorporate into their day is a nap. In early toddlerhood, between one and two years of age, naps happen at least two times per day. Once they are closer to age two, they switch to one nap per day until finally, after toddlerhood, the nap goes away. Even though every child stops napping at a different age, most toddlers nap during the day, and these are not short naps. At one year of age, more than nine out of ten toddlers sleep between two and four hours during the day, and by four years of age, eight out of ten preschoolers are still napping one and a half to two and a half hours per day.[39] All toddlers need is to be provided with an opportunity to nap, and they will do it. It simply involves having a quiet time built into their day with a proper space and lighting.[40]

And why do toddlers nap each day? Of the many benefits they get, one of the main ones is consolidation of learning at a time of rapid brain development. To illustrate this, a group of researchers at the University of Sussex examined how toddlers learned words, a critical task at this age. They worked with forty-eight three-year-old children in their preschools over the period of a week and read stories to them. Half the children were read three different stories while the other half were read the same story three different times. The stories were timed such that half the children took a nap after story time and the other half did not. The children were tested on word comprehension immediately after story time, two and a half hours later, twenty-four hours later, and one week later. As suspected with repetition at any age, the toddlers who heard the same stories had better word retention. Interestingly, however, taking a nap after the stories had a strong effect on their performance. So much so that the children who read different stories and napped did just as well as the children who heard the same story and did not nap.[41] The children that did the best were by far those that read the same story and then napped. Different studies have also been done with nap deprivation in toddlers and have shown that children are, not surprisingly, less effective in engaging in difficult tasks when they have not napped.[42]

For adults, a modified approach is recommended: Take a nap in the early afternoon and keep it under thirty minutes. This is also known as a power nap. It can help with wakefulness, enhance performance, and improve learning ability.[43]

To summarize, set a bedtime that will get you at least seven hours of sleep each night and stick to it, even on the weekends if possible. At least an hour before this time, put away your phone and turn off other screens, including your computer or tablet. To reduce the urge to check your phone while lying in bed, leave it outside the bedroom. Once you have done this, choose two activities that you will do in the same sequence each night. One can be hygiene related, like bathing or brushing your teeth (or both), and the other is any other type of quiet activity such as listening to music or writing down your thoughts on paper. Finally, end your evening with reading. Although it may be difficult, try to fit in a short nap in the afternoon, even if it is just on your days off to start.

Witness the Fitness

Despite the benefits of exercise we know about, it can be challenging to find both the time and energy to do it regularly. The more we put it off, the harder it becomes as we get heavier and do not have it built into our regular schedule. Toddlers, on the other hand, never seem to have an excuse not to be active, and they truly stand out when it comes to being a model for exercising regularly. Try walking by a park with a three-year-old, if they were not already begging you to go. As soon as they see a play structure, they run toward it and start climbing and jumping. They continue to challenge themselves with increasingly difficult physical maneuvers and find fellow athletes at the park to maintain motivation. When injuries happen, it is usually a brief setback before resuming the training circuit. I have seen countless toddlers even push through the pain of a fracture and soldier on. They push themselves to the point of exhaustion, and only then are they ready to take a break. And you can bet that toddlers do not take a day off or plan ahead to exercise three days a week. They do it instinctually every day. That is the kind of dedication to exercise that would truly benefit us all. In fact, when slightly older children have been tested, their fitness level is close to that of trained adult endurance athletes.[44]

Think for a minute how many hours you are sedentary during your day—sitting at your desk, sitting on the couch, or driving. Inactivity is commonplace, and we do this for hours at a time, often in half-day stretches before getting up and moving. For a toddler, however, things are the opposite. In fact, it is recommended that toddlers should be inactive for no more than *one hour* at a time.[45] Yes, at least once every hour they should be up doing leapfrogs, running, and dancing. Even if you try, it is quite a challenge to get a toddler to sit for an hour since they have the internal drive to move. This is important because the recommended time for being active in both toddlers and preschoolers is an accumulated total of at least three hours per day.[46] Most of us are lucky if we can do that in a week.

Unlike adults, where health guidelines are set and often not adhered to, toddlers do incredibly well in meeting their exercise targets naturally. In one of the best studies to date measuring child activity levels, researchers in New Zealand attached accelerometers around children's waists and kept them on twenty-four hours a day for up to seven days. Accelerometers are sensors that measure movement. Your Fitbit, for example, has an accelerometer to track your steps. How these researchers managed to keep these around the waists of 380 children for that long deserves an award in itself. With these accelerometers they were able to measure sleep time, sedentary time, light physical activity, and moderate-to-vigorous physical activity. After a week of measurements in hundreds of children, the two-year-olds were found to engage in light to vigorous physical activity for nearly five hours a day; the three-year-olds just over five hours daily; and the five-year-olds, five hours and twenty minutes daily. Taking the five-year-olds and accounting for the ten and a half hours they slept, 40 percent of their time awake was spent doing some form of activity. And that was every single day.[47] One of the key differences between adults and children is how much sedentary time they have while awake. In the previous study, two-year-olds were shown to have nearly seven and a half hours daily of sedentary time. British adults, on the other hand, have been shown with accelerometers to be sedentary for nine and a half hours a day on weekdays and nine hours on weekends.[48]

For most of us, spending as much time as toddlers do being active each day is impossible. Nevertheless, it is still something we all need to prioritize. Even if your work is mainly sedentary, try to get up every hour and move around. Other suggestions at work include walking meetings or a twenty-minute chair workout at a certain time each day. No matter what your current level of exercise is, any increase will be helpful and, hopefully, that will motivate you to gradually increase it even more.

Toddler Teachings
Eat when you are hungry, not for any other reason.
When you feel full, stop eating! You do not need to finish what is on your plate. If someone tries to tell you that you need to eat "one more bite," squish the peas and create abstract art instead.
Turn screens off one hour prior to bedtime. There will be time to watch cat videos tomorrow.
Have a set bedtime routine. If you can convince someone to put lotion on you, even better.
Demand a bedtime story. If that does not work, read to yourself.
Make taking a nap a daily certainty. Power naps are for winners.
Any free time you have is a chance to exercise, even if that means simply taking a walk. Do it every day.

Chapter 2:

Kindness

No matter what you do,
I will share my stickers.

Often in the ER we need to ensure children stop eating for a variety of reasons. Sometimes they come in with severe belly pain and we think they might need surgery, and other times they are vomiting so much that we need to treat their nausea first before we slowly have them try drinking and eating again. For anyone, especially a little person who eats only when they are hungry, this is often one of the worst experiences in the hospital as it can last several hours while we wait for blood test results and an ultrasound. Yes, some of them do become irritable, like anyone else who hasn't eaten, but what is remarkable is what happens after I go back in the room to follow up sometime later. Their parents are waiting at the edge of their seats, both for the good news that everything is okay and for the word that their child can eat again. They immediately hand their toddler a favorite snack, which is always crackers, and a big smile instantly comes across the toddler's face. But despite not having eaten in several hours, and having their favorite snack in front of them, the first thing that comes to a toddler's mind is sharing. Somehow, they are magically able to detect that I too have not eaten for seven hours since my shift started. As I sit beside them to do one last belly check, I am sometimes even offered the first cracker out of the packet, or at least the third one after it has been licked. For me, these are heartwarming moments, but for toddlers, it is just normal behavior. There is no group of people kinder and more generous than toddlers.

Without knowing it, toddlers are enhancing their own wellbeing through their acts of kindness, and the same is true for adults. Spending money on others, for example, has been shown to increase happiness in the giver, an effect that is universal and has been demonstrated in both high- and low-income countries.[1] Not only that, researchers at the University of British Columbia showed that for older adults with high blood pressure, spending money on others compared to on themselves led to significantly lower blood pressure.[2] However, the benefits of kindness do not necessarily have to involve an exchange of money, as even performing simple, daily acts of kindness has been shown to increase life satisfaction as measured by a research tool designed to assess people's lives overall.[3] The benefits also extend to the office setting. In a meta-analysis of thirty-eight different studies, researchers at the University of Arizona examined organizational citizenship behaviors. These include altruism, courtesy, and are generally things people do in the office that are positive and not necessarily part of their job description. The study demonstrated a relationship between these behaviors and a number of positive individual and organizational outcomes including managerial ratings, productivity, and efficiency.[4]

Despite the benefits, according to the World Giving Index, only about 35 percent of the world's population in 119 countries surveyed gave to charity in 2021. As we might expect, people in high-income countries had a higher giving rate than those in low- and middle-income countries. However, people in low- and middle-income countries had higher rates of helping a stranger and volunteering their time. Less than a quarter of the world's population was found to volunteer. The most generous nation was Indonesia, where nearly two-thirds of the population volunteer their time. In the United States, this number is closer to one-third.[5] These numbers are certainly skewed negative as the World Giving Index only includes adults. If toddlers were included, at least for helping a stranger, the numbers would be much higher for every country.

Compared to toddlers, adult kindness is inconsistent for most people. Adults are generally kind to colleagues and family members most of the time but not all the time. Some adults are kind to strangers, but others are not. If someone has acted selfishly, only few adults would be kind to that person, and sometimes adults are kind only because they need something from the other person. Ideally, we want to get to the point where we are kind for the sake of being kind, no matter who the other person is, how they are acting, or what they have done. To learn this, we need to turn to our toddler teachers who demonstrate kindness in all these situations.

In 2015, internet personality Meir Kay wanted to see what would happen if a parent gave a child a dollar to buy ice cream from an ice cream truck. After being given the money, young children are seen skipping toward the truck with a look of anticipation and excitement. As the children get close to the truck, however, they notice a homeless man sitting against the wall, holding a cup. Consistently, what happens next is both remarkable (for us) and normal for young children. As they see this man, they don't even have to think and they give the homeless man the money with a huge smile. They feel so good in doing this that they then run back to their parent and give them a hug. Only one little girl in the video buys an ice cream, but then she immediately walks over to the man and hands it to him. Helping a stranger is not only what they want to do; toddlers and young children know that this is also what will make them feel good.[6]

After observing the incredible generosity and kindness that toddlers have toward others, I am convinced that if they, or someone with a toddler mindset, were policymakers, many of our social injustice issues would be diminished or resolved. There is no way a toddler would accept living in a comfortable house while their classmate slept in the cold outside, or feast on Cheerios while a stranger did not have anything to eat. This is true even if it came at the expense of that same toddler having a lower standard of living or less food. They have an inherent bias toward fairness and naturally share resources, even at a cost to themselves. Whether they obtain additional resources by working with a partner, by luck, or being given the resources by an adult, they have an aversion to having more than others. Inequity is a big problem for toddlers, and they will attempt to equalize resources by sharing.[7] Beyond what I have observed, I am even more amazed by toddlers after diving into the research on the kindness and empathy of toddlers. As we will see in this chapter, not only will they help strangers but also neutral robots, antisocial people, and selfish people. And they do it without any expectation of something in return. They don't even need a thank-you. This is just who they are.

Kindness Toward Strangers

Toddlers have an incredible, innate ability and drive to share with others. This may not be immediately apparent when you see one child argue with another over a plastic duck, especially if there are dozens of other plastic ducks around. However, I can assure you this does not reflect their true character. Spend enough time with them, and you will see them offer half-eaten food, their toys, and even what adults would consider garbage, to everyone around them with a big drooly smile. They are givers in the true sense of the word.[8] This observation is backed up by a considerable amount of research, and what makes it more compelling is that these experiments were done with strangers rather than people the toddlers knew.

We'll start with an important experiment done at the University of Washington using food. Food is a good way to test kindness, as its value increases the hungrier someone is, and this can be manipulated by the experimenter. In this study, one-year-old toddlers were placed in a room with their parent. After some time, an experimenter (a stranger to them) came in, dropped a piece of fruit onto a tray, and then simply looked at it. This group was referred to as the non-begging group. The other scenario was that the experimenter came in, fumbled with the fruit before dropping it, and then tried to reach it but could not. This group was referred to as the begging group. The toddler was positioned such that they could reach the fruit and then had to decide what to do with it. Results showed that most of the toddlers in the begging group gave the fruit to the stranger but only one did in the non-begging group. If the toddlers were simply returning something that was dropped, they would have done this in both groups. Instead, they were specifically responding to the fact that the stranger wanted something. This is the first point, that toddlers are perceptive of others' needs.

In the next phase of the experiment, we can start to see the picture of toddler altruism building. In this part, the researchers waited until it was time for the child to eat before repeating the same procedure. And keep in mind, as a one-year-old you do not have the ability to get your own food so whatever shows up in front of you is all you have. We all know what it is like to feel hangry, but if you truly want to see hangry, observe a toddler who is late to receive their rice puffs. Prior to the experiment, the fruit was rated as "highly liked" by the toddlers' parents and included all their favorites: bananas, blueberries, grapes, and strawberries. This time, the toddlers clearly had a reason not to share the delicious fruit since they were hungry, but still, the toddlers ate the fruit less than one quarter of the time. Those who gave away their fruit didn't even have to think about it and did so in an average of 1.55 seconds![9] It is also important to note that they did so without any verbal prompts or reciprocation. These toddlers chose being kind to a stranger over satisfying their own hunger.

The kindness that toddlers exhibit goes well beyond humans, often to their own detriment. I have lost count of the number of toddlers I have cared for in the ER that were bitten by an animal. Sometimes the cuts are so severe that I need to sedate the child so that a plastic surgeon can repair the wound. Other times we need to administer the rabies vaccine over multiple days. This happens invariably because the child was trying to play with a dog they met (or a cat, squirrel, fox, etc.) and offer them a treat or toy. Toddlers will walk up to any animal and try to be their friend. It does not matter to them if the beast is five times larger than they are and clearly not friendly. They will simply wear their usual smile and attempt to play. And the goal to be friendly and play does not stop there. They even befriend inanimate objects such as dolls, stuffed animals, or Popsicle sticks with glued-on googly eyes.

One Australian research team examined the issue of toddler kindness toward nonhumans in a group of three-year-olds. In this study they used a NAO humanoid robot. This robot stands two-feet tall and has arms, legs, and lit-up eyes. It has movable joints and is able to do simple tasks such as walking and picking up items, and it has built-in microphones and speakers to allow it to communicate under user control. There are also various settings to make the robot lifelike. First, the researchers set the robot in a high-autonomy mode or a low-autonomy mode. Using the high-autonomy setting, the robot would speak more like a human, while using the low-autonomy setting, the responses were more robotic. Second, the researchers adjusted the sociability of the robot to be either friendly or neutral. These were differentiated by the way a robot would speak. For example, set to high autonomy and friendly, the robot would say, "Hello! My name is Kira. Welcome to the Babylab!" In the high-autonomy and neutral mode, it would say the same thing but without any expression. In the low-autonomy mode, the robot would say, "My ID number is 19469233," and again, friendliness was varied by changing the way the robot spoke.

Children were then placed in a room with a xylophone and the robot set to one of the four modes. After some time to introduce and get to know the robot, the robot began to play the xylophone. The robot was then programmed to drop the stick, look for the stick for ten seconds, look alternately between the stick and the child for ten seconds, then exclaim, "My stick!" and continue looking between the child and the stick for another ten seconds. Children were assessed during this thirty-second period. They could decide to return the stick, play with it, or really do anything they wanted. Looking at the data together from all four modes, half the children helped the robot within that time frame. More importantly, there was no statistical difference if the robot was friendly or neutral or had high or low autonomy.

This is an important experiment as it goes deeper into the mind of a toddler so that we can see how they feel about people, animals, and inanimate objects. In the final part of the study, a researcher sat down with each toddler and showed them pictures of items in four categories: children, animals, vehicles, and robots. They then asked a series of questions, including, "If everyone left and nobody is around would [item] feel lonely?" The majority of responses were yes for all the objects, including vehicles, even though most toddlers correctly answered that vehicles cannot breathe.[10] This gives us great insight as to why they are so universally kind.

What these and other studies show is that altruistic behavior in toddlers extends beyond people they know. Strangers, robots, and even cars all have feelings and should be assisted when in need. Nobody should be lonely. They do not even care if the person, robot, or object they are helping is friendly. Their natural state is to be kind and generous, no matter what.

By befriending inanimate objects, toddlers have uncovered something that only now, with the latest research, has been shown to potentially benefit adults. Using fMRI (measuring brain function), German researchers have shown that adults have similar brain responses if they are shown either a human or a robot given affection or hurt.[11] In the future, this could have implications for creating robot companions, especially for people who live alone. This will, however, take some time as current companion robots are not yet designed in a way that make people feel less lonely.[12]

Be Kind When Others Are Not

So far, we have established toddlers' kindness toward strangers and nonhumans. This kindness holds true even under more difficult circumstances, such as the recipient not being friendly or, in more extreme cases, when toddlers have not yet eaten and the sharing involves food. In this section, we will look at how toddlers react to others who are either selfish or antisocial. It is worth noting that antisocial can mean different things to different people. Here, in the child research context, being antisocial simply means that a person lacks consideration for others but is not necessarily doing things that would harm others. *Prosocial,* a term also used in the research we will examine, means that a person is helpful and demonstrates positive behaviors. As we go through these experiments, think about what you would do if you were in the toddler's shoes. Given the option, would you choose to be kind to the person who has been nice to you? How about the person who acted selfishly? Perhaps the way toddlers behave might influence you to think about who should be treated kindly.

Most people prefer to help others who they deem as good or who treat others well. Ideally, it would be nice if we were willing to help anyone in need, whether we have positive or negative feelings about them or their behavior. One experiment with toddlers ages one to two years looked at how they respond to inconsiderate people. In the first phase, the children were placed in a room to watch the interaction of three different people: an experimenter, a prosocial actor, and an antisocial actor. First, the experimenter rolled a ball to the prosocial actor and then said, "Roll it back," while clapping. The prosocial actor rolled the ball back. The experimenter then repeated this procedure with the antisocial actor. However, instead of rolling the ball back, the antisocial actor simply put the ball in her apron, even as the experimenter held her hands out and looked at the ball and her hands alternately. The actors were not given the prosocial/ antisocial labels explicitly, but this demonstration showed the children what type of people the actors were.

In the next phase of the study, a beanbag was "accidentally" pushed onto the floor where the child was, halfway between the prosocial and antisocial actors. Both actors reached toward the beanbag and looked at the child and beanbag alternately and the child had to decide if they wanted to help and, if so, who they wanted to help. For the analysis, the children were broken down into three different age groups. Overall, most children helped at least once and for the two younger groups there was no difference in which actor the child helped first. It was only in the oldest group that prosocial actors were helped first. Even so, the little helpers in all age groups were willing to help both actors at least once. The authors conclude that young children's willingness to help is not completely dependent on their social evaluation of that person, and one hypothesis as to why that might be is that helping assists in building relationships, and this is a "dominant objective" for young children.[13]

These studies add more to the picture as we get a better understanding of the true nature of a toddler. They want to help others, and the younger they are, the less it matters to them if others are prosocial or antisocial. And even older toddlers will still help people who are antisocial. These findings are based on what the toddler observes one person doing to another, so the next question is, how do the toddlers respond if the antisocial behavior is directed at them?

In a study from Spain, toddlers were partnered with an unfamiliar adult and played a sticker game. In this game, the child or adult pulled one of two levers. Pulling lever one would give only the person who pulled the lever a sticker while pulling lever two would give each person a sticker. What the researchers found was that even if the adult consistently pulled lever one and acted selfishly, taking all the stickers for themselves, when toddlers were given a chance, they would pull lever two more often so that each person would have a sticker. The authors summarized it well by saying that toddlers have a "basic tendency to be nice to others," and not even other people who are "repeatedly selfish toward children can erode it." They did not retaliate against others who were selfish toward them, and they did not try to behave nicer to get a reward from the other person. They simply saw an opportunity to be kind and seized it.[14]

As adults, we know that this tendency to be kind even when the other person is selfish doesn't last, and we can start to see the beginning of this in later toddlerhood. To see how age might influence toddler behavior, researchers from Harvard University and the Max Planck Institute for Evolutionary Anthropology in Germany studied two groups of toddlers, ages two and three. They set up two games for the children to participate in with puppets. Within these games there were times when one partner needed help reaching certain objects and other times when sharing was required. When it was the puppet's turn to help or share, the puppet did one of three things. It either helped/shared with the child, did not help/share and remained silent, or did not help/share and explicitly told the child, "No, I don't give you any cubes."

As you might be able to guess by now, the results showed that toddlers in both age groups almost always helped, and it did not matter to them how their partner behaved. For the sharing task, the results were similar, with two-year-olds demonstrating no difference in sharing based on their partner's behavior. For the three-year-olds, the results were mixed. There was no significant difference in sharing if the puppet was silent but didn't share. These toddlers only shared less if the puppet was vocal about not sharing. The researchers offer one possible explanation for this, which is that the toddlers were giving their partner the benefit of the doubt when their intentions were unclear. Overall, the authors summarize these findings as a model in child development where "reciprocity is secondary." The youngest toddlers start off completely prosocial and do not discriminate when others act selfishly, but as they get older (and eventually become adults), this sadly changes.[15] It's unfortunate because if we could focus on kindness and giving people the benefit of the doubt, then we would also have better relationships, like toddlers do.

Toddlers and Racial Bias

In our discussion of how toddlers act kindly toward others, it's important to discuss racial biases, as this is such an important issue for many people. In the United States, 76 percent of both African Americans and Asians and 58 percent of Hispanics report experiencing discrimination because of their race or ethnicity.[16] I'm not going to argue that toddlers are color-blind, as they do detect race and certainly have racial preferences for their friends, for example.[17] Here, I'm simply focusing on one aspect, and that is helping behavior, related to our discussion on kindness. It's fascinating to see how little emphasis toddlers put on race, and this provides another area where we can learn from them. I will note that the literature in this particular area is relatively sparse, especially compared to the other sections of this chapter establishing how toddlers behave when it comes to kindness, but it's an important discussion, nonetheless.

To get a better understanding of racial preferences that young children may have, and how these might change over time, researchers at the University of Chicago and Harvard University designed a series of experiments to test white babies, two- to three-year-olds, and five- and six-year-olds. In the first experiment with the infants, researchers found that they had no race preference accepting toys. In the second experiment, toddlers ages two and three were told that they were part of a giving game. The toddlers had to give presents to either a Black individual or a white individual on the screens in front of them by placing the present in the boxes that were in front of the screens. In the end, the toddlers gave presents equally to the people of both races. When a third experiment was run with five- and six-year-olds, these children had a clear race preference for their own race.[18] What we see here, and has been confirmed by other studies, is that this racial preference develops later, at the end of toddlerhood.

An experiment from Lehigh University also explored the theme of race in toddler responses and produced a surprising result. This study included nearly a hundred white and Hispanic toddlers who were split into two groups, one-year-olds and two-year-olds. The most interesting part of this experiment sought to measure *empathic distress,* a term used to describe what it feels like to share and inter-nalize another person's suffering.[19] In the study, the experimenter, either a Black or white woman, was playing with a wooden peg and mallet toy set. At one point she intentionally missed the peg, hit her thumb, and said, "Ouch! I hurt my finger." The children's reaction was then captured on three dimensions: empathic distress, arousal, and engagement. For one-year-olds there was no difference in how they reacted and who they helped. For the two-year-olds, they also showed no preference for who they helped, but for empathic dis-tress and arousal, there was a clear difference in favor of the *Black* experimenter. This was a surprise and contrary to the researchers' hypothesis of what they thought would happen.[20]

So, while toddlers do have racial awareness and preferences, when it comes to sharing and helping, they are much more equitable, especially the youngest ones. It's only near the end of toddlerhood and later childhood that this impartiality starts to erode.

Kindness Motivation

The question then arises, Why are toddlers so kind? Are they doing it so others will be nice to them, or so they can get some favor in the future, as adults often do? Do young children think this way? To test this, a team of researchers led by faculty at the University of Michigan set up an experiment in which children would have to make decisions on giving away one of the most prized child com-modities: stickers. To make the decision even more challenging for the children, two different types of stickers were used: a brightly col-ored fish and a yellow circle. Before starting the experiment, each child, ages three to seven, was given one of each sticker. Then, the child, the experimenter, and an adult "competitor" were brought into a room. The experimenter said aloud, "I wonder which sticker you're going to give me, and then I can choose who to play my game with." The experimenter then received a sticker from the child and then from the competitor.

What the experimenters were testing here was something called strategic giving. That is whether the children share the nicer sticker in order to influence the experimenter to choose them to play the game. Like adults, the five-year-olds and seven-year-olds did engage in strategic giving by using the fish sticker as an opportunity to be able to play the game. The only group that did not do this were the three-year-olds. As the authors point out, since there is a large body of evidence demonstrating how prosocial young children are, the interpretation of this finding is that toddlers are simply not thinking about what they will get in return when they give.[21]

While strategic giving is part of being an adult, and even an older child, it may be something to be aware of when we do it and instead try to extend our giving beyond any benefits we may receive.

If the studies so far have not convinced you that toddlers are naturally the kindest people on earth, a few additional data points may persuade you. Not only do toddlers not engage in strategic giving, but other research done with Dutch and Chinese toddlers demonstrates that they don't even get a boost of happiness from being thanked.[22] It only comes from the act of giving itself. And a German study confirms that they are not significantly responsive to praise. There was no difference in how much three-year-olds shared if they were praised or not. The researchers do note that it was difficult to tell any differences because toddlers share so much naturally that there is a "ceiling effect," at which they can't share much more.

This same study also examined what would happen if toddlers received rewards for sharing. Wait for it. Their sharing *decreased* when they received rewards. The authors conclude that toddlers are "genuinely intrinsically motivated to share resources with others," and receiving rewards "might have replaced children's inherent fairness inclination."[23]

So if toddlers aren't strategic givers and are not motivated by praise, then the question remains, what do they get out of giving so much? The answer may lie in how they feel when they give. A study from the University of British Columbia examined a group of one-year-olds to determine how happy toddlers feel when they give. Researchers used Goldfish crackers or Teddy Grahams (also my personal favorites) and a puppet. Both the child and the puppet had a bowl in front of them, and the puppet would say, "YUMMM," whenever they were given a treat. The experimenter started by magically "finding" three treats and giving one to the child, one to the puppet, and the third to the child, asking him or her to give the last one to the puppet. Finally, the experimenter simply asked the child to give a treat to the puppet from their own bowl.

To measure the child's feelings, the researchers did something clever. They recorded their faces throughout the interactions, and their facial expressions were analyzed for happiness. Not only were the toddlers happier when giving treats to the puppet rather than receiving them themselves; astonishingly, they demonstrated higher levels of happiness when they gave away their own treats rather than the "found" treat![24] There is something much deeper for toddlers when it comes to giving. Their highest level of happiness comes from giving what they have to others, over and above anything else.

Warm Glow and the Peak of the Hierarchy of Needs

The happiness we feel from giving to others is not something that fades. It is still there into adulthood to varying degrees for each of us. It even has a specific name: warm glow.

Warm glow is a model developed by economist James Andreoni, who argues that people's motivation for giving is not purely altruistic; there is an emotional benefit for them.[25] This has further been supported by neuroimaging studies that demonstrate that the reward system in the brain is engaged when people give.[26] Furthermore, the feel-good neurotransmitters oxytocin and vasopressin are released when giving.[27] These are the same neurotransmitters released with sex, food, and drugs. No matter what the motivation is, giving to and helping others makes us happier.

The other interesting part of giving to others is that the happiness we derive from it doesn't fade like other things that make us happy. In the phenomenon known as hedonic adaptation, we derive less happiness from repeated exposure to the same thing. So, for example, that new car you just bought initially gives you a spike of happiness, but this then drops to a baseline level over time. This is different from what happens to us with repeated giving. Researchers at the Booth School of Business, University of Chicago, and Kellogg School of Management, Northwestern University, ran an experiment where adult participants would either receive the same amount of money each day or give this amount to another person each day. After five days they found that happiness declined over time in the group receiving the money but did not decline in the group giving the money. In a second experiment, participants either won money for themselves or for a charity they supported. In this experiment, their happiness level declined at half the rate if the money was going to charity rather than to themselves.[28]

There is a different type of happiness we can derive from giving that goes beyond the in-the-moment pleasure we get from most things. This type of happiness gets more at how we feel about ourselves and the type of person we want to be. This is why it's less fleeting, and we will get back to this in the next study we will discuss.

The link between well-being and giving has intrigued researchers for decades, and hundreds of studies have been done on this topic with varying results. But perhaps the most comprehensive study was a meta-analysis published in 2020 that was able to get at the most important and interesting details of this relationship, and it's worth spending some time on this. The analysis was led by researchers at the University of Cambridge and included an incredible 201 studies with nearly 200,000 adults. When combined, the authors demonstrated what they describe as a modest relationship between prosocial behavior and well-being, but it was the sub-analyses that provided the most useful information. First, researchers were able to show that there was a stronger correlation between kindness and eudaemonic well-being rather than hedonic well-being. Hedonic refers to our subjective feelings and is an outcome of something we do. Eudaemonic happiness is different as it arises when we feel we are achieving our potential. It is the process of discovering and fulfilling our true nature that gives us happiness. And those familiar with Maslow's hierarchy of needs may recognize this as the peak: self-actualization.[29]

Getting back to the study, there were three more important findings. First, the authors found a stronger link with psychological functioning rather than malfunctioning. In other words, the warm glow we discussed was seen here again, and giving was correlated with a more immediate psychological boost when helping others. This link is stronger than that of preventing negative psychological outcomes, such as anxiety and depression. Second, informal helping was linked to more well-being benefits compared to formal helping. Small daily acts, which are more casual and don't necessarily follow rules and schedules, were shown to have a higher correlation with well-being. This is not to say that formal volunteering did not have a positive effect—it did; it was just that informal helping showed a stronger effect. And third, there was an age effect with younger and middle-aged adults demonstrating a higher correlation with overall well-being when they were kind. The authors hypothesize that this might be because younger adults are finding their "meaning and purpose in life—a measure of eudaemonic well-being." And for older adults, there were other benefits. For them, physical well-being showed the strongest link, nearly double the effect size for retired compared to non-retired older adults.[30]

Giving and being kind, no matter how it's done, will help others and can boost your own happiness. Kindness toward others is also associated with higher self-esteem and self-efficacy.[31] Practically speaking, there are three broad ways to do this. First you can simply donate money. It could be a cause you're passionate about or an organization that does meaningful work. Perhaps you are a pet lover and want to donate to an animal shelter. For larger charities, you can use sites such as Charity Navigator and Guidestar to get a better sense of how much of your donation is going to the beneficiaries versus administration. Second, you can sign up with a volunteer organization. There may be an organization in your community that you are aware of, or, if you want to be inspired, volunteer matching websites such as

VolunteerMatch and JustServe can be a good place to start. And you can find both in-person and virtual volunteer opportunities. Interestingly, studies have shown that when you give money to charity or do formal volunteering, it can give you a happiness boost equivalent to an annual raise of tens of thousands of dollars.[32,33]

Donating money and formal volunteering are excellent ways to get a warm glow, but as we also saw, small, simple acts directed toward friends or strangers are all it takes. These opportunities are all around us but sometimes are not as obvious. Thankfully, the volunteer matching websites noted above can also help you find kindness tasks. A search in my area on VolunteerMatch yielded results such as "Help a neighbor in Mississauga with a homemade meal" and "Help a disabled senior with lawn care in Etobicoke." On a macro level, this behavior helps improve entire societies. And while we are not quite at the level of toddlers, adults continue to make significant progress. Despite the global COVID-19 pandemic and economic hardships, in 2021 more than three billion adults around the world helped someone they didn't know, an all-time record.[34] And finally, one last added benefit is that kindness has been shown to be contagious, so the benefits extend well beyond you and the person you are directly helping.[35] Follow the toddler lead. Be kind.

Mind Control

Although simple, informal acts of kindness are easy to do, sometimes we need a nudge to get started with a behavior change, even if we know that change is good for us. For many things we want to improve about ourselves, that initial hurdle can often be challenging. For kindness, however, there is a surprisingly easy solution. We just have to think about it.

Kindness toward others provides one of the best examples of self-perpetuating behavior. We can get ourselves into a wonderful positive cycle of doing good, which is then reinforced by others and how we feel so that we do it more. When others see this, or are around us when we are kind, this helps them be more prosocial. Alternatively, by being around kind people, we are more likely to be kind ourselves. Kindness can be so powerful that a physical act isn't even necessary for us to receive a benefit. In 2021, researchers at the University of California, Riverside, conducted an experiment with more than five hundred adults divided into four groups. Group one was instructed to perform three kind acts for someone else in the next twenty-four hours. Group two was asked only to think about previous kind acts they had done. Group three was asked to both perform kind acts and think about previous kind acts, and group four was not given any specific instructions. All participants were followed for three days and completed a series of psychological measures. As expected, performing kind acts increased well-being outcomes, but surprisingly, so did only recalling them. In fact, there was no significant difference in well-being between the groups who performed the acts, only recalled them, or both performed and re-called them.[36] Clearly, there are benefits to performing kind acts that cannot be had by only thinking about them, but this provides an easy way to test how it makes you feel as a way to encourage yourself to do more.

Along the lines of thinking about kind acts and how this can boost your well-being, let's dive into an even more powerful mind trick. If thinking about simple acts of kindness we performed in the past is helpful, imagine if we thought about an entire time period when we were at our peak level of kindness. As we've clearly established in this chapter, that time was toddlerhood, and one group of researchers explored what would happen if we went back as far as we could in our memories. In an incredibly thoughtful and profound study conducted at Harvard University and the University of North Carolina at Chapel Hill, two researchers examined how childhood memories themselves can affect present prosocial behavior. They conducted a series of five experiments with hundreds of undergraduate students. In the first experiment, one group was asked to write down positive memories they had from childhood, and another group was asked to write down their memories from a recent trip to a grocery store. They were then given a helping request from the experimenter, which they were told was "pilot testing for another project." Nearly 50 percent more participants in the childhood memories group offered to help compared to the grocery store group. In the next four experiments they manipulated certain aspects of this experiment to see if this behavior was more broadly applicable. The results were astonishing. People who thought about their childhood memories were more generous monetarily, even when compared to other personal positive memories in their teenage years. They also held others to higher ethical standards after recalling their childhood.

Most stunning was the last experiment, in which there were three groups. One group wrote down positive memories of childhood, another group wrote down negative memories of childhood, and the third control group wrote down positive memories of their teenage years. Compared to the control group, participants' positive and negative childhood memories "led to a heightened sense of moral purity and promoted participant's likelihood to help." So even the participants who wrote down their negative childhood memories were more likely to help than those who thought of positive memories at a different point in their life. Memories are funny in that we cannot often recall an entire scenario. Instead, we remember parts and use related information to form a picture in our minds. Despite what people think of toddler behavior, they are seen as innocent. So thinking about our own childhood activates what we think about young children in general, and this in turn allows us to act in a more prosocial way. Your own younger self is the best role model you have for kindness. Practically, the best way to make this experiment come to life for yourself is to simply follow the directions given in the experiment and do a little journaling:

> Please think about your childhood and good memories you have from it. Please write a few paragraphs describing them and one event that you still remember to this date. Please provide as many details as possible so that another person reading what you wrote could understand how you felt at that time.[37]

For those of you who journal, this would be an excellent prompt to use weekly or monthly. If you don't journal, give this short exercise a try. What will likely come out from thinking about these memories are moments when you and others were kind to one another. It may be the time you recall when a parent taught you to bake cookies or the pet you spent so much time taking care of. Whatever the memories are, this exercise puts you in the frame of mind of the kind person you were, and it is this mindset that you can then carry forward in your present life. And what I like about this exercise is that it gets directly to the message of this book. Our own younger selves have a lot to teach us. We will come back to this type of exercise later in Chapter 5 on play and Chapter 7 on mentorship. The toddler mindset is the kindest mindset.

Born This Way

Taken together, it is clear that toddlers are simply good people who are kind in a wide range of situations and without expecting anything in return.[38] This is their natural state. They don't share, give, or act kindly to get happiness in the moment; it is more about who they are at their core. They do it informally, in multiple environments, and with different types of people. Because kindness defines them, they naturally live in a place where they are able to realize their human potential nearly all the time and achieve eudaemonic happiness. This is not to say that they don't also experience a warm glow, they do, but to achieve the ultimate form of happiness, both types are important.

We may think that parents and caregivers teach children how to help others and be kind, but this is simply not true. Felix Warneken, professor of psychology at the University of Michigan, has spent more than a decade researching toddler altruism. After doing many experiments with both toddlers and chimpanzees, he concludes that a toddler's willingness to help has "deep evolutionary roots" and developed well before social norms or culture could have influenced their behavior. He gave a wonderful TEDx talk titled "Need Help? Ask a 2-Year-Old," which I highly encourage you to watch. In it, you will see these experiments come to life.[39]

There's something special about giving and being kind that toddlers have tapped into. The results of the adult studies reveal so many of the benefits of toddler-like kindness, and we continue to discover more. If we all acted as givers more of the time, the way toddlers do, we would be happier, have better relationships, and get closer to fulfilling our individual potential.

Toddler Teachings

Assume everyone is your friend, no matter who or what they are. They could all use your help in some way.

It is always best if both you and your stranger friend can get stickers, rather than just you alone.

No matter how other people behave, stick to what you know: kindness.

There is no need to be nicer to someone just so they will play a game with you.

Small, informal acts of kindness are just as important as formal volunteering or donating money.

Kindness will make you happier!

Think and write often about your toddler self.

Chapter 3:

Laughter

Knock, knock . . .

It's impossible to walk by a group of toddlers and not hear nearly constant laughter. Everything is funny, from different facial expressions, animal sounds, bodily noises, and of course, peek-a-boo. Toddlers can see the humor in almost every situation much better than adults. They understand how life should be: mostly fun with some serious time rather than the opposite. And even the issues that are serious can usually benefit from a bit of humor. Not only does laughing help toddlers enjoy their lives more, but there are also many other reasons why increasing laughter can help them and all of us—from improved learning to lower blood pressure.

We know that smiling and laughter are evolutionarily important for individuals and groups as this is a trait we share with chimpanzees. Most importantly, smiling and laughter play a role in social bonding.[1] In humans, these begin at a very young age, well before we are able to do many basic things, such as sitting up. Most babies start to smile in their first month of life, followed by laughing by three months of age.[2] By the time children reach toddlerhood and start to say words, they are already well practiced in the art of laughing and joking with their family and friends. The fact that smiling and laughter emerge and then develop at such a young age points to the importance of humor in our lives. Humor helps us cope with stress, make friends, learn, and be creative.[3] Perhaps this is the reason toddlers excel in all these domains.

One of the sad parts of getting older is that we all go over what has been termed the "humor cliff." A 2013 Gallup study of 1.4 million people in 163 different countries showed that the amount we smile and laugh per day starts to fall dramatically at age twenty-three. It does start to rise again but not until age eighty, and it never reaches the peak we started at.[4,5]

Although the amount toddlers, and children in general, laugh per day has been widely misquoted and carried forward from older studies, two things are clear. One, they laugh a lot, and two, they laugh more than adults. It is commonly said that children laugh 300–400 times per day, but this is incorrect. The original quote comes from a book published in 1994 titled *Living Wonderfully*, in which psychologist Robert Holden wrote that children smiled 300 to 400 times per day and laughed 150 times per day.[6] For a more objective number, a study published in 2019 compared how much toddlers ages three to five years laughed with how much early child educators (a generally happy and cheerful group of people) in the same preschool laughed. In this study, researchers examined seventy-seven hours of video recordings in two Swedish preschools over one and a half years. The video captured everything a toddler would do in a typical day, including eating, drawing, circle time, and the all-important free play sessions (more on that in Chapter 5). The researchers wanted to know who was laughing and to whom it was directed, so the first thing they did was remove the instances where someone was laughing to themselves. Of note, and not surprisingly, these instances of self-chuckling out loud were all children. In the remaining instances of more than one thousand episodes of laughter, the researchers found that 86 percent of the laughter was from children and 14 percent was from adults, that is, it was six times higher in children. This figure, however, is skewed because the teacher-to-child ratio was not one-to-one. So a more important measure is child-to-child laughter over time. In this study, without adults around, this occurred nearly one time per minute, or more precisely, fifty-four times per hour.[7] Compare this with a study of adults in which participants were recorded during an interview and found to laugh on average, twenty-three times per hour, similar to other studies in adults.[8]

Another important finding from the study with toddlers was that when adults were around, they laughed less, about thirty-three times an hour. This is still higher than the adult average. So, while the quote that children laugh 300–400 times per day is incorrect, if they were left to interact only with other children all day, they would probably get close to that level. There are obvious reasons that explain why children laugh more without adults present. Mainly, when adults are around, children are more likely to be engaged in goal-directed activities; however, the question remains: Why is this difference so large? One part of the explanation is that toddlers can see humor where adults cannot. In the study, when a child had laughter directed toward an adult, half the time the adult either smiled but did not laugh or had no response.[9]

Toddlers are like aspiring comedians who see the world as a comedy club. It is their goal to make everyone around them laugh. They encounter different crowds as they practice and develop jokes, and unfortunately, they don't get as many laughs from big people as they do from little people. Not only that, but the big people aren't making many jokes or laughing much themselves. What do toddlers do then? They stick to the crowd that understands them, laughs at all their jokes, and always comes back for more. They will still try to make everyone laugh but have a preference for other toddlers who are able to see how funny everything is. It is challenging to understand why every adult does not break out in laughter anytime a rubber duck is placed on one's head, or there is a sound that remotely resembles a farting noise.

Learning Through Laughter

"Lala-lala lala-lala Elmo's song. Lala-lala lala-lala Elmo's song." Without reading anything more, most readers can immediately hear the high-pitched voice of the famous bright red Muppet. Elmo, as most people know, is a character on *Sesame Street*, the longest-running children's show in history with more than fifty seasons. Many of you may also remember the show from your own childhood. At its core, *Sesame Street* is an educational program, and humor is one of the primary ways it helps young children learn. Joey Mazzarino, head writer for the show, has been quoted as saying, "If it's not funny, we don't do it."[10] This can be seen in almost any *Sesame Street* clip, but as an example, let's look at how Elmo and James Marsden teach the word *"engineer."* In this clip Mr. James explains that the word *"engineer"* means to design and build something. Elmo then proceeds to engineer an automatic spaghetti server consisting of a block of wood and a plank. A bowl of spaghetti is placed at one end, and then Mr. James strikes the other end, launching the spaghetti in the air, which eventually comes down on his head. They both have a good laugh and repeat, "Engineer."[11]

Sesame Street has remained popular for decades among young children because it offers them an opportunity to learn in a fun way. One of the central themes of this book is that toddlers are highly proficient in learning new things, so it is understandable that humor is connected to improved learning given how much they laugh. The good news for you is that this extends well beyond toddlerhood all the way to older adulthood. To illustrate how laughter helps with learning, researchers from two universities in France took fifty-three one-year-olds and taught them a new task with and without laughter. They placed a toy duck in the room and then showed them a cardboard T-shaped tool that acted as a rake to bring the duck closer. Of note, a handful of smart cookies figured out how to use the new tool before the demonstration and were then excluded from the experiment. The rest were divided into two groups. In one group the researcher demonstrated how to use the tool, and in the other group, after using the tool, the researcher threw the duck on the floor and smiled to make the child laugh. They then had the toddlers attempt to use the tool. For the children who were not made to laugh, only 25 percent were able to use the tool correctly. However, in the toddler group that did laugh, more than 90 percent were able to use the tool successfully.[12]

Of course, there are many explanations for this finding as the authors discuss. First, there could be individual differences, such as toddlers who laugh more have better social skills and find it easier to interact with adults. However, it is also possible, and this is backed by research with adults, that this effect is connected to dopamine release, which comes with laughter. Dopamine, which is the brain's reward hormone, is what can motivate us, and it also plays a role in learning and memory consolidation.[13] Many studies in adults demonstrate the relationship between humor and learning. This is true even for topics that are difficult or dry. For example, students at Sam Houston State University in Texas described statistics as one of their "dreaded" courses. So researchers chose this course and had students watch three recorded statistics lectures. There were two versions of each set of lectures. One version had a humorous story to start and other bits of humor inserted at various points in the lectures. The other version of the lectures had these segments seamlessly cut out. Students were not told which version they were watching. In the end, the students who watched the humorous version recalled and retained significantly more information when tested.[14]

The data supporting the use of humor as a learning aid extends throughout adulthood to older adults. For people ages eighteen to thirty-four years, humor helped them remember and share political information.[15] For older adults, between sixty-three and seventy-four, watching a twenty-minute humorous show prior to a standardized short-term memory test improved learning ability and recall.[16] To further strengthen this finding, the authors then repeated their study and this time included additional older adults with diabetes. Similar results were found, and for both studies, they also found lowered levels of the stress hormone cortisol in the humor group compared with the control group participants.[17] We'll talk more about how helpful laughter is in lowering stress later in the chapter.

One of the other ways laughter helps with learning is it allows for an immediate connection with another person. Feeling this connection and comfort not only helps the relationship between the person teaching and the person learning, but it can also help with subjects that are particularly challenging as the material itself may cause anxiety. Humor facilitates learning through several other mechanisms including reducing stress while simultaneously increasing attention, motivation, and alertness.[18]

In the formal classroom setting, humor not only aids learners, but it has also been shown to improve teaching evaluations of instructors, as long as the jokes are not offensive or inappropriate.[19,20] All of us are teachers in some way, and incorporating humor can almost always be beneficial. Although most academic research focuses on the use of humor for teaching subject material or to test memory, using humor outside the classroom setting has also been studied with training elite gymnasts. Through interview data, recordings, and observation, research from the University of Oklahoma and Georgia State University provides insight into how the functions of humor are more generalizable in teaching. As in other studies, humor was noted to help "bond people together," relieve and manage stress, and make corrective feedback easier to digest.[21] If you are in the role of instructor or learner, humor is helpful.

As a learner, you can use humor to your advantage to learn and remember things better. It is one of the tricks of advertisers who want you to remember their ads more than the others.[22,23] If you're lucky, you can find humorous delivery methods of material you want to remember better. For example, for the daily news and political information, it would be better to watch it presented by a late-night comedian such as John Oliver or Bill Maher.[24] If the material that you want to focus on does not exist in a humorous format, you'll have to do the work yourself. Options include creating a funny mnemonic,[25] acronym, or rhyme, or making some other type of humorous association. Another option is to simply engage with a humorous audio or video clip before you start learning.

So the next time you want to learn new information or skills, remember something important, or are teaching, adding humor will certainly help. Bringing giggles to everything, like toddlers do, can focus your mind and make you more comfortable, exactly the state you want to be in to maximize learning.

Shared Laughter and Making Friends

Making new friends as an adult is hard. It's challenging both at work and outside work. It takes time to meet people and get to know them. It can be tough to even start a conversation or think of the right thing to say, often because we are too self-conscious. But friendships are critical, and shared laughter can help build those friendships. Multiple studies have shown that people with strong social networks live longer.[26,27]

On average, working people spend about ninety thousand hours at work over their lifetimes.[28] Given this incredible amount of time, it's important to cultivate better relationships in the office. A survey of three thousand American workers found that the average number of friends people have at the office is five. Most people they work with are considered coworkers while nearly a quarter are either strangers or even enemies. About a third were either at-work-only friends or real friends.[29] Ask a toddler how she would characterize every person in her class, including her teacher: 100 percent would be friends.

Toddlers have many techniques to make friends quickly. As we discussed in the last chapter, one technique is being kind in every situation no matter what the other person does. Other toddler approaches include sharing a cookie, inviting a new person to play a game, or simply giving a warm, awkward hug or a high five. But by far the most common strategies employed by every toddler are smiling, laughing, and creating as much humor as possible.

When my daughter graduated from her infant class to the toddler class, I remember dropping her off in the new classroom for her first full day there. Although she knew some of the children and had been briefly introduced to the others, it was a different environment with different teachers. I could tell she was nervous. Instead of her normal confident self as we tottered toward her infant room, she held my hand tighter as we turned the corner on our way to the toddler room. She kept pointing to her old class as I explained to her we were going somewhere new. As we entered the class there were eight children all staring at her. I could see it on their faces, and there was no confusion on their part as to why this new person was there. This was a new friend. With big wide steps they all moved toward her, each with huge smiles and dripping noses, and then circled her to welcome her. Some said a few words, some waved, and one little boy gave a gentle touch on the arm. It took less than thirty seconds for one of them to start giggling, and soon enough they all were. I said a quick goodbye knowing she was going to have a wonderful day filled with laughter.

Laughter is important in building relationships for several reasons. First, it makes people more relaxed, which we saw helps with learning, and we'll discuss some of the physiology in the next section. Feeling more relaxed allows people to open up as they feel more comfortable, and this is one of the key building blocks of relationships. In fact, laughter has even been shown to encourage people to share personal stories that they otherwise would not. In one experiment from Oxford University, 112 people ages eighteen to thirty-one who did not know one another were shown one of three videos. There was a comedy routine intended to make people laugh, a golf instruction video as the neutral scenario, and scenes of animals from *Planet Earth* to elicit positive feelings but not laughter. The participants did this in groups of four, and after watching the video, they were asked to write down five pieces of information they would like to share about themselves to get to know one another better. As rated by others, the person making the disclosures revealed significantly more intimate information if they were in the laughter group compared to both the neutral group and the positive affect group.[30]

Feeling more relaxed and open is of course helpful for relationships, but laughter goes much deeper. Studies have shown that people who laugh together have perceived similarity with the other person. To them, it's a mutual connection in which the other person understands them more. And these perceptions of feeling more comfortable and being similar to another person are then tied to relationship outcomes such as satisfaction, liking, and affiliation.[31]

Shared laughter with others is one of the most powerful things we can do to build deeper and more meaningful relationships. Toddlers do this consistently, helping them make friends with ease and maintain those relationships. Any way you can find to incorporate more laughter with people will help you make stronger bonds, and it is certainly worth trying.

Laughter Is the Best Antidepressant

One of the arguments I've heard about why it's so easy for toddlers to be happy is that they don't have the stress of being an adult.

While it's true that toddlers don't have financial or work stress, they have to deal with their own stressful situations. Some of these may seem trivial to an adult, but for them, they are quite significant. Take for example the lovey, that wonderful, worn-down, rag-like item that used to look like a rabbit (or "rarat" as my daughter says). Loveys are much more than toys to young children; they provide friendship, comfort, and emotional support.[32] Not having one's lovey, especially when entering a new situation, can be stressful for a toddler. And this is just one example. Toddlers also have to deal with bigger changes such as a new caregiver at day care and sometimes at home, which can be incredibly difficult. Still even with these and other daily stresses, toddlers remain largely playful and continue to laugh throughout the day.

The body's physiological response to stress is critical to understanding why laughter is helpful in mitigating it. When you feel stressed, several hormones are released into your bloodstream; the most important ones for this discussion are cortisol and epinephrine. The brain, via its command center, the hypothalamus, sends signals to the adrenal glands, which sit on top of your kidneys. These hormones then circulate throughout your bloodstream. At first, epinephrine is released, and you feel the effects immediately as your heart beats faster, your blood pressure increases, and your breathing rate goes up. After this, as the epinephrine decreases, the adrenal glands then release cortisol. Cortisol decreases all the functions that are unnecessary when dealing with a stressful situation such as lowering your immune response and digestive system function. Importantly, it also sends signals to regions of your brain that control mood, motivation, and fear.[33] In the short term, these effects go away as the stressful situation decreases. However, for many people who have ongoing stressful situations, this response can stay activated, leading to chronic stress. This in turn leads to many health problems including anxiety, depression, headaches, and others.

The good news is, laughter has been shown to decrease levels of these and other stress hormones.[34] This fact, along with all the other known benefits of laughter, has led some researchers to test out various forms of laughter therapy with promising results thus far. A meta-analysis published in 2019 looked at ten different studies that included 814 adults. These studies looked at a wide variety of patients living in different parts of the world who utilized a diverse set of humor interventions. In Australia, Elder Clowns visited nursing home residents. In Japan, Korea, and Iran, adults with chronic diseases (COPD, breast cancer, and Parkinson's disease) participated in laughter activities such as laughter yoga. Two of the studies, from China and Israel, included schizophrenic patients. In China, these patients underwent humor skills training, and in Israel, they watched comedies. Taken together, what these studies demonstrate is that laughter interventions are effective in decreasing anxiety and depression, as well as improving sleep quality in adults.[35]

Stress is caused by different factors, many of which are beyond our control. Laughter provides a simple way to decrease this stress as the benefits of decreasing stress hormones are felt immediately. While you may not think peek-a-boo is hilarious anymore, there are other things that likely fit with your comedic tastes, and it's important to increase the amount of humor in your life as much as possible.

Laugh More, Live Longer

Toddlers do nearly everything right for health. As discussed in Chapter 1, they sleep well if on a schedule, do not overeat, and exercise regularly. It turns out their laughter also keeps their bodies healthy, and you too can reap these benefits by laughing more. Laughter has been shown to have both short- and long-term cardiovascular benefits. Multiple adult studies have demonstrated that watching funny videos produces immediate increased heart function and higher blood pressure, similar to what exercise does.[36] After these immediate effects, the healthy longer-term effects can be a decrease in heart rate and blood pressure. One study from Japan had elderly people who attend "Gashu-en," an elder day care center, watch a stand-up comedy routine for half an hour once a week. After these sessions, the participants had significantly lower heart rates and blood pressures.[37]

Some of the most robust data on the long-term health effects of laughter comes from Norway in a study of more than fifty thousand adults and included a fifteen-year follow-up. In this study, adults were asked to participate in an extensive health survey that included a validated Sense of Humor Questionnaire (SHQ). The most important part of this was whether people easily recognized humor in their lives or, in other words, could find humor wherever it was presented. The researchers then went back to examine the health status of these people, ensuring that they captured things known to affect health, such as exercise, smoking, and BMI. The results were astonishing. For women, those who scored higher on the SHQ had a lower risk of death from any cause. For specific diseases, they also found an association between higher SHQ scores and lower rates of death from cardiovascular disease for women and infection for both men and women.[38] Understanding that there are many humorous things in our world, like toddlers do, actually decreased the risk of death and disease. And while not as robust, another large study from

Japan, with more than twenty thousand participants, found a significant decrease in heart disease and stroke in people who laughed daily compared to those who never, or almost never, laughed.[39]

Taken together, studies that demonstrate the immediate positive physiologic effects of laughter coupled with the longer-term studies demonstrating associations with decreased disease and death are compelling. This is especially true since we know the beneficial effects that laughter has on our hearts, and this has been linked to a decrease in cardiovascular disease. Laughing at anything remotely funny or silly, like toddlers do, is one of the easiest and best things you can do for your health.

More Giggles

The question then remains: How can we follow the toddler example and inject more humor into our lives? The first step is to gather more friends (or at least one). We all laugh more with others rather than alone, although laughing while you are alone is also an important step to increase your overall daily laughter. To demonstrate the effect of laughter in groups, researchers from the UK had toddlers ages two to four watch cartoons either alone, in pairs, or in groups of six to eight children. The children who had at least one partner laughed eight times more than when they were alone and smiled nearly three times more. And there was no significant difference if the toddler was with one friend or several. The researchers observed that often it was the laughter of one child that made another laugh, and in a larger group, it was a "chain reaction." They would look at one another when laughing to encourage everyone to laugh. Some toddlers went so far as to attempt to engage the researchers who were standing behind a privacy screen.[40] Toddlers just will not stop until everyone is laughing. Shared laughter is also important for adults, and studies demonstrate that adults too laugh more when others are present. Often, we can't help but laugh when others are laughing as we have less voluntary control over laughter compared to speaking. Even recorded laughter can make us laugh.[41]

After you have a partner, the next step is to try a few different types of humor to see what works for you. Toddlers, being masters in this area, have been known to utilize a variety of methods to ensure their days are filled with laughter. One study in two- and three-year-olds documented seven different ways toddlers produce humor by themselves. The first was object-based humor such as putting underwear on their head. Second was changing labels for objects like holding a cat and calling it a fish. Third was conceptual such as saying a dog has five ears. The next type was classified as taboo topics and included things like licking a parent. Some toddlers used physical humor to demonstrate funny bodily actions like silly walking. Finally, the last two were the classic tickling/chasing and peek-a-boo.[42]

For you, perhaps your coworker shouting a made-up word repeatedly, or giving you a good tickle, isn't what will make you laugh, but there is certainly something for everyone. There are comedy clubs, humorous books, podcasts, TV shows, and social media. It just takes some exploration to find out what makes you laugh, and then you will be motivated to engage with it regularly. This is easy to do through social media, or, if you prefer, you can sign up for a daily e-mailed joke. For me, not surprisingly, I enjoy watching funny toddler video clips. The day I am writing this my daily chuckle came from a clip posted on Twitter of a toddler named Maisie who walked around her neighborhood introducing herself to every insect she saw. You can see her lean over or squat near anything that moves and say things like "Look, bug! I'm Maisie." This continues in various other locations until she is sure that all the bugs in her home and neighborhood know who she is.[43]

And finally, if your favorite TV shows or podcasts aren't helping you get those daily chuckles, there is always simulated laughter.[44] Unlike spontaneous laughter, where you are laughing in response to something you see or hear, simulated laughter means you make yourself laugh, like a fake laugh. This may seem like an odd thing to do, but there is good evidence that it works well. In fact, in a large review of twenty-nine different studies, the authors concluded that for depression and anxiety, simulated laughter was more effective than spontaneous laughter.[45]

There are two ways to do simulated laughter: alone or in a group. A few techniques have been described in research studies, but basically, anything that helps you generate more laughter for longer periods of time will help. If you are alone, the first technique is laughing with yourself, acknowledging a mistake, and pointing and laughing at yourself. The next is lion laughter, where you stand in front of a mirror, open your mouth wide, and do a laughing roar. Finally, there is crying laughter, where you lean forward and cry and then laugh as you lean back.[46] To get the benefits of simulated laughter you want to try to laugh for at least three minutes, twice a week for six to eight weeks. If simulated laughter alone doesn't work for you, there are also group sessions that allow you to do it with a trained instructor. The most popular are laughter yoga and laughter meditation. And with the numerous benefits of laughter programs, it is also important to note there are very few downsides in case you are hesitant. In a review of forty-five studies that included more than 2,500 participants, only three people in a single study using laughter yoga reported any discomfort. From laughing so much, these people experienced a higher heart rate, dry mouth, and feeling breathless. None of these required any medical intervention.[47,48]

With all the benefits that laughter can bring, prioritizing laughter each day should be as important as improving your diet and sleep. Luckily this is much easier to do, especially if you are fortunate enough to have some mini laughter mentors in your lives.

Spending Time with Little People

As you know by now, I'm an advocate for spending time with toddlers, for all the lessons they can teach us. Many of them are contained in this book and will be brought to life if you observe them. None of the lessons, however, will immediately jump out at you and improve your life faster than the laughter a toddler can provide. I can guarantee they will make you laugh in a short period of time, and anything silly you say will be met with toddler belly laughter rather than a blank, slightly confused stare an adult might give you.

The benefits of spending time around young children is probably best exemplified in older adults who live in retirement homes. In what they called a social experiment, faculty members from the University of Bath and the University of Brigham wanted to see what would happen if they consistently surrounded elderly people with preschoolers. To do this, they set up a preschool within a retirement community in Bristol. This brought together ten four-year-olds and eleven people in their late eighties for a six-week program. Baseline cognitive and physical function were measured in the elderly residents and then repeated at three and six weeks. At the end of the program, the residents showed improvement in both physical activity and mental health.[49] This by itself is good news, but what was perhaps the best part of surrounding elderly people with children was the happiness these preschoolers brought to everyone.

What's so wonderful about this experiment is that it was filmed and turned into a TV show titled *Old People's Home for 4 Year Olds*, first in the UK and then in Australia. These clips, which are available online, beautifully encapsulate everything I have written about. You can see how the young child's natural state has such a powerful effect on the retirement home residents. Children engage their new friends in games, dancing, and singing all with big smiles and plenty of jokes. Laughter naturally flows from children to everyone around them. At one point, to understand them a bit better, each child is asked what love is. Young Max doesn't even need to think about it before he says it's "a great leaping of joy in my heart."[50]

Joy is what toddlers believe in and what they bring to others.

Toddler Teachings

A good chuckle before learning will help you remember information, even for the most boring subjects.
Smiling and laughing with others is the easiest way to get more best friends.
At least twice a week, start a tickle fight, a spontaneous game of peek-a-boo, or some other type of laughter therapy. It's good for both your physical and mental health.
If you don't have a friend to laugh with, try simulated laughter.
Spend time with people who like to giggle, like toddlers.

Chapter 4:

Reading

Story time, all the time!

Toddlers don't particularly like going to see their pediatrician for regular checkups, mainly because they know what almost always happens: shots. Afterward, doctors will try to offer them some sort of reward for their bravery, such as stickers, crayons, or a lollipop, but the only thing I have seen that will make them instantly forget about their boo-boo is a book. When I was doing my pediatrics residency more than a decade ago, I worked at the Windsor Street Care Center in Cambridge, Massachusetts. This clinic provides a variety of medical services and, within pediatrics, serves twenty-five thousand patients, who come from diverse socioeconomic backgrounds. Thanks to the nonprofit Reach Out and Read, we had an entire closet filled from floor to ceiling with books for babies, toddlers, and older children. At every routine well child visit, children and their parents would get to choose a book to take home. And there are eleven of these visits from birth to age five. I still remember the excitement the toddlers had as they ran toward the magical closet. Once the doors were opened, their faces beamed with pure awe. Without understanding the profound effects of reading, they knew that books were special. For them, books allowed entry into new worlds and were a preferred method to satisfy their natural drive to learn new things.

Unfortunately, like the humor cliff we discussed in Chapter 3, there is also a reading cliff we go off as we age. Research from the National Literacy Trust in the UK shows that at age five, more than half of children read daily outside the classroom. This then drops to about one in five by the time they are teenagers.[1] In adulthood, the level of daily reading for personal interest stays low until about age fifty-five, when it finally starts to increase. Adults ages sixty-five and over have the highest average.[2] This level, however, never reaches that of a five-year-old. There is no data for children under five because at this age, they are not reading like the rest of us, but they certainly engage with books as much as they can. Whenever it is playtime with my two-year-old daughter, the top three activities in order are: read a book, make a puzzle, blow bubbles. In fact, her first full sentence was "I want to read a book." She reads so much that she even wore out her board book copy of Bill Martin Jr. and Eric Carle's *Brown Bear, Brown Bear, What Do You See?*[3] after flipping through the pages multiple times daily for more than a year. How many adults can say they wore out a book from reading it too much?

Clearly since you are reading this you are not in the category of the nearly one in four adults who have not read a book in the past year.[4] But you are also probably not in the category of aggressive toddler reader who needs to replace books. In this chapter, we will discuss why it is important to develop toddler-like reading habits. Not only does reading provide specific developmental benefits to toddlers, but many of these also translate to adults, such as improved cognitive functioning and building vocabulary. As we will see, reading can have the power to influence behavior in both adults and children. Perhaps most importantly, we will also review why reading is so important for adults long-term as it can provide important brain exercise to protect against dementia. Finally, we will explore the concept of deep reading, discuss the different ways you can consume books, and help you decide which method might be best for you.

Toddler Reading and the Drive to Learn

I should note here that although we discuss toddler *reading* throughout this chapter, it may not mean what most people think it means. Toddlers are not looking at the letters in a book, sounding them out, and then understanding the specific words. They go through different stages of rapid development between the ages of one and five, and only after that do they generally recognize familiar words in print and can read simple words. By age six to seven they can read familiar stories.

So while toddlers are not reading by its strict definition, we can still learn a lot from them by how much they make books part of their lives. Between the ages of one and three is a special time when all toddlers discover their love of books. It is during this period that they start to build their own little libraries and know the names of their books. They also decide on a favorite book and request to read it repeatedly. At this age, they learn to turn pages themselves and can answer questions about the books, as well as finish sentences in books they are familiar with.

At age three, they are ready to do everything themselves, and when it comes to books, they will explore books independently, imitating the action of reading a book aloud. At age four they understand how print is read, from left to right and top to bottom, can name some letters in the alphabet, and retell stories.[5] While these are the textbook developmental steps that toddlers and preschoolers progress through in their journey to read, what they do in practice also includes trying to get every adult around them to read stories and go through as many books as they can each day.

One of the reasons toddlers love to read goes back to one of the foundational concepts we have discussed, and that's learning. Learning is one of the most powerful drivers of toddler motivation. Specifically, they don't just want to learn facts; they also want to know how things work. Toddlers will ask questions persistently about new tools so that they can better understand what they are used for.[6] Four-year-olds have also been shown to prefer getting information from adults who they deem to have more knowledge about certain objects.[7] The title of "little scientists" given to them by the renowned Swiss psychologist Jean Piaget describes them perfectly.[8]

So when toddlers and preschoolers discover books, they are instantly drawn to them because they can learn how things work. This was demonstrated in a study published in 2020 from Vanderbilt University and the University of Texas at Austin, where researchers sought to learn what type of books toddlers prefer. For this study, forty-eight three- and four-year-olds were read two different animal books. The first was *What Do You Do When Something Wants to Eat You?*,[9] which contained information on how an animal's body part was important for survival. The second book, *Biggest, Strongest, Fastest*,[10] contained factual descriptions. Of note, these books were written by the same author and had similar pictures. Each of the books were read to the children by an experimenter. Children were asked comprehension questions on the books and asked which one they preferred. They scored similarly for comprehension but clearly preferred books that provided more explanations.[11]

If we can understand how strong this drive to learn new things is for toddlers, then it makes perfect sense why they are doing everything possible to engage with books. Spending more time reading is a profound change that we can all make and comes with enormous benefits as we will see later in this chapter, including potentially prolonging our lives.

The Reading Brain

Unlike kindness and sharing behavior, which has evolutionary roots as we discussed in Chapter 2, reading is a relatively recent phenomenon in human history and is not hardwired at birth. Writing was invented about 5,400 years ago in Babylon, and until recently, only a small percentage of the human population was able to read. Despite this, as we saw in the introduction in our discussion of neural pathways, our brain can rewire itself to learn new things. Reading provides an amazing way to do this as it connects different areas of the brain used for other functions, including vision, language, working memory, and attention.[12]

Researchers have used fMRI to demonstrate areas of the brain that are activated by reading in both children and adults. And there is good news: No matter what reading level someone starts at, the brain can adapt and engage different regions, even for disadvantaged children. In a study from Cincinnati Children's Hospital, researchers examined twenty-two four-year-olds from households that earned less than $15,000 per year. In the study, the children listened to stories through headphones, without any images, while they were in an fMRI machine. They then had shared reading time with their mothers with *The Little Engine That Could*,[13] and this interaction was scored on a quality scale. Ultimately, the researchers found nine different areas of the brain that were activated in these children when they heard the stories. They also found that those preschoolers who had access to more books at home, had more reading time with their mom, and had higher-quality reading time all had higher activity of these brain areas. This study not only demonstrates the importance of reading for young children as their brain is maximally capable of rewiring but also demonstrates that even small changes in reading accessibility, such as having more books and spending more time reading, were associated with differences in brain function.[14]

Similar work using fMRI also has been done with adults in France demonstrating that you can still change your brain regardless of when in life you learn to read. In this study, researchers examined ten illiterate people, twenty-two people who became literate as adults, and thirty-one who became literate as children. They found that all the literate people, no matter when they learned to read, had increased brain activity in areas responsible for writing, visual responses, and speech recognition, compared to those people who were illiterate.[15] So even later in life, learning to read or reading more continues to reorganize the brain to form important connections.

Reading Benefits for Toddlers

"I want to be a panda!" exclaimed Arya. It was a bit of an odd response to my question, "What do you want to be when you grow up?" but for a good six months now she has not changed her mind. It turns out she learned about pandas from a book her class read in day care. Since that time she enjoys rolling on the ground, pretending to eat bamboo, and hanging over the arm rest of the couch on her stomach, like a panda would do on a tree branch. And while I'm fully supportive of her goal to become a panda, what is fascinating to me is the power a single book had on her thinking. Not only did she learn facts, but it actually changed her behavior.

In the process of rewiring our brains, the benefits of reading go well beyond learning. While there are some shared benefits between adults and toddlers, such as increasing vocabulary and improving comprehension, reading has also been shown to benefit toddlers and adults in different and interesting ways. The principle, however, remains the same. The more reading you do, the better it is for you. In this section, we'll start with some studies on toddlers to see how reading has the power to shape behavior, and then, in the next section, we will move on to adult studies to see how the effects of reading go well beyond knowledge acquisition and behavior change.

For children in general, self-control is one of the most important predictors of long-term success. There have been many studies that have demonstrated this, but perhaps the best data comes from the Dunedin Multidisciplinary Health and Development Study. This study started by following 1,037 people born in 1972 in Dunedin, New Zealand, and is still ongoing. In one of the publications from this study, researchers looked at how self-control had affected these people's lives by the time they were in their thirties. As children, they had been assessed for self-control at age three, five, seven, nine, and eleven by researchers, teachers, parents, and the children themselves. At age thirty-two, and after controlling for a wide variety of factors, the researchers found that self-control was a predictor of better health, more wealth, and decreased criminal activity.[16]

Given that self-control is so important in one's life, it is fascinating to see what young children do when they read a book centered on the exertion of willpower. In a study done by researchers at the University of Pennsylvania and Stanford University, eighty-six four- and five-year-olds participated in a story-time session. The children were randomly assigned to be read one of two versions of a book with a character that either conveyed the idea that self-control can be energizing or not. After the story, the researcher left two gummy bears in one pile and three gummy bears in another pile, and the children were given a bell. If they rang the bell, the researcher would come back, and they could receive the smaller treat. If they did not ring the bell, and the researcher came back on their own, they would get the larger treat. The children who heard the story about willpower being energizing, not only used more effective self-control strategies (covering their eyes, turning away from the treat), but they were also able to wait an additional three and a half minutes.[17]

While the power to influence willpower is remarkable, even more interesting is the power of reading to influence eating behavior. Eating vegetables is hard for both toddlers and adults, and most of us do not eat the recommended amount each day. Toddlers would rather practice their fine motor skills by squishing peas or give themselves a new sensory experience spreading hummus over every part of their face. Tricks to get them to eat more vegetables such as covering them in ketchup or the classic airplane coming in for a landing are only sometimes successful. Adults simply avoid vegetables because of the many options to eat something that tastes better (and has many more calories). For toddlers, at least, there is some hope in that books can influence the type of foods they eat. In a fascinating study from the University of Reading, UK, scientists enrolled 127 one- and two-year-olds. Their parents were asked to choose one vegetable that their child refused to eat and that they wanted their

child to eat. The toddlers were then randomly assigned to either receive a picture book of their target vegetable or not. Parents read the
books to the children every day for two weeks, and then there was
a two-week taste exposure phase where the vegetables were offered.
Compared to the group without a book, children who read the book
about the vegetable were found to not only like the vegetable more
after three months, but they also ate more of that vegetable.[18]

For toddlers, reading not only has the power to improve brain
function in ways we would expect, such as increasing vocabulary
and improving language skills, but it can also influence their behavior in surprisingly positive ways.

Reading Benefits for Adults

So far, we have touched on several important benefits of reading
for adults, including creating new neural pathways,[19] improving vocabulary, and improving sleep as we saw in Chapter 1. But there are
countless other advantages of reading. The research on this topic is
similar to sleep research in that the more work is done, the more
benefits we learn about over time. As you will see, the theme of this
section is how reading, like we saw in toddlers, can influence our
minds. But unlike toddlers, where we see several language benefits as
well as positive behavioral changes, reading for adults is even more
powerful because it can protect our brains from the changes we don't
want.

Before we get into how reading protects our brains, we'll first look
at the data on how it can influence our behavior in a positive way,
like it does for toddlers. Most of the data here comes from studying
how reading influences us to become more empathetic, and the
strongest data is for reading fiction. As cognitive psychologist Keith

Oatley from the University of Toronto explains in a review article, reading fiction allows the reader to essentially be in a simulator. He points to studies that show, for example, when a character in a story pulls a cord, the areas of the brain in the reader that are associated with grasping light up on fMRI. When we read about characters, especially in literary fiction, we can become emotionally involved and understand experiences that aren't part of our daily life. In this way we develop a better social understanding of others.[20] Oatley points to his team's previous research done after adult participants read either fiction or nonfiction, which showed that exposure to fiction was more positively associated with the Mind's Eye Test.[21] In this test, users are shown pictures of other people's eyes and need to match words describing emotions to these photos. This is a measure of empathy. And other research has shown that participants who read fiction had the strongest social cognitive performance.[22] In other words, they can better understand what other people are thinking and feeling.[23] Overall, it's clear that reading fiction improves our understanding of others and our ability to empathize with them.

This idea hits home for me whenever I read one of my and Arya's favorite books, *Love You Forever*, by Robert Munsch.[24] This book was published when I was a toddler, in 1986, and I remember reading it with my mom. It has since sold more than 30 million copies. In the story, a mother watches her son progress through life stages and at each one, holds him in her arms and sings a lullaby. Eventually, the mother becomes too old and sick to do this, so her son holds her and sings it instead. Although I have tried, I have not been able to read this book to Arya without crying, and almost immediately after, I always call my mom.

In addition to changing our behavior to become more empathetic, regular reading also has the power to protect our brain from deterioration. One of the most difficult parts of aging is the change we all undergo in how we think. Our brains rapidly develop throughout toddlerhood, and although the pace of this slows down, we continue to expand our thinking abilities until about the age of thirty. After that, these abilities slowly decline with age. Imaging studies have shown that there are areas of our brain that decrease in size as we get older. At first, the changes we experience from this decline are unnoticeable, but the more we age, the more they are apparent. We have more difficulty with multitasking, attention, and word finding. For some people, this can be even more challenging as they have a faster cognitive decline than what would normally be expected for their age. This can be either mild cognitive impairment (MCI) or dementia. With MCI, your ability to do everyday tasks, such as cooking and getting dressed, are not affected. With dementia, your ability to do these tasks is affected. Dementia can also come with other issues such as personality changes, forgetfulness, and repetitive questioning.[25]

MCI is very common, especially in older adults. The American Academy of Neurology estimates that by age sixty, between one in twenty and one in ten people have MCI, and by age eighty, it's one in every four people. People with MCI have a higher risk of progressing to dementia.[26] Luckily there are some things we can do to decrease our risk of suffering from MCI and dementia in the future. Most of these we discussed in Chapter 1 and include better sleep, a better diet, and regular exercise. Additionally, quitting smoking is helpful. Besides taking care of our physical health, it's also important to keep our brain active, and the easiest way to do this is by reading.

One of the best studies that has looked at the protective effect of reading is a study of adults over sixty in Taiwan. This study included nearly two thousand older adults followed for fourteen years after collecting baseline data from them. The authors had initially asked participants how much they read, and several other questions including education level because this is a known protective factor against dementia. They found that over the long-term, those adults who read at least once a week had a reduced risk of cognitive decline, and this was true no matter what their educational level was. In this study, reading counted if participants read books, magazines, or newspapers.[27] And while they didn't ask about the amount of time people spent reading in a day, previous research in Taiwan has shown this number to be at least an hour among older adults who read.[28]

While this correlation doesn't imply causation, as there could always be unmeasured factors that explain it, we do know that reading is mental exercise for the parts of the brain most vulnerable to the aging process. These include working memory, episodic memory, and executive control.[29] So it makes sense that engaging these parts of your brain will keep those neural connections stronger for a longer period of time.

While protecting against dementia is incredible, the benefits of reading may go well beyond that, to increase our life span. In a twelve-year study with more than 3,500 participants over fifty, researchers at the Yale University School of Public Health analyzed a survey dataset where people were asked about how they spend their time doing a variety of activities, including reading.[30] In order to tease out if the type of reading material mattered, participants were specifically asked about reading books, newspapers, and magazines. Overall, the researchers found an incredible 20 percent reduction in death for those who read books compared to those who did not read books. And a couple of other findings are fascinating. First there was a dose-response relationship, meaning that the more people read books, the lower their risk of dying. Next, the survival effect was greater for books compared to reading newspapers or magazines. And, importantly, this effect of reading books persisted for both genders, different education levels, different levels of wealth, levels of depression, and other important factors. In research terms, this is a "survival advantage," and all it took was reading thirty minutes per day.[31]

How to Get Lost in a Book

An obvious question that comes to mind from the longevity study is why was there a greater effect for books compared to newspapers and magazines? What is it about books that make them potentially more beneficial? The answer is not in the material itself; it's how we can better immerse ourselves with books compared to other media. The more we can engage with the material, think about it, and process it, the more neural connections we can form or strengthen. This is how we can exercise our brains, and toddlers do this all the time.

Going through a book with a toddler is an entirely different experience than if you were to go through it on your own. Each page requires careful, slow reading (or sometimes singing) of the text, often to the point the child memorizes it. The pictures require explanations, pointing, and touching. Sometimes you will get a few pages in only to have the toddler flip back a few pages as the connections between different parts of the story are formed in the toddler mind. There are questions along the way about new words they hear, something in the story that is unclear, or perhaps an image they might not be familiar with. Finally, when you reach the end of the book, about twenty times longer than it would have taken you to read it straight through, the request (or demand) inevitably comes, "Again!"

Although tedious, toddlers are onto something here. The

deliberate process of truly engaging with a book, asking questions, and making connections is an act known as "deep reading." And while the entire process of deep reading goes well beyond that to include deductive reasoning, analogical skills (making comparisons), reflection, and insight beyond what a toddler brain has been developed to do, they have the right idea.

In an article published in *The Guardian* titled "Skim Reading Is the New Normal. The Effect on Society Is Profound," Maryanne Wolf, Director for the Center of Dyslexia, Diverse Learners and Social Justice at UCLA, discusses how our ability to read is changing. Since reading and synthesizing information is not ingrained but rather adapted, these abilities will continue to adapt with the latest reading culture. Wolf is concerned about reading processes that are "fast, multi-task oriented and well-suited for large volumes of information, like the current digital medium." If this is the type of reading we continue to do, skimming short online articles and spending hours on e-mail, our brain circuitry will adapt to this. This can lead to "cognitive impatience," where we no longer have the endurance to read longer texts, and more importantly, we diminish our ability to critically analyze text and comprehend the complexities.[32,33] This is more of a problem with digital reading where readers do more scanning and skimming of text[34] but can be applicable to anything we read.

Deep reading is so important that there is even a course on it at Maastricht University called Project Deep Learning. In this month-long course, a single text is used, and students are encouraged to read slowly, reread, and think about what they are reading. The purpose of the course is to "understand and ultimately enjoy a particular text to the fullest extent possible."[35] While it would be wonderful to go to the Netherlands and take this course, there are ways you can train your brain to do deep reading at home if you are not already practicing this. The method Wolf used herself was to sit in an environment with no stimulation, including screens, for twenty minutes each night and read a physical book. She says it took discipline and nearly two weeks to retrain her brain. After this initial period she was able to increase her deep reading to twenty minutes in the morning and twenty to forty minutes in the evening.[36]

While this method may not be ideal for you, there are some things that might help. First, if you can, use a physical book. While it is still possible to do deep reading on a screen, you will likely have more success with physical books. As Wolf explains, "There's a psychological assumption that when we see a screen, we assume it moves fast."[37] Next, like sleep, you must eliminate all distractions, especially your phone. Keeping it out of sight, in another room is best. Then, set a minimum time and not a minimum number of pages. You want to read carefully, and it does not matter how many pages you get through. The important part is that you spend time reading without distractions. Anywhere between twenty and forty minutes is good to start, and then you can slowly build up to longer reading sessions if you have time. Next, it's important to be consistent. If you can develop a deep reading habit daily, as part of your nighttime routine, that would be ideal. If you can't set aside time for reading daily, try for at least two to three times per week. And finally, try to engage with the book as much as you can. There are many ways to do this. For some people this may mean highlighting and rereading passages. Other people create book summaries, which they refer to. And some people like to discuss books in a book club or with a friend. And of note, the book can be any genre, fiction, or nonfiction.

No matter how you do it, keep in mind that deep reading is

challenging and takes time to develop. You will end up reading fewer books overall, but the ones you do, you'll understand better, which will be more rewarding in the end.

Digital, Print, or Audio?

So far, we have established that the lessons from toddlers about reading often, reading with purpose, and deep reading can have a significant impact on improving and potentially prolonging your life. That being the case, the last question we need to address is how we should consume a book. With so many options available, it's sometimes hard to choose between audiobooks, printed books, and e-books. And depending on what your goals are, how you are able to fit books into your life, and what is the easiest to do, you may have different preferences in different scenarios. But let's discuss these in more depth so you are able to make an informed decision on what to choose.

We'll start with audiobooks because, by the very nature of how we consume them, they are quite different from books we read. Audiobooks also have less comparative data and research behind them, which we can review briefly before we get to other types of books. For research purposes, the simplest and most direct way we can measure how much we get out of a book in any format is by measuring comprehension. For audiobooks, the research has been quite mixed with some studies reporting better comprehension with audiobooks and others reporting that reading was better. The best way to sort out how all the data looks when put together is with a meta-analysis, which was conducted at the University of Dakota. In this study, educational psychologist Virginia Clinton-Lisell compared forty-six different studies with more than 4,600 participants. Most of the studies were done with adults, but secondary and elementary students were also included. Text passages, both in print and electronic were compared to identical material presented in audio format. The studies included both narrative and expository text. In the end, although the modalities performed similarly for comprehension of the basic facts and information, reading outperformed listening for understanding the underlying meaning of the text and general comprehension beyond the basic facts. There was also a benefit noted when the reading was self-paced, compared to listening to the same text.[38]

So, while audiobooks are an important and useful way we can gain information, it may be that it is better to be reading in order to go beyond the basic level of comprehension, if that's your goal. It's also helpful to set your own pace, something audiobooks allow you to do to some degree, but reading text allows you to change in the moment. Another, perhaps more important, thing to keep in mind is that the people being studied in these experiments do their reading and listening in controlled, quiet, and undistracted environments. While this is hopefully how we are able to read books, it's often the case that audiobooks are listened to while the user is doing something else, such as driving or walking the dog, and so the comprehension gap between reading and listening would likely widen.

Now, let's turn our attention to electronic books. As I've argued in this book, we can learn many lessons from toddlers, but focus might not be one of them. Giving a toddler an e-book is a perfect example of this. With all the colorful buttons, switches, lights, and animal noises such as "moooo," almost any toddler would rather sit there and mash the buttons to hear fun sounds rather than go through the story. Adults are not that much different and are easily distracted by electronic devices. This is not to say e-books are not useful. There are, of course, many advantages to e-readers including portability, capacity, adjustable text size, translation, and the fact that it is easier to search for information. And, if you are used to reading electronic text and read more because of it, then that's fantastic, and you should keep it up. However, for those of you who use e-readers and read physical books without a strong preference, you may find after this brief review of the evidence that reading physical books is the preferred way to read.

For toddlers, we know that they have a preference for physical books. In a national survey from the nonprofit BookTrust in the UK, parents were asked what their children from birth to age eight prefer to read. They found children preferred physical books 76 percent of the time when reading for pleasure and 69 percent of the time when reading for educational purposes when compared to both simple e-books and interactive e-books. Some of the reasons given why children like physical books were that they like turning pages, they like to have ownership of print books, and they like choosing books from the library.[39]

More compelling than preferences is data we have from a 2019 videotaped study conducted at the University of Michigan. Researchers sought to understand what happens when toddlers interact with their parents with physical books compared to e-readers. In this study, thirty-seven two- and three-year-olds, along with a parent, were videotaped reading print books, basic electronic books, and enhanced electronic books that included sound effects or animation. What they were capturing on tape were all the positive interactions toddlers and parents have with each other while reading a book, such as "What is that?"; "Show me the cat"; and "Great job, you're turning the page!" Of course, being with a toddler also came with negative directives such as "You can't keep pressing the back button" and "Don't rip the book." And no toddler interaction would be complete without off-topic discussions (a toddler would argue these are very much on topic) such as "You can have your goldfish later" and "We are going to the store after this." Subsequently analyzing all these interactions, the authors found that compared to electronic books, toddlers who read a print book with their parent demonstrated more verbalizations, had higher quality interactions (measured by a scaled score), and had a higher level of collaboration in their discussions.[40]

What we can say from this study is that toddlers show us how much more they are getting out of print books. Aside from childhood preference, a print book offers more opportunity for questions and engagement.

As with audiobooks, the data on adult comprehension of e-books has been mixed, and again we will turn to a meta-analysis, as these types of studies can combine years of data, in multiple contexts, with different types of people. In 2018, researchers from Spain and Israel conducted one such analysis. To ensure they were drawing from high-quality data, the researchers only included studies that involved adults who read alone and silently, where the reading material was similar in terms of content, structure, and images, and where there were no text features that only digital material could provide, such as hyperlinks. In the final analysis, the researchers used fifty-four studies published over an eighteen-year period and included an astonishing 171,055 participants.

Overall, the study found that people who read printed material had better comprehension than those who read electronic material. There were a few other interesting findings, as well. First, when participants were time constrained, the advantage of reading printed material increased. Second, the type of reading material mattered. Readers had higher comprehension reading printed materials if the text was informational or a mix of informational and narrative. Finally, and perhaps most interesting, is that over the study period, 2000–2017, the advantage of paper-based reading increased. We would think that as people were exposed to more screen reading over time, they would adapt and get better, but this was not what the authors found. Furthermore, the age of the participants did not matter, so younger "digital natives" did not have an advantage.[41]

Although the authors weren't looking for a specific cause of the advantage of reading printed material in their study, they do point to the *shallowing hypothesis* as one potential explanation. What this hypothesis says is that because most of our interactions with digital media, on screens, consist of brief interactions and immediate rewards, it may be difficult to use those same or similar devices for harder tasks. The authors also point to previous research that demonstrates the more adolescents use digital media, the lower their text comprehension.[42]

While this data is strong, it should be acknowledged that some people do better with reading comprehension after reading digital passages. And although it was a small study, research has shown that those who generally do worse with reading comprehension when reading digital text can improve with practice.[43]

Reading should be enjoyable and done as much as you are able to. If you like reading physical books, wonderful, you will likely comprehend more. On the other hand, if you are someone who spends time highlighting, rereading, and making notes with electronic material more than print, then this is likely more beneficial. It's also possible that maximizing comprehension is not your goal for what you are reading, and that's okay. Some people will choose a mix of printed reading when they want to retain more information and digital reading when they are simply reading for pleasure. The fact that you are reading is what matters most.

Toddler Teachings

Whenever you are given the option of a prize or reward for yourself, choose a book. The benefits are endless.

Try to make reading a daily habit, especially at night. Aim for at least twenty to forty minutes of undistracted story time.

Mix up your reading between make-believe and real stories. Make-believe can help you learn about how others feel and make you more empathetic. Real stories will teach you more about the world.

Slow down when you read. Feel the pages, pause, go back if you need to. Make some scribbly notes. This type of deep reading is important for keeping your brain engaged.

If you can, pick up a real book. Audiobooks and e-books are fun and are still good for learning, but physical books will help you comprehend more.

Chapter 5:

Play

Having fun equals a better life.

While most of us are busy at our regular jobs throughout the day, toddlers keep themselves busy playing. While play is obviously different from work, toddlers arguably get a lot more out of how they spend their time than we do (and are far more engaged). This may not be immediately obvious because when we think of play, we think of having fun. Toddlers do too; however, they also use play for a wide variety of other purposes critical for their development. Play changes both the structure and function of the developing toddler brain. It facilitates learning and improving memory while also decreasing the body's stress response. Play in children has been shown to improve math skills, language, social development, peer relationships, and physical development, among others.[1]

Just as toddler play enhances brain function in a wide range of areas, the same is true for adults who are more playful. Playful adults report being happier and having better coping skills. Research in adults has also shown that while highly playful adults have the same stressors as others, they are able to react to them differently, and it is easier for them to overcome those same stressors. Additional research shows that being playful makes adults more attractive to potential romantic partners and is associated with long-term relationship satisfaction.

Sadly, play is another activity, like reading and laughter, that falls away after toddlerhood, but there are many reasons to bring it back into our lives. So let's discuss why play is so helpful to perhaps convince you that you should be playing more. We will first start with toddler play in a typical day care setting and see some examples of what play is doing to develop their skills. We will then discuss the benefits you can have by integrating more play into your own life. Finally, we will end by examining some of the barriers that adults might face when trying to integrate play into their lives and a simple bedtime routine that may help bring play back. After understanding the benefits of play, hopefully you won't see play as silly or a waste of time. The only thing silly would be if you didn't spend some time being playful each day.

It's Not Just a Game for Toddlers

If we look at a typical day care classroom, with all the toys for children to play with and an outdoor space for them to do the same, it may seem on a superficial level that toddlers are there to have fun. This is only partially true, as there is so much more going on. Let's take the example of two-year-old Arya spending an hour playing at day care to see what her brain is doing and how she is benefiting from her time spent playing. In this example, she initially gets free playtime, and then her teacher steps in for some guided play. Observing her fascinating behaviors can help us understand her better and how her play session is shaping her brain, beyond the fun she is having along the way.

To start, Arya walks over to an area with some simple objects and picks up a wooden rod. Remembering one of her favorite books in which Clifford the Big Red Dog helped put out a fire, she pretends the rod is a firehose and walks around putting out fires to help people. As we have seen, she is wired to do kind things for other people, and at the time, putting out fires seems like a good way to start. Most importantly she puts out the fire in the reading corner as books are the most valuable physical items in the room for her and her friends. As she marches around, she tells Jackson and Reggie what she is doing, and they join in to help, each holding a different section of the firehose as they carry it around the room. Soon, all the fires are put out, and there are high fives all around.

What Arya is doing here is called object play. At the most basic level, through exploration and handling of the object itself, she is learning about its physical properties. She can understand how heavy it is, how it moves through space, and that it might knock down other objects. Standing at three feet tall, she figures out that she can use the rod to reach higher objects. This type of spontaneous discovery is invaluable as she prepares to tackle bigger challenges as she gets older. With the wooden rod, she is also learning about the use of symbolic objects and abstract thought. Today, this rod is a firehose, but maybe tomorrow it will be a tree, or a rocket ship for squirrels. With the involvement of her friends, Jackson and Reggie, Arya also used the play session to develop her communication and language skills. This type of play with others is called social play and allows children to learn to cooperate, negotiate, and develop rules—all critical social skills.[2]

Next, it's time to head outside! As Arya steps out onto the mini-playground area, she meets some new friends, Sally and Kosta. The three of them decide to go up and down the slide. Each time, they try something a bit different to prove to themselves that they can do it and to show their friends. Sometimes it's pushing off with their hands to gain a bit of speed, other times it's a small jump at the beginning or the end. This type of outdoor play does a few things. First, as we talked about in Chapter 1, it provides exercise, crucial to any human's well-being. Next, it allows them to take risks and further develop their motor skills. And similar to other types of play, Arya is practicing important social skills such as taking turns.

As the children all eventually come outside, their teacher, Ms. Lauren, then attempts to gather them in a circle for a game of Simon Says. It takes about five minutes to stop the adventurers from running and jumping around in all directions, but eventually Ms. Lauren gets them all to the same place. All it really took was to alert the kids that a new game was starting, which they all wanted to play. She starts the game and says, "Simon says, touch your forehead." Arya touches her forehead and looks around. Looks like everyone is with her. Next, Ms. Lauren says, "Simon says, touch your hair." Arya pats the top of her head. Smiles all around. Then Ms. Lauren says, "Touch your chin." Arya immediately does but then realizes her error. There was no "Simon says" before the command, and she'll have to sit out this round until the next one. This fun game, a type of guided play, allows Arya to develop her executive functioning, one important part of which is inhibitory control. In addition to inhibitory control, guided play sessions that include games with rules can improve other executive functions such as attention control, working memory, problem-solving, and planning.[3,4]

The play session wraps up, and the children head inside for a well-deserved rest and story time, which they are all eagerly awaiting. In that one-hour example of both free and guided play, Arya not only had multiple bouts of laughter (with all the benefits that come with that), but she also did a considerable amount of physical exercise and developed multiple different areas of her brain. Play is a powerful tool to improve well-being, and it is far too underutilized by adults. Even if it only provided fun and laughter, that would be worth the time invested, but it can do so much more, and in the next sections, we'll discuss all the benefits you can get from integrating play into your life.

What Does It Mean to Play?

Play is easy to recognize in toddlers. They spend so much time doing it, it gets mixed into just about every aspect of their lives. They play when they are exercising, they play while they are eating, and generally try to make every activity into a game. They are both playful, as a character trait, and spend time playing, and we will discuss this difference more. For adults, since play happens so much less, it's a bit more difficult to define play. This is, however, important if we want to integrate it into our lives more. One of the reasons adults don't play as much as they used to is that we think in a goal-directed way. Play seems silly, not meeting an objective, and for some, a waste of time. So that's where we should start. Play is an activity that does not have an end goal such as building muscles when strength training. Although there are many benefits to play, which we will discuss, we should acknowledge here this important aspect of play. There is no specific goal. If we are to play more, this is something we have to learn to be okay with. Over time, doing activities for enjoyment and without goals is something we will increasingly seek out.

That's the next piece that's important to play. It is enjoyable. If you are not having fun, then you aren't playing. In line with that, play is also something that you are motivated to do because you like doing it. It has to be voluntary. Some guidance or ideas are perfectly acceptable, but if you would rather not be doing the activity, then it's not play.

Finally, play involves active engagement. This can be with others, with the environment, or with some sort of instrument such as a paintbrush. So watching TV, the way most adults spend their leisure time, would not count as there is very little, if any, active engagement.[5,6] And unfortunately, the US Bureau of Labor Statistics shows that for American adults, who have a little over five hours for leisure activity each day, nearly three hours are spent watching television.[7]

With all these aspects in mind, play is quite freeing. Without any objectives for the activity, being completely voluntary, and allowing us to engage in different ways, play allows us to use our imagination more, create our own rules (or have no rules), and simply have fun. Just thinking about what play is perhaps has already brought to mind some of the potential benefits.

Lastly, we need to spend a bit of time discussing playfulness. This is different from play itself, although closely related. Playfulness is the way we act in certain situations. Most importantly it allows us to reframe situations so that we can experience them as entertaining, intellectually stimulating, or personally interesting. Playful people can use these skills to make challenging situations easier by decreasing tension.[8] Expressed as a behavior, playfulness becomes play. René Proyer, a German psychologist, provides a useful framework for thinking about playfulness and breaks it down into four categories. His model, called the OLIW model, is an acronym representing the four major aspects of adult playfulness. It has been turned into a research measurement tool and used in multiple studies that we will discuss further. For our discussion, it can help us in understanding what playful people do. More importantly, as we discover the benefits of play in this chapter, we can think about areas we excel in and want to bring out more or perhaps areas we want to improve. These categories may bring to mind playful people you know, not just toddlers, and you can learn from them as well.

The O in OLIW stands for *other directed*. This means that the person behaves in a playful manner around other people. They help cheer others up, tell funny stories, and joke around in a way that makes other people feel more relaxed. The next aspect of adult playfulness is *lighthearted*, meaning the person doesn't take things too seriously, is more spontaneous, and doesn't make complicated plans. The third aspect is *intellectual*, described as enjoying thinking about problems and being creative with solutions. And finally, W stands for *whimsical*. These individuals are "amused by oddities and have a preference for extraordinary things and people."[9,10]

Although the OLIW model was developed for adults, toddlers would score very high in an assessment as they incorporate lightheartedness and fun into everything they do. They are always trying to engage others in their play, and *whimsical* describes just about every toddler I have ever met. For adults, the playful state of being as well as the act of playing have incredible benefits, which we will now discuss for the remainder of this chapter.

Playtime Will Decrease Stress and Increase Well-Being

With all the play that toddlers engage in, there are certain risks. Running toward pretend fires with a wooden rod can sometimes lead to falls and cuts. Putting a magic bead in your ear because it's the ideal hiding spot means sometimes it will get stuck. Outdoor play on structures many times the size of you can lead to worse falls and fractures. But that's okay. The benefits of exercise and play far outweigh the risk of injuries, most of which are minor.[11] And the emergency department is always available to deal with any of these issues. Interestingly, one of the ways we at the hospital deal with all of these play-based injuries and what helps children feel less stress when they see us is more play.

The pediatric emergency department can be one of the scariest places for children and caregivers. There are any number of unpleasant things that have to happen, such as sharp needles in your skin, gross medicine that needs to be swallowed, or tweezers in your ear or up your nose to retrieve those magic beads. Despite this, most of our patients who need painful and stressful procedures leave happy. This is largely thanks to a team of child life specialists. These unique health care workers have an incredible job with the goal of decreasing stress and anxiety for children while they are in the hospital. Using a variety of evidence-based techniques, child life specialists help children and parents understand what is happening and make the experience as easy as possible.

One of the techniques used by child life specialists is therapeutic play. This can involve dolls to explain procedures, a game that describes what will happen to the child next, or it can be physiological, like when toddlers reach up to the stars to ensure their elbow reduction was successful. Play in the medical setting has been shown to decrease anxiety, fear, emotional distress, and negative physiological responses such as a higher heart rate or blood pressure.[12] I can tell you, listening for a wheeze in tiny lungs is so much easier when we play three little piggies, and the child, as the wolf, is attempting to blow down houses represented by a finger in front of them.

The data on play to decrease stress spreads well beyond the hospital and for all age levels. Although the research is largely correlational, it extends to a wide number of findings related to well-being in adults. Besides decreased stress, playfulness is correlated with happiness, positive affect, and life satisfaction.[13-17] More playful adults are not only less stressed overall, but being more playful in general is protective against higher levels of stress in objectively stressful situations. This goes back to how being playful allows us to reframe situations, which can mean they become less stressful.

The global COVID-19 pandemic is a good example of a highly stressful situation that affected individuals differently, and there is research examining the question of whether playfulness made a difference. In a 2022 study, research conducted at Florida International University examined over eight hundred American adults to see how playfulness interacted with stress during the pandemic. Research questionnaires were used to measure playfulness, stress, and coping. The study showed that understandably, participants were stressed by the pandemic. However, what they also showed is that people who identified themselves as playful, or said that others would identify them as playful, perceived less stress and had better coping strategies compared to people who said they were not playful. There was also a positive relationship between being more playful and the perception that the stressful situation could be managed rather than the perception of helplessness. The authors describe playfulness as a "beneficial psychological resource" that helps us mitigate stress when it enters our lives.[18]

One of the critiques of the studies we've discussed so far in this section is that they all rely on self-reported data. The individual in the study is reporting on how playful they are as well as on the other factor being studied, such as happiness or stress. As you can imagine, these are difficult to assess and highly subjective. Given this is the case, Proyer published a study in 2018 where he was able to get around this issue by using peer-reported data as well as objective fitness data when he and his colleagues examined the relationship between physical fitness and playfulness. More than five hundred adults ages eighteen to seventy-eight were enrolled. As in other studies, the participants rated themselves on playfulness and in this case, physical fitness. However, about a quarter of the participants also had a romantic partner, family member, or close friend rate them as well. Participants then performed several physical fitness challenges including hand-grip strength testing, a sit to stand test, stair climbing, and additional tests to measure flexibility and coordination. Overall, the researchers had two important findings. First, when comparing self-reports to peer reports, they largely agreed, adding validity to self-reported data on playfulness. And second, overall, playfulness was positively correlated with higher levels of activity, cardiorespiratory fitness, and health behaviors leading to a more active lifestyle.[19]

As we touched on earlier, an important note here is that all the studies in this section were cross-sectional, meaning that a relationship was found between playfulness and a specific measure of well-being at a certain point in time. We can't determine whether playful people are more active, or more active people are more playful, for example, but certainly there is strong evidence that they go together. The fact that playfulness is correlated with such a wide range of well-being measures, and that at least in part we can objectively measure these outside of self-reports, further supports the notion that being more playful is good for you. In the next section, you'll see even stronger evidence for the importance of play as we discuss creativity and a simple yet powerful experiment that can help you form this link.

Use Play to Inspire Creativity

If you spend a bit of time around toddlers, you will see something amazing in the way they live and interact with the world. Not only do they thrive on unstructured playtime, but they can take any situation and turn it into a game. They are creative masterminds, and these two functions, play and creativity, build on each other. The more time they spend playing, the more creative they become, and the more creative their games are, the more they will spend time playing and developing them. As we saw in our example with Arya, a wooden rod became a firehose used to put out fires. Many parents, friends, aunts, and uncles will tell you, often the best gift for a toddler is the box the toy comes in. Sure, the toy makes noise and has flashy lights, but it is limited in what it can do. A box can be an unlimited number of things from a tall seat to a 3D mural using their paint set to a castle if they stack a few more boxes on top, and beyond.

As you might expect, if you were surrounded by a group of these highly imaginative little people all day, they would challenge you to be at peak creativity. In order to keep toddlers engaged, early childhood educators (ECEs) need to constantly think of new and exciting crafts, games, and stories; they have one of the most creatively demanding professions. Since the skill of integrating creativity into games and play is part of the training and formal assessment process for ECEs, they are an ideal group to research to learn more about this link. In 2018, Proyer and his team in Germany examined nearly two hundred ECE students and looked at how they performed in their own training, as well as what they did for leisure on their own time. The researchers found that using the OLIW model, ECEs who had higher grades, which in part formally measure their creativity, scored higher on intellectual and whimsical playfulness compared to those with lower grades. Outside work, there was a positive association between the global playfulness score and the number of hobbies they pursued. And perhaps most interesting, when researchers looked at a subset of nearly fifty ECEs, they found that those who scored highest on whimsical playfulness had the most innovative hobbies as assessed by two independent raters. These included activities such as playing the oboe and making Zentangle drawings, a type of abstract art created with patterns.[20] This is fascinating because if you walk the halls at any day care or preschool, you will see, in my opinion, the most beautiful abstract art. On my fridge I have kept a special painting that Arya made consisting of blue circles, red lines, green thumb prints, yellow dot patterns made with raw broccoli, and some scattered macaroni glued on. It doesn't look like anything, and when I ask Arya about it, all she says is "I made it." A true artist response who wants to leave the interpretation up to the viewer. Toddlers have natural creativity, and it comes through in every activity they do, largely because they can incorporate play so well.

Turning back to adults, if I had to think of the one activity that most resembles toddler free play, it would be improv. Also called improvisational theater, this is an activity that forces adults to be spontaneous, silly, and playful. It's not easy for anyone to do because we are not used to having minimal structure and so few constraints on our activities. For many of us, being silly is something we have long forgotten. Improv, however, is a fantastic way to bring out our inner toddler to both play and be creative.

To test how improv might unlock adult creativity, researchers at Lund University in Sweden performed a study in which they brought improv to the workplace. They had a total of ninety-three participants from nine highly diverse fields, including software engineers, government legal department employees, and human resource managers. Fifty of the participants were in the experimental condition where they took part in three two-and-a-half-hour improv sessions over a five-week period. The sessions consisted of games to build improvisation skills, and there was a "high level of playfulness" throughout. The remaining forty-three participants in the control group did not receive any intervention. Group creativity was measured by assessing the ability of the group to generate creative ideas for a new multi-tool and was scored by independent judges. All participants underwent this assessment before and after the intervention period. After controlling for baseline scores, researchers found significantly higher creativity scores for the teams in the improv group compared to those in the control group.[21]

While it's probably asking a lot of both employers and employees to do improv sessions at work, what if we could make dreaded meetings more playful and boost creativity? The same group from Lund University answered this question using some innovative methods to stimulate play in meetings. Similar to their other study, they had participants from a wide range of organizations. In the experimental group, there were 164 participants making up eighteen meeting groups, and in the control group there were forty-one people making up five meeting groups. These were their regularly scheduled meetings to discuss work, and researchers did not interfere with that. All they did was, halfway through the meeting during a break, place items on the conference table. In the control group, they received a bowl of fruit and dark chocolate. In the experimental group, one of four fun items was randomly selected for the table. There was colorful children's candy, toy guns with foam darts, self-adhesive mustaches, or instructions to play a game in which people would throw up their hands and shout "life is fantastic" when they noticed another person in the meeting touching their face in any way. In both groups, participants rated themselves and the meeting at the halfway point, when the items were introduced, and at the end of the meeting. At the end of the experiment, the researchers found that for the experimental group, the score they called the "meeting creativity climate" showed a significant increase while in the control group there was no change. The meeting creativity climate was measured by five criteria: collaboration, openness of the meeting, openness to new ideas, engagement, and participation. As an added bonus, the experimental group also showed an increase in playfulness and productivity, and the control group did not.[22]

A playful attitude exists within each of us, and sometimes all we need is permission or a nudge to get us going. Otherwise, many adults have great difficulty scheduling time to play. Ironically, because play has been missing in so many of our lives for so many years, it can be hard to even think of what to do when you finally make some time to play. Thankfully, there is a simple solution, and it involves your inner child.

Measuring creativity is challenging, but there are validated research tools to do it. One is the Abbreviated Torrance Test for Adults (ATTA). This simple test asks participants to do three things, for three minutes each. First, participants are given a "just suppose" . . . scenario: They are given a hypothetical situation and are asked questions about it. For example, "Just suppose you can walk on air," and then list problems that you might run into. Next are two drawing tasks that involve simple lines and triangles, and the test-taker must complete the drawings and give it a title. Participants are scored in a number of areas including fluency, flexibility, originality, and elaboration.[23] It's interesting to see that this research tool to assess adult creativity measures how well adults can perform natural toddler behavior. Toddlers regularly engage in "just suppose" scenarios in their mind, such as walking on clouds and flying. Creative drawing tasks are a toddler favorite and something they do daily.

Using this creativity test, researchers at North Dakota State University conducted a study with undergraduates to see what would happen to creativity if they simply thought about their childhood. There were seventy-six participants, and first they were given a writing task. In it they were told that school was going to be canceled on a particular day, and they had to write for ten minutes on what they would do. The students were randomly assigned to an experimental group or a control group, and the only difference was that the participants in the experimental group were told "You are seven years old." After seven minutes of writing, the participants were interrupted and given the ATTA. Overall, the group that was told to think like a child were more creative and produced more original responses. Here are two samples illustrating what two different participants wrote:

Control Condition (Thinking like yourself)

I would go back to bed for a while if school was canceled. I would then get up, check my e-mail, call work to see if they needed me to do anything there, and since they probably would I would go to work until I was done. I then would go home to finish any homework or other things around my apartment, such as cleaning. I would try to get a workout in somewhere or do something outside if it was nice . . . .

Experimental Condition (Thinking like you are a child)

I would start off by going to the ice-cream shop and getting the biggest cone I could get. I would then go to the pet store and look at all the dogs. After that I would go visit my grandma and play a few games of gin. Then she would make me cookies and give me a huge glass of milk. I would then go for a walk, where I would meet up with my friends and would play in the park for hours.[24]

Which one sounds like a better day to you? And which path would lead to a happier, healthier version of yourself (minus the ice cream and cookies)? These paragraphs nicely summarize the underlying thread of the argument of the book. Both thinking and then acting like toddlers have enormous benefits. When the authors of this study went back and looked at all the writing samples together, they found one main difference. Thinking as an adult produced more responses involving obligations while thinking like a child focused more on desires, especially playing with friends. Obligations are important, and of course, we shouldn't neglect these, but adult thinking is often far too focused on these obligations at the expense of play and spending

time with friends. Play is a way of life for children, especially toddlers, and thinking like a child might be a good strategy to try next
time you are planning how to spend your free time outside work.
You could start employing this strategy for half a day on a weekend.
If it works well, this could expand into a full weekend day or two and
maybe even an hour or two on weekday evenings. If you are lucky
enough to have a toddler in your life, feel free to ask them to plan for
you, and they will give you plenty of fun ideas to choose from.

Using Play to Start Romantic Relationships

Whether at the beginning of a new relationship or when looking
at couples who have been together more than fifty years, we can see
the importance of play. At the start, people send signals to potential
partners involving eye contact, smiles, a touch, and humor. We call
this flirting, but what people are actually doing is being playful. In
the long-term, we see how playfulness is essential to relationships by
keeping that spark alive with shared activities and adventures and
jokes that only the other partner understands. As we discussed in
Chapter 3, shared laughter makes people more comfortable, open,
and gives them an immediate sense of connection, which is critical
in building relationships. Similarly, playfulness can help with the
same things, and beyond decreased stress and increased creativity,
adopting this attitude can assist in both finding love and maintaining
relationships long-term.

Since laughter and play are so closely related, it makes sense that
play has evolutionary roots. As we saw in Chapter 3, smiling and
laughter develop naturally at an early age and are shared functions

with other animals. Similarly, we can see play in animals all around us. Dogs chase one another around, otters juggle rocks, and dolphins blow bubble rings. In humans, there are obviously different functions of play throughout one's life, and after childhood one of these is relationship building, specifically for romantic relationships.

How play relates to adult relationships has been put forth as a theory by professor Garry Chick at Pennsylvania State University. In his signal theory of playfulness, adult playful behavior sends messages to potential mates. Specifically, males signal nonaggressiveness through play and females signal youth and the ability to bear children.[25,26] Chick has conducted extensive research on this topic, and in one study, he examined the importance of play in attracting potential partners with 254 college students between the ages of eighteen and twenty-six. They used a survey to ask about sixteen traits that the students would potentially find attractive in a partner and asked them to rate each one on a scale of one to ten from "not desirable" to "extremely desirable."

Taking both genders together, "playfulness," and the associated traits of "sense of humor" and "fun loving" all ranked in the top five. The other two traits in the top five were "kind and understanding" and "healthy." These preferences for having a playful partner beat out "attractive," which ranked tenth, "college graduate," which ranked eleventh, and "good earning capacity," which ranked twelfth. In terms of importance of each of the traits, the authors noted that none of the playfulness traits were ranked lower than four out of ten and the only other trait that was rated to be as important was intelligence. Even if Chick's hypothesis as to what specific messages partners receive when the other person is playful is not entirely correct, there is clearly a benefit to playfulness when attracting others.

So playfulness is important to potential partners and may help in getting that first date, but what happens over time? It turns out, playfulness is also related to longer-term relationship satisfaction. Proyer, who developed the OLIW model, conducted an experiment where he tested aspects of partner playfulness and different aspects of relationship satisfaction. His study had more than 200 hetero-sexual couples who were in a relationship between three months and thirty-seven years. Each member of the couple in the study com-pleted an online questionnaire. Out of the four facets of playfulness described in the model, three were correlated with higher relation-ship satisfaction: other-directed, intellectual, and whimsical. As the authors expected, other-directed playfulness showed the strongest correlation, particularly for engaging in maintaining the relation-ship, future orientation, fascination, and sexual satisfaction. As the authors point out, this makes sense. Acting in a playful way toward others can make them feel good and "strengthen social bonds."[2]

So far, the work discussed in this section is limited by smaller sample sizes and only representing people who identify as hetero-sexual, and either male or female. A larger study published in 2019 from the University of São Paulo, Brazil, included nearly 1200 people and had individuals identifying as cisgender, transgender, and non-binary. Only 60 percent of the people in the study identified as ex-clusively heterosexual. Most participants were in their twenties and thirties. In this study, participants were given the OLIW question-naire to measure playfulness and asked about previous short-term and long-term relationships they had had in their life. A short-term relationship was defined as casual dates without an expectation of staying together, while a long-term relationship did have an expecta-tion of remaining together. In their analysis, what the authors found was fascinating. First, playful adults had more partners, and second, different types of playfulness were used by different genders to compete for mates.[28]

As a final added bonus, playfulness can help in the bedroom. Although preliminary, there has been research specifically looking at adult playfulness and sexuality. In a study published in 2022, Proyer's team studied more than one thousand adults asking them both playfulness questions as well as questions on sexual traits and practices such as sexual restraint, sexual sensation seeking, and BDSM (bondage, discipline, sadism, masochism) practices. They found a relationship between various sexual traits and playfulness, in particular whimsical playfulness, and they also found that people who engage in BDSM are more playful than people who don't engage in those practices.[29]

Taken together, these studies have important limitations as we discussed previously in that the data comes from self-reported preferences and practices. Nevertheless, this growing body of research points to the importance of play in relationships, both as a trait that signals something positive to a potential mate and something that allows couples to interact in a way in which they feel more comfortable and happier over time.

More Playtime

With all the benefits of play, as well as the enjoyment factor, it's probably clear that play is something lacking in our lives. It sounds like a simple thing to do, to go and play more, but for adults this can be incredibly challenging for a few reasons. Let's explore some of those barriers so we can figure out how to get over them.

First, and most importantly, adults don't feel they have permission to play, as if it's somehow not acceptable. Even if we have the time, we have this idea that we talked about before: that we need to be doing something "productive." So this is the first step to getting more play. Understanding that you don't need anyone's permission to play. Yes, there are benefits, but you are allowed to play simply to enjoy yourself. This issue, unfortunately, follows us all the way to senior adulthood. In a study published in 2022 from Ariel University in Israel, researchers examined the impact of medical clowns in residential homes for older adults. Using observational and interview data the authors concluded that one of the main benefits of having a clown was that it gave "legitimacy" to playing. Once the seniors felt as though it was okay to play, they enjoyed themselves with one resident saying, "It's a time in which one doesn't think about problems in life or the fact that one is alone." Sadly, some residents did not participate in play with the clown, and when asked why, one participant said, "It's for [the] elderly or for children." Keep in mind that this person was over seventy.[30] So if we don't give ourselves permission to play right now, we may never get there.

One of the other issues holding us back from spontaneous play is that adults spend a lot of time thinking about the future and what needs to be done rather than living in the present like toddlers do. It's often difficult to live in the present moment when the future causes so much anxiety, but there is at least one temporary solution. In 2019, researchers from the University of Warsaw studied hundreds of undergraduate students to see if their thinking would change if they either thought about their own childhood or took the perspective of a child. In order to measure their orientation to the present, they used a research tool designed to assess present moment enjoyment. A total of four experiments were conducted, and each had an experimental and control group. What the researchers found was that recalling memories from childhood, as well as taking the perspective of a child, made adults more present oriented. In one of the experiments, they didn't even make the child or adult position explicit. In this version, they gave participants thirty sets of five words and had them form sentences. In the experimental group, half the sentences contained childhood-related words such as "naïve" while in the control group, the sentences only contained adult-related words such as "work," "boss," and "document." Even in this experiment the mere presence of words reminding people of childhood made them more present oriented.[31]

So far, for more play, we know we need to give ourselves permission and be more present oriented, which can happen simply by taking the perspective of a child. While these are more related to mindset, let's end this chapter on what you can do practically to add more play to your life. In 2021, Proyer and Chick teamed up with two other researchers to test whether they could stimulate playfulness in adults. They enrolled more than five hundred adults ages eighteen to eighty-four in an experiment in which they were randomized to one of four conditions. Each of these conditions involved spending fifteen minutes before bed thinking about what had happened during the day, how they felt, who was involved, and then writing it all down. In the first group, participants had to write about three playful things that happened to them that day; in the second group, participants were asked to use playfulness in a way they were not used to and write about it; in the third, they had to count all the playful things that happened during the day whether they were involved or not; and finally, in the control group, they were to think about childhood memories and write about them. Each group did this for seven days.

The participants were followed at two, four, and twelve weeks, at which they rated their playfulness, happiness, and depressive symptoms on validated scales. At the end of the experiment, the authors found that, for all time points and for all three playfulness conditions, participants scored higher with respect to playfulness and happiness and lower on the depression scale compared to the control group. It is also worth noting that some participants chose to continue the exercise beyond seven days. While this contributed to some of the observed effects, excluding them from the analysis showed the same overall result.[32]

Being a more playful person has a multitude of benefits, but most importantly, it simply allows you to enjoy your life in the present moment. We need to give ourselves permission to play regularly and not worry about how this is going to affect the future. This is much easier said than done but starting by simply reflecting on play at the end of the day, as well as trying to engage in playful moments in ways you are not used to, can improve your well-being.

Toddler Teachings

Anytime is playtime, and aspects of play can be incorporated into everything you do. Little reminders of play can help get you started.

Give yourself permission to have unstructured play sessions. Every moment of your life does not need a goal. Go have fun!

To be more present, creative, and enjoy some time playing, think of what your child self would do.

Being more playful sends signals to others that you are the type of person they may want to get to know better.

Spend some time each evening reflecting on play during the day. These observations can help you try out new forms of play and use them more often.

Part II:

A Gold Star at Work

Chapter 6:

Teamwork

Let me help you with that.

Many business leaders and professionals regard toddlers as cute oddities, but in fact, these professionals could learn a lot from toddlers as they consistently demonstrate some of the most important teamwork skills useful in any type of workplace. The mechanisms that both enable and motivate us to cooperate with others develop at a very young age. Infants begin taking turns with adults, for instance, when rolling a ball back and forth. By age two, children are able to engage in collaborative tasks, and by age three these shared goals turn into commitments. Three-year-olds expect their partners to follow through on joint tasks, and if they don't, these toddlers will employ a variety of strategies to get their partners back on track.[1]

Great teamwork skills come naturally to every toddler. Without even being asked, they will start participating in the most boring tasks if someone else is doing it and do so happily. In my home, after dinner cleanup is met with excitement and enthusiasm by Arya, who readily grabs the Swiffer each night to make sure all the food she dropped during dinner is swept up. While this usually means the food simply gets spread out and squished on the floor in more areas, I certainly admire the effort.

The drive to work with others is something all toddlers share. Another great example is fifteen-month-old Thomas Pethick, who lives in a small town in British Columbia. His family owns a clean water business that involves daily drop-offs of empty water jugs. In a video posted on TikTok by his mom, you can see Thomas head out to the delivery truck on a snowy day as soon as it arrives. The water jugs are as big as him, but he grabs two at a time and hauls them to the indoor storage area. When he has some downtime, he grabs a shovel and starts shoveling snow. This video was incredibly popular, with more than 33 million views, and all it showed was normal, everyday toddler behavior.[2]

Working with others on various tasks is something almost all of us need to do. For some of us this is almost exclusively what we do in various teams. Over the last two decades, time spent by workers in collaborative activities has increased by 50 percent or more, and at many organizations, 80 percent of an employee's time is spent in collaboration.[3] Often, in a leadership role, it is our responsibility to make sure everyone is working efficiently toward a common goal. Inevitably, team dynamics come into play, which can both positively and negatively influence team members. These dynamics are important to pay attention to as they can influence outcomes.[4] How we react in various scenarios can either guide the team on a path toward success or may hinder the objectives of the team. Negative team dynamics can often be challenging for adults to navigate, and seeing how toddlers do it with ease can be both inspiring and motivating. As we will see, they love cooperative activities. Even after completing a task, their tendency is to reset it so that they and their partner can do it again.[5] As experts in this field, we can learn from toddlers by seeing what they do, proactively, to help decrease negative team dynamics. This chapter will focus on five key toddler teamworking concepts that can help improve any team.

Before we begin, this is a good opportunity to acknowledge the work of Michael Tomasello. Tomasello is a professor of psychology and neuroscience at Duke University and the codirector of the Max Planck Institute for Evolutionary Anthropology in Germany. He has dedicated his entire career to understanding cooperation, communication, and social cognition in young children. The majority of the research in this chapter comes from his lab, and I highly recommend watching his keynote address given to the Association for Psychological Science in 2019 titled "Becoming Human: A Theory of Ontogeny." In his talk, Tomasello has video clips from many of the research projects described throughout this chapter that show how wonderful toddlers can be as team members.[6]

Clear Communication to Reengage a Team Member

When a coworker disengages from a project or doesn't stay on task, we react in a wide range of ways, some of which are more helpful than others. One option is to simply ignore that person and finish the project by yourself or with another team member that continues to work. Another option is to confront the person who stopped working. A third, kinder option would be to guide the person through the task. It is their expertise that may help bring the entire project together, and there may be a reason they were chosen to be part of the team in the first place. For toddlers, working together with others comes naturally. As we saw in Chapter 5, they are intrinsically playful, meaning they can reframe tasks into games. That being the case, when someone starts a game with them and stops midway, they are flabbergasted. It doesn't make any sense to them why someone would do that, and they will do everything they can think of to try to get that person back on task.

In this section we will focus on one study in detail that highlights several important findings of how toddlers cooperate and reengage their partners. As with most toddler skills, their methods are both simple and effective. The study was published in 2006 and involved thirty-two toddlers between one and two years of age.[7] In the study, experimenters first set up four tasks for the toddlers. Two were problem-solving tasks, and two were social games. Each task required that two people perform it either with different actions (complementary) or the same action (parallel). For example, the problem-solving task with complementary actions was called Elevator. In this task there was a cylinder that moved up and down with an object inside. To get the object, one person had to push the cylinder up while the other person retrieved the object. It was not possible for one person to do both functions, as there were screens set up so that one person had to be on the opposite side. After ensuring each child knew how the task worked, the experimenter and the toddler would start the task, and then, suddenly, the experimenter would stop what they were doing for fifteen seconds.

Puzzled by why someone would stop in the middle of a task they were working on with a partner, the toddlers had a few choices. They could either follow suit and stop the task, try to do it themselves, wait for their partner, or reengage their partner. Overall, the most frequently observed behavior was reengagement, and they did this in a few interesting ways that provide two good lessons. First, there was clear communication. The toddlers would both address their partner and communicate the goal or task. For example, in toddler language with a male stranger, they would say "Man!" Secondly, they used words to draw attention to the shared goal. For example, saying "Ball!" in a task in which the goal was to retrieve a ball from an apparatus. Another example of clear communication employed by the toddlers to get their partner to reengage was to give them instructions. They did this both with referential gestures, such as pointing at the apparatus, or simple verbalizations. For example, "Lift it," "Take it out," and "Open." Toddlers did not fault their partners. And as any kindhearted person would do, they were also sure to include "Please."

Direct communication is often all we need to do when working in teams. It may be the case that your teammate does not know their role or perhaps simply missed a calendar invite for a deadline or meeting. There may have been a miscommunication about what needs to be done. Clear instructions, without blame, can often bring that person back on track. And don't forget to say "Please."

The second strategy the toddlers used to reengage their teammate was to go a step further, beyond communication, and gently assist them. For example, one of the problem-solving tasks involved retrieving a toy that was inside a tube. There were handles at each end, and both teammates had to pull their respective handle to release the toy. In this task, when the adult disengaged, some toddlers held the handle and pushed the entire tube over to their teammate to help them. They tried everything they could to help their partner understand what they were supposed to do, and actually do it. This is another strategy we might want to try when it comes to teammate disengagement. Perhaps your partner didn't understand the initial instructions and guiding them through the process another time might be all they need.

For adult teams, poor communication is a serious problem. In a report titled "Communication Barriers in the Modern Workplace," published by *The Economist* in 2018, more than four hundred executives, managers, and staff participated in a survey on workplace communication. Poor communication was identified as a primary factor responsible for a variety of workplace problems. The most common issue was added stress reported by more than half the respondents, and the second most common concern identified was a delay or failure to complete a project. Survey respondents said this happened 44 percent of the time. Overall, the most cited stressful situation at work was having unclear instructions from a senior colleague or manager.[8]

For joint tasks, toddlers think differently than adults. They are more process focused and oriented on the act of working together rather than outcome focused. In the toddler study discussed previously, researchers noted one unexpected observation. Once the toddlers had met their objective for the task, they did not stop. They put the object back in its original position. Out of thirty-two toddlers, thirty of them did this and the researchers conclude that "their attempts to return the object are indicative of their interest in continuing the cooperative activity, which to them is rewarding in itself."[9] So if a team member stops the task, reengaging that person is what toddlers will gravitate to. They do this in a number of ways and, most importantly, first with clear communication addressing both the person they are talking to and explaining the task. If that doesn't work, they go a step further and gently assist their partner.

Rolling with the Punches

Even with the most highly skilled team there are always bumps along the way. Things happen beyond our control, and it's important that we recognize what we can fix and what we can't. As we saw, toddlers act in a way to maximize cooperation. They are also problem solvers, want to make sense of roadblocks, and act in a way that both is "morally relevant"[10] and moves the task forward. What this means is that they have a strong sense of fairness and seek to understand their teammates before deciding on the next course of action. In this section we'll see how toddlers react in two different, unexpected scenarios: first, when they start a joint task and realize their partner is incorrectly doing the task, and second, when the apparatus the toddler and their partner are working on breaks.

In this next experiment, researchers wanted to see what toddlers would do if things didn't go as planned with their partner. This time, instead of an adult, the toddlers had a child partner. The apparatus they used can best be described as a rectangular table, like a pool table, that sat on the ground. A rope was stretched out across the table with one end going to each side. To complete the task, two people had to pull the rope via a handle, which would in turn roll marbles out of the table. The children could then redeem the marbles for stickers. The subjects were the toddlers being tested while the partners were the children who were trained to act in a certain way. Researchers set up three scenarios. The first was a selfish condition in which the partner was trained to detach the handle and use that to open a box to get stickers only for themselves. (As we know from Chapter 2 on kindness, toddlers would never do that on their own, so they had to be tricked into thinking that this was the point of the game, and then they complied.) In the second scenario, called the ignorant condition, the partner was trained to pull the rope from the side of the box rather than from the front, so that the marbles wouldn't roll out. It would appear to the subject child that their partner was making an effort but doing the task incorrectly. And finally, in the third scenario (accidental condition), the handle was rigged to break.

For the purposes of this discussion, we'll focus on scenarios two and three. This experiment had 144 three-year-olds. Half of them were subjects, and half of them were the trained partners. During each of the conditions, researchers looked to see the types of behaviors and verbalizations the toddlers had. This ranged from protesting, teaching, and tattling to normal, irrelevant toddler muttering such as "Blue is a nice color." Toddlers also had their emotional arousal measured when things didn't go as planned from zero, no behavioral change, to three, signs of extreme agitation, frustration, or anger.

Let's start with the emotional arousal results since, as we discussed in the introduction, it's something toddlers have a bad reputation for. Yes, tantrums are real, and sometimes extreme, but it's helpful to see how toddlers react in a situation that doesn't go their way but is one in which they understand and have the means to communicate. We will focus on scenario three in which the apparatus breaks. When this happened, toddlers most often simply stated what happened: "This broke." More importantly, they showed little frustration, not even reaching an arousal level of 0.5 on the 3-point scale. Contrast this with adult reactions to equipment failures. The most easily recognized one is computer rage, which perhaps you or someone you know has experienced.[11] In the United States, more than a third of adults surveyed who experienced computer problems in a six-month period reported lashing out at their computer including using profanity or striking it with their fist or an object.[12] Toddlers understand that equipment failures such as these are largely beyond their control and there is no point in either getting angry or blaming an object.

The next important point in this study was brought out in the "ignorant" condition. In this part of the experiment, the toddlers in the study recognized that their partner was trying to do the task, but they were doing it incorrectly. Sure, their frustration level went up, reaching just below 1 on the 3-point scale, and some protested, "No, not like that," but most importantly, there were two areas where toddlers scored higher in this condition compared to the other two scenarios. First was what the researchers termed "neutral tattling." In this case, toddlers communicated that the game did not work, but they did it without blame. They said things such as "We didn't do it." Second was teaching and guiding their partner through the task, "It goes like this," "Get your rope," and "Heave-ho!" The authors commented that toddlers used teaching to turn "ignorance into knowledge, which presumably will result in more cooperative behavior."[13]

While it is human nature to assign blame when things go wrong,[14] the importance of establishing a workplace culture that does not blame individuals is highly valuable. This type of workplace encourages trial and error and allows for innovation.[15] Some of the most elite teams in the world, such as the Mercedes-Benz F1 racing team, operate this way because it allows them to "get to the root of the problem and then make sure it doesn't happen again," says Mercedes team principal Ian James.[16] And in his book, *The Blame Game*, organizational psychologist Ben Dattner argues that blaming at work "shuts down or prevents learning."[17]

When things don't go as planned during teamwork, toddlers take the time to understand why things aren't working as they should and then act accordingly. When their partner seems to not understand what to do in a task, what they say is most often neutral, and what they try to do is teach the other person to work cooperatively. When it's the actual piece of equipment that's the problem, there is no point in blaming others or getting angry; they simply acknowledge the problem and move on the best they can.

A Respectful Way to Leave a Project

For a variety of reasons, sometimes it is impossible to finish a project and keep our obligations to others. Since toddlers have such a strong sense of commitment to teamwork, they expect no less of others, and in the toddler universe there is certainly a right way and a wrong way to leave a project. Even when approached by a teammate who is asking permission to leave, some toddlers are taken aback. Why would anyone leave a project before it was finished, after they had committed to working on it together? It's confusing.

In the next experiment we will discuss, researchers sought to learn how toddlers would react if their partner, a puppet in this case, broke off a commitment to work together. They initially had 144 three- and five-year-olds in the study; however, half of them had to be excluded. There were some technical issues, such as a camera malfunction, and exclusions for reasons that we might expect of young children, such as not wanting to be in a testing room alone or being scared of the puppet. Some reasons, however, were surprising and speak to how genuine and caring toddlers are. Eight toddlers in the study refused to agree with their puppet partner leaving the task. They were so committed to teamwork that they had to be excluded. Also, in the second part of the experiment, an additional twenty-eight toddlers had to be excluded because they continued to wait for their partner to return after they had left and didn't restart the task on their own. They were sure that someone leaving a project would come back eventually. And I'll also note that none of the children were excluded for not starting the task. As long as they were not scared of the puppet, every toddler wanted to be involved in the joint task and agreed to do it.

Now, getting back to the experiment, toddlers were first introduced to a puppet friend. After getting to know them, the toddlers learned that the puppet was the same age and gender, lived in the same city as the child, and liked to play. What a coincidence! The special task they were assigned was a modified version of the elevator task discussed previously. One partner pushes up a cylinder, and the other person can then retrieve objects. In this case it was beads. After a commitment to work together with an "Okay" and a high five, the work began. It did not last long. As the child pushed up the cylinder so the puppet could get the beads, the puppet decided to leave. They did this in one of three ways. They would either tell the child they forgot something and ask if it was okay to leave, tell the child the same thing and simply leave without asking permission, or simply leave without saying anything.

The researchers measured whether the toddlers protested, how long they waited before restarting the task on their own, and whether they felt the puppet should get a bracelet at the end for their work. The analysis demonstrated that if the puppet abruptly left, toddlers protested more and waited longer for them to return "as if they could not believe that the partner could just quit." They also felt that a partner who had left was less deserving of the reward, although notably, more than half the toddlers said their partner who unexpectedly quit should still get a bracelet. In situations where the toddlers were notified but were not asked permission by the puppet to leave, they felt this was more acceptable than simply leaving but not as reasonable as asking permission. As the authors point out, for toddlers "the main point is that the underlying social dynamic in joint commitments is mutual respect among partners" and "asking permission to break a commitment is maximally respectful, whereas notifying can be a bit presumptuous (depending on the circumstance), and just leaving is typically disrespectful."[18]

Toddlers understand that once we agree to work with someone, it carries a lot of weight, and we should do everything we can to honor that commitment. It demonstrates respect for the other person and the high level of work ethic that all toddlers have. There are times when we do need to leave a project, and if this happens, this should be done by agreement with your partner. Although it is acceptable to simply notify them, it is preferable to have that discussion. And while this is what toddlers firmly believe and how they act, other people may not always be as respectful. If this happens, other people still deserve kindness, as the toddlers demonstrated through their willingness to share rewards. As we saw in Chapter 2, holding grudges is not the toddler way. There is, of course, some balance of fairness when it comes to rewards, and we will discuss that more at the end of the chapter.

The idea of having open and respectful communication when leaving a project or a job may seem obvious but is not always the case. Harvard Business School professor Leonard Schlesinger emphasizes that the beginning and end of a professional relationship are the most important stages. When leaving a job, you must be sensitive, plan carefully, and assist your team with the transition. And while two weeks is the norm, he suggests giving closer to a month's notice of your departure to have the opportunity to collaborate with the team on what the best use of your remaining time should be. "You want your former boss and colleagues to feel nothing but positive about your professionalism," he says.[19] In an article published in *Nature* in 2022, a spokesperson for the US National Institutes of Health's human resources department had similar advice in that you should "use your departure to build bridges, not burn them," and "give your supervisor plenty of notice of your departure." It is also recommended that the meeting with a supervisor or manager happen in person. Thinking about your next position, if you need to take documents or files from the job you are leaving, make sure you have permission and only take copies. And finally, to be as helpful as possible, make yourself available to the colleagues you are leaving by providing them with your updated contact information.[20] All these recommendations maximize respect for other people, like toddlers aim to do.

Giving Everyone a Voice

Sometimes when we work in teams, especially in a leadership position, decisions need to be made that may seem unfair to certain members of the group. As fairness experts, toddlers are acutely aware of this. But they also know that compromise is important, and in observing their reactions to different scenarios in which they are treated unequally, we can get some tips on how we can manage teams better if we are put in the situation of making those decisions.

For this next experiment, an important business meeting was arranged between a toddler, a cow puppet, and a pig puppet. One hundred sixty toddlers ages three to five participated. When the toddler entered the boardroom, the chief pig officer (CPO) and the chief cow officer (CCO) were seated comfortably on their cushions, and they started with the usual formalities of getting to know the newest member of the team. During the course of the meeting, miraculously, another person found a treasure chest that was filled with stickers and dropped it off in the room. The stickers were to be distributed among the three participants, but it was only the CPO or CCO that got to decide how this was done. Each time, unfortunately, the toddler was left with the least number of stickers. The CPO and the CCO tried this multiple times with each toddler in one of four ways. First, they simply ignored the child and took more stickers. Second, they asked the child their opinion but still took more stickers no matter what the child said in response. Third, they both asked the child their opinion and offered the justification that it was the CPO's birthday, so he should get more stickers. And in the last scenario, the child was also asked for their agreement based on this justification.

The researchers then measured both the quantity and types of protests heard by the children. The most important finding was that the toddlers protested the least when they were extended the courtesy of being asked their opinion, given a justification for the decision, and asked for their agreement. There was only one other scenario where toddlers protested very little, and that was in three-year-olds when they were ignored. As the authors point out, this is likely because at that age, they are used to adults making decisions for them, but when they were asked their opinion, they certainly had a lot to say! By far the most important thing for toddlers of both ages when they protested was that they wanted to assert their personal choice. When referring to the larger pile of stickers, for example, they would say: "But I wanted that side!" The next most common type of protest was to use language to demonstrate consequences of a particular decision: "But then I'll only get one sticker!" Less often, but still important, the toddlers protested the process of how the decision was made, and others highlighted moral or fairness issues.[21]

There are some important lessons here for leadership. First, if there is a decision to be made that is objectively unfair, then allowing everyone to voice their opinion, giving justification, and asking for agreement is the kinder approach that allows for greater acceptance. And second, it is important to recognize that some team members are so used to having decisions made for them that they may never speak up. These team members might be the ones with the best ideas, and for that reason as well, we should consider all opinions with any major decision.

This idea of giving people a voice has also been tested in adults. There have been similar findings in that they are also more willing to accept an unfavorable outcome if their voice is heard. Importantly, research with adults shows that there is a strong effect of giving people a voice in the unfair distribution scenario whether they expect their opinion to change the outcome or not.[22] In one of the largest studies to date on this topic, researchers at the University of Michigan studied garment workers in India. They worked with a large company with more than one hundred thousand workers and randomly selected two thousand workers for the study. For context, the workers recently learned that their annual raises would be lower than expected. Half the workers in the study were given the opportunity to anonymously give feedback on their job, including on their supervisors. The group that was allowed to voice their opinion showed a 20 percent decrease in the probability of quitting six months after the survey compared to the other workers.[23]

Critically important here is that this is not to say that giving people a voice should be used as a method to exploit employees. Toddlers would absolutely disagree with this and would say there should be pushback. For toddlers, fairness is paramount, and in fact, three toddlers in the experiment discussed in this section had to be excluded because they stood their ground and refused to agree with any unequal distribution. In an exit interview with a neutral cat puppet after the experiment, the majority of the toddlers said no to the question: "Would you play again with the cow and the pig?" Unfair behavior should be called out in a variety of ways. When given the opportunity to voice their opinion, toddlers not only rely on personal choice but also point out to leadership the consequences of a particular decision, are critical of the process of the decision-making itself, and appeal to moral and fairness issues.

Aside from the issues of fairness and morality, standards that toddlers hold to the highest degree, teams also simply function better when everyone is given a voice. In a study by researchers from MIT and Carnegie Mellon University, 699 people working in small teams were given a variety of tasks to work on together. These tasks included things such as solving visual puzzles and negotiating over limited resources, something we will dive deeper into in the next section. In the analysis, what they found was remarkable. There was a general collective intelligence factor they called the "c factor." More importantly, this factor was not related to either the average intelligence of the group or any individual's intelligence. So having a team with the smartest people did not lead to the best outcome. Instead, the c factor was correlated with social sensitivity and "equality in the distribution of conversational turn-taking." In other words, giving everyone an equal voice and being sensitive to their feelings gave the team the best possible chance of success.[24]

This idea, of being sensitive and giving everyone a turn to speak, ties into the broader concept of psychological safety, which is the "belief that one can speak up without risk of punishment or humiliation."[25] In 2015, Google embarked on an intensive project to learn what makes up an effective team. They called this Project Aristotle and it involved more than two hundred interviews, examining over 250 attributes of a wide range of teams at Google. What they found, similar to the MIT research, was that who was on the team was less important, and how the team members interacted was far more important. In fact, they found that psychological safety was the most important factor when creating the best team. The next two most important team dynamic factors included dependability, and structure and clarity.[26,27] Both, as we have seen earlier in this chapter, are what toddlers strive for. In joint tasks, there is nobody more committed and dependable than a toddler, and what they want more than anything is to make tasks clear to their partner so that they can work together to finish the project.

Above All, Be Fair and Respectful

As we've discussed toddlers in detail over the last five chapters, some common themes have emerged that get at the core of who they are. These are attributes that describe them in any situation and hold true no matter how they are tested. Words that come to mind from our discussion so far are *kind, curious, committed,* and *determined,* among others. And after reflecting on how they perform in teams, *fair* would also be on this list. Toddlers always act in a way that is fair to others. They don't assign blame right away when their partner is not performing their task and instead try to understand the situation to determine the next course of action that is fair to everyone. When decisions are made, they want to have a voice and want everyone to have a voice, as that would be equitable. Because the data is so highly supportive of the toddler ideal of fairness, rather than go into one study in detail, let's touch upon a few different studies to understand what fairness means to a toddler. As we will see, what they really want is for everyone, including themselves, to be treated with respect.

In a review article published in 2019 summarizing all the research to date on this topic, toddlers are shown to demonstrate an innate and strong sense of fairness.[28] In previous chapters, we discussed some of the evolutionary roots of toddler behavior, and here again this can serve as an explanatory model. At some point in early human history, our ancestors learned that collaboration was the best way to ensure everyone was fed. In order to find solutions that satisfied different people with different needs, we developed a sense of fairness. Maintaining this fairness helps us to maintain relationships, and at the heart of why toddlers want things to be fair is that they want good relationships.

The way this idea has been tested is by seeing how toddlers distribute rewards that they obtain when working together. In these scenarios there are two ways that there could be unequal distributions. The first, called disadvantageous inequity, is when a toddler gets fewer rewards than someone else, and the second, advantageous inequity, is when that same toddler gets more of the reward than others. Multiple studies have shown that starting at three years of age toddlers avoid both types of inequity. They don't want less than others after working together, but more importantly, they also don't want more than others who have helped them. The rewards were gained because they worked together with another person, so it naturally flows that they should share equally. If they are given more than their share, they either reject the reward or simply accept it and then share it. It also doesn't matter to them who their partner is; it could be an animal puppet, an adult, or another toddler, they act the same. The immense worldwide problem of pay inequity we have, where women earn 37 percent less than men in similar roles,[29] is not acceptable and would never exist in toddler world.

In their quest to get the fairest distribution of rewards, toddlers also take into account how much people worked on the project. Since they are such good observers of all the tiny details of life, evaluating their partner's contribution, as well as their own, comes easy. While not perfect, as everyone has some self-serving bias, toddlers will try to give more of the reward to the person who worked the most, even if it's not them. In one study, children recognized the projects in which they had contributed less and, therefore, kept fewer stickers for themselves and gave these to their partner.[30] The same distributive behavior has been shown when they receive toys[31] or tokens.[32] And on the extreme end, when there is a free rider in the group, toddlers disapprove of anyone intentionally not contributing to the group and want to make sure they don't get equal rewards. They also, understandably, don't feel strongly about working with that person again.[33] Importantly, however, their strong sense of kindness we discussed in Chapter 2 often overpowers their sense of fairness. Although they share less with free riders who have contributed nothing to obtaining a particular reward, they still share nonetheless, just a bit "less equally."[34]

Their sense of fairness also allows toddlers to deal with issues on splitting up rewards when conflicts arise, without expensive lawyers or mediators. At the extreme end, toddlers have been tested in scenarios in which they are given the opportunity to monopolize rewards. Still, when given this opportunity, their tendency is to share equally, and this holds true across different types of rewards and when rewards have different values.[35] However, if one toddler happens to take more, a pair of toddlers almost always share equally in the end when the disadvantaged child points out the unequal distribution. As the authors of the review article write, "The key point is that children were not just expressing a preference for equality, they were expressing resentment against inequality and a normative judgment that they should not be treated that way."[36] There are no big arguments or meltdowns. Since they are so fair-minded, they think everyone is this way and most often simply point out an unfair distribution "trusting the partner to decide to do the right thing."[37] They act similarly whether they themselves don't get an equal distribution or they see a third party in the same predicament.[38]

In the end, what this all comes down to, and is perhaps the most powerful underlying lesson from toddlers when working in teams, is that everyone deserves respect. It is respectful to follow through on joint commitments. If you need to leave a project, then you should respect your partner enough to have a discussion. If you see someone who is not performing properly on the team, the best way to approach this is in a respectful teaching mode. And finally, when it comes to distributing rewards, everyone must be treated with respect. The easiest way to do this is to distribute rewards equally; however, if someone has worked on a project more, they should get more. And if rewards must be divided unequally, then it is respectful to ask others' opinions, give justification, and allow them the opportunity to speak their mind.

The Ultimate Team Member

In this chapter, we have seen all the ways that toddlers make great team members and how we can improve in our own interactions. I'm sure we would all love to work with someone as committed, fair, and respectful as a toddler. But what does the literature on adult teams show us about what makes a high-performing team? This question was best answered by the MIT Human Dynamics Laboratory in a *Harvard Business Review* article titled "The New Science of Building Great Teams." In likely the most comprehensive and detailed examination of what makes great team members, computer scientist Sandy Pentland from MIT sought to determine the most important characteristics of team members that produce the best results. He and his colleagues conducted multiple studies across a seven-year time span in more than twenty organizations and included 2,500 people. In these studies, they had each of the employees wear electronic sociometric badges that collected information on communication. These devices are about the size of a cell phone and are worn around one's neck. The badges are able to pick up body language (moving arms, hand motions, nodding), body positioning, and the speaker's tone of voice. The badges are also able to track who people talk to, how much they speak, and where they have their conversations. In the studies, the researchers also measured a host of other factors that would be important to measure for each employee, such as skill level based on job-specific metrics. For example, for call center employees this would include how many issues they were able to resolve, the average time spent on each call, and customer satisfaction.[39]

Interestingly, when all the factors were analyzed and measured against dollar productivity, it was team communication that was the most important factor for the success of the team. It was so important that all the other factors combined, including intelligence, personality, skill, and what was said, were equivalent to the importance of how people communicated. When the researchers then looked at exactly what parts of communication were important, they found three specific dimensions, all of which are exemplified by toddlers.

The first key element of communication, critical to its success, is energy. This is an easy one for toddlers as we have seen. They readily say yes to group work and love it so much that they will reset tasks to do it again. For adults, bringing energy to the team, as measured in the MIT studies, meant having more exchanges and being more engaged with colleagues—for example, even a simple yes or nodding your head in conversation. They also found that higher-energy teams have more face-to-face communication, so it's important to prioritize that when possible. Next most valuable are videoconferences and telephone calls; however, the more people that are on these calls, the less effective they are. And finally, as expected, e-mail and text messages are the least valuable.

The second important part of communication shown in the data was engagement. Again, as we have seen with toddlers, they are a model for engagement, not only showing the highest level of dedication to joint commitments, but also doing everything possible to ensure their team member returns to a project when they disengage. This is also related to our discussion on giving everyone a voice, as it keeps people engaged. In the MIT studies, this is exactly what was shown. Teams who heard from more team members and allowed everyone to participate performed better. In one business example, teams made less profitable decisions when there was only partial engagement from team members. It is critical that all team members participate, and as a leader, a key question from the MIT dataset is: How can [leaders] get them more involved?

Finally, the third most important dimension of communication was exploration. You may intuitively know from any observation of a toddler that *explorer* could easily be added to the list of characteristics that define them in every situation. We will revisit this in detail in Chapter 10 when we discuss risk-taking. For now, what this meant in the MIT studies was that team members who engaged in exploration had more communication with other teams. They sought outside connections, which led to innovation and new perspectives.[40]

The data on communication style is so powerful, in fact, that it can be used to predict success without knowing anything about the team member or what they are saying. In one of the studies conducted by Pentland, he had a group of executives wear the sociometric badges at a party. Five days later, there was a pitch competition in which these executives presented business plans. Using only the data from the party, without knowing what was said, the study predicted the winners of the contest with 87 percent accuracy.[41]

Toddlers function extremely well within teams because, as we discussed, their goals relate to the process of working with others rather than the outcomes. This allows them to focus on clear communication and helping their teammates when needed. And we can see how important this is from adult research as well. Team communication is the most critical factor for success. Like toddlers do, keep the three *F*s of team communication in mind whenever you are working in a group: energy, engagement, and exploration. These will guide you to be the best team member you can be.

Toddler Teachings

When it comes to teamwork, a verbal commitment or a high five means a lot.

Above all, respect your team members. This will guide all your interactions to ensure team success.

If someone on your team disengages from the project, they may not have understood their role. Try to clearly communicate with them, directly but politely. Remember: "Man, please lift it."

If your partner is doing a task incorrectly, the best way to complete the project is to gently assist them by showing them what needs to be done. "Heave-ho!"

When there is equipment failure, nobody is at fault. Calmly acknowledge what happened and move on. Swearing at a piece of equipment will not fix it.

As a leader, one of your primary responsibilities is to ensure you hear from everyone. The best teams are the ones on which everyone is given a voice.

Who you have on your team is important but not nearly as important as how you communicate. Energy, engagement, and exploration make for the most successful teams.

Chapter 7:

Mentorship

Show me the way, and I will work harder.

O ften when I go to day care to pick up Arya, I stand by the doorway for a short while to observe her. I find it heartwarming to see how her early childhood educators, Ms. Kristin and Ms. Roop, guide her in every activity she does. Without telling her specifically what to do, they will give her some options of what would be a good activity for her to try next, knowing exactly areas in which she needs to improve. If it's a new task or something more challenging, for instance, when Arya first learned to use scissors, her teachers will do the activity alongside her so she can see both what needs to be done and learn how important it is to keep trying if she can't get it at first. And finally, Arya knows she can always ask for help if she needs it and does so often.

"Daddy Pig!" is what I most often hear when Arya finally spots me standing at the doorway. It's not my preferred name, but I have learned to live with it for now. The name comes from one of her favorite TV shows, *Peppa Pig*, which chronicles the adventures of a little British pig and her family. Although this show is mildly entertaining, I much prefer to watch *Ms. Rachel—Toddler Learning Videos* with Arya, another one of her favorites. Rachel Griffin Accurso is a teacher by training and now a YouTube megastar among toddlers with more than 5 million subscribers. She initially started making videos to help her one-year-old son with speech delay, which then rapidly gained popularity.[1] Now she has an entire library of videos teaching toddlers new words and songs. What is wonderful to see with Ms. Rachel is how encouraging she is, something all toddlers thrive on. At every step of her teaching, she sprinkles in "Good job!" "Wow!," and "I'm so proud of you!"[2]

Although the relationships children have with their educators and parents are not formal mentorship roles, they can nevertheless provide valuable lessons to us as they bring out many important aspects of adult mentor-mentee relationships.

Many top performers across all disciplines have a mentor. A mentor is someone with experience in your field who is there to guide you, motivate you, and offer their own expertise. Having a good mentor can often propel you forward in your career by assisting with decision-making and helping you network. Sometimes, however, we get so caught up in the business of daily work that we don't put in the effort to foster these relationships or have them at all. This is unfortunate, as there is strong evidence of a wide range of benefits of having a mentor, including improved productivity, higher motivation, and improved career recognition.[3]

Toddlers don't really care about these specific benefits. However, since toddlers are dependent on adults, they offer a unique, magnified view of what this type of relationship can offer. In this chapter, we'll start with a discussion of some of the general benefits mentors can provide and then review qualitative research on what makes a good mentor-mentee relationship. This can help if you are in either position of mentor or mentee. After this, in the bulk of the chapter, we will get into some specific toddler studies that demonstrate how mentorship is useful, especially as it relates to persistence, and then discuss the literature about adult mentor-mentee relationships.

The Benefits of Having a Mentor

Even if you decided to ignore all the other advice in this book and chose a life of crime, this is the chapter for you. In 2006, researchers at the Université de Montréal published a study titled "Mentors and Criminal Achievement." In this project, they interviewed nearly two hundred inmates in five Québec prisons and found that "the presence of a criminal mentor is pivotal for achievement over one's criminal career." Mentors helped criminals have higher earnings and lowered their risk of getting caught."[4] No matter what you do professionally or otherwise, mentorship matters.

Like in other types of relationships, simply having a mentor-mentee relationship does not guarantee good outcomes. It depends a lot on the relationship itself, and we will get into some elements that may help this. A good mentor-mentee relationship, however, has been shown to have a number of benefits. Across several research studies, mentees in the workplace have been shown to have better work attitudes, higher subjective and objective career success (career satisfaction and promotions), higher job performance, lower job turnover, and even better interpersonal relationships outside the mentor relationship. And there are benefits to being a mentor as well. While this has not been studied as extensively, mentors have been shown to have higher job satisfaction, better job performance, and less career plateauing.[5]

In addition to these important benefits, we should also highlight how mentorship on both sides is related to salary. In 2006, Gartner, a technology research and consulting firm, conducted a study for Sun Microsystems to evaluate their mentorship program. In this study they looked at ninety-five mentor-mentee pairs and compared them to more than one thousand employees in the control group that did not have formal mentorship. Over a five-year period, it was shown that 25 percent of mentees had an increase in their salary compared to only 5 percent in the non-mentored group.[6] More recently, both unpublished data examining a large business with over 7,500 mentored and non-mentored employees[7] as well as a published study on mentorship in academia[8] found that having a mentor is associated with higher salaries. Furthermore, research from the University of South Florida has shown that being a mentor is also associated with a higher salary.[9]

Despite the benefits of mentorship and the recognized importance of this type of relationship, many people still do not have a mentor. In a 2019 survey of three thousand American adults ages twenty-one to sixty-eight who work full-time, only 56 percent said they ever had a professional mentor, and only slightly more than a third said they had a current mentor. There was also wide variation by industry. In science-related fields for example, 66 percent of respondents reported having a current or previous mentor, whereas in finance, skilled labor, and health care, that number was less than 50 percent. Despite these low numbers, three out of four respondents overall said they consider mentors important.[10]

What all this information tells us is that having a great mentor or mentoring someone else can be incredibly beneficial. And while most people recognize this, there are barriers to both starting and maintaining those relationships. If you're lucky, your workplace may have a formal mentorship program in place, and that can be a good place to start. However, many people don't have this benefit, so it's important that you seek out a mentor. This person may be at your workplace, but they could be in a different department. They might even work somewhere else and be in an entirely different industry. Conferences or other regional and national work-related events can be a good place to meet potential mentors, and e-mentoring is certainly a possibility.[11] These informal connections can be equally or more effective than formal mentorship in structured programs. It all depends on the relationship that is built and the commitment on both sides.

Finding that person, either mentor or mentee, is the hardest step, but once you have that, there are certain things both parties can do to ensure a successful mentor-mentee relationship. Researchers at the University of Toronto and the University of California, San Francisco, conducted a study in which they interviewed fifty-four faculty members and asked them questions about mentorship. Through the course of these interviews, five broad themes emerged as characteristics of successful mentoring relationships. First, there needs to be a bidirectional nature of the relationship so that the mentor can also benefit. This can be as simple as a thank-you or a formal acknowledgment. Next, there should be mutual respect, especially for the mentor's expertise and the time given. Third, there should be clear expectations on the mutually agreed-upon outcomes, and both mentor and mentee should be accountable to each other.

Fourth is the importance of having a personal connection. Sometimes, even with similar interests, that connection isn't there, which doesn't lead to a successful relationship. And lastly, there should be shared values around their approach and commitment to the work they are doing.[12]

While it is challenging to find the right person, having a mentor or mentee can have significant positive impacts on careers, and it is well worth the search to find that person. This can also mean that you have more than one mentor in some cases, and that can be helpful too. In the rest of this chapter, we'll look at some specific aspects of how mentors can help us, and at the same time we'll offer some guidance if you are in the mentor role instead. Much of this work comes from the Leonard Learning Lab, where professor Julia Leonard studies toddler learning and persistence in the Psychology Department at Yale University. Through a series of fascinating studies, we will see how toddlers change their behavior as a result of how adults act and speak, and overall, how the right mentor can help us all excel in the workplace.

Offering Guidance on the Best Project to Choose

Why won't she jump? I remember thinking to myself as I observed Arya in her gym class. As we discussed, toddlers love to exercise, so every Saturday includes an hour at the toddler gym where she can run around and play with her friends. One activity at the gym involves the children running up a soft ramp, about as tall as them, and then jumping off onto a gymnastics mat. One by one, I would see all the kids run up to the edge and do all sorts of jumps with laughter and smiles. Not Arya, however. She would run up the edge of the ramp, turn around, and lower herself down gently. This continued for quite some time, and even jumping on the spot was something she would not do.

It's always a bit concerning to see your child unable to do something other children can, so we talked to her pediatrician and educators and then worked together to guide Arya on specific activities that would help her jump. At home, we normally have a five-to-ten-minute dance party each evening after dinner cleanup. Instead of her favorite songs, such as the "Party Freeze Dance Song," we started dancing to "Hop Little Bunnies." At day care, her teachers set up a series of games with targets on the floor that would help her practice. These were spaced out gradually with little improvements each day. Over time, this worked, and Arya now loves jumping around, including every morning on my bed when she wakes me up with an Arya-original dance called "The Bouncy Castle Dance."

Having a third party focused on your development is valuable. They may see areas that you need help with that you may not see and offer guidance on the activities you should prioritize for maximum improvement in areas that you know you need to get better at. We can't do it all, and most of us are in positions where we have too many things to do at work and need to prioritize. Others are fortunate enough to have control about which projects they say yes or no to. In either case, a mentor can be invaluable in helping us prioritize what to tackle next. We don't want to do things that are too easy and will not build skills (although sometimes we have to), and at the same time we don't want to take on projects we can't handle.

In a series of three experiments from Yale, researchers sought to understand the types of tasks that preschoolers and slightly older children would be more persistent with. In the first experiment, sixty-six children ages four to six participated. Each child sat at a table with a tree that had a pulley device. They were told that an egg had fallen out of the tree, and it was their job to put the egg on a metal platform and slowly raise it up via a pulley. What they didn't know is that the experiment was carefully controlled with a hidden magnet that the researchers could turn on and off to make the egg stay on or fall off the platform. The children were randomly assigned to one of two conditions. In the first condition the egg fell off the platform at increasing heights: 8 inches, 10 inches, 12 inches, and finally 14 inches. In the other condition, the egg fell out at 14 inches each time. At the end of four trials the children were all asked if they wanted to play with the tree again. Children in the first condition, where the egg fell out at increasing heights, were more likely to continue with the challenge compared to the constant group, even though all children reached the same level. Increasing performance was motivating, and stagnant performance was demotivating.[13]

Young children are rational and are motivated by their own internal gauge of improvement over time. Adults also thrive in this type of scenario in which they can see their progress over time. Studies in adults using unlearnable tasks show that they eventually steer away from these and are motivated by tasks where they can see their own progress.[14] Sometimes it's easy for us to see our own results over time and compare, with sales numbers, for example. However, these simple metrics may not give us the entire picture, and there are some skills for which our progress is more difficult to track and get feedback on. This is where a mentor can come in, encouraging our own persistence by guiding us to tasks that offer growth over time, and guiding us away from tasks that not only don't offer this but that we will eventually abandon anyway and waste a lot of time in the process.

We also know that adults, even though they can accurately predict learning over time, misestimate certain features. In another experiment from Yale, but this time with adults, more than 150 people were recruited for a series of three experiments. This was an online game called Lollitoss in which participants would capture lollipops that moved back and forth at the bottom of the screen and launch them at a target. Overall, the participants were able to predict how their learning would progress, with less errors over time. However, the issue was that people overestimated their starting performance and underestimated their rate of learning.[15] This could potentially be detrimental when we want to see progress over time. If we start off thinking we will be better than we actually are, then initial progress can get buried. Similarly, if we think we are progressing more slowly than we actually are, there is also a risk of abandoning the project. A mentor, as a neutral third party, can help us see the progress, relate their own experiences, and also set realistic expectations of how good we can expect to be with a new task.

Leading by Example

While offering direct guidance on our career choices is incredibly important, it is equally important for a mentor to lead by example. This is especially true when it comes to motivating a mentee to consistently work hard. Staying persistent is what can help us achieve our biggest goals. Often, people give up on large projects (such as writing a book) prematurely. A mentor can help us stay persistent by demonstrating what they do day-to-day.

In a study published in 2017, researchers sought to understand what toddlers would do with a new task after they observed an adult working on a different task. Think of a mentor-mentee relationship in which both parties might be in related fields but working on different projects. This study included over one hundred one-year-olds that were split up into three groups. The first group of children, called the Effort group, observed an adult perform two different tasks: opening a box to retrieve a toy, and removing a key chain from a carabiner. All along, the adult would narrate what they were doing, "Hmm . . . I wonder how I can get my toy out of here? Does this work? No, how about this . . . ?" After thirty seconds in each case, the adult was successful in the task. The next group of children, in the No Effort condition, observed an adult complete the same tasks in ten seconds without any of the narration and minimal effort. And in the final condition, the Baseline condition, the children didn't see any modeled behavior. After this phase all the children were given a new toy, which was a music box with two buttons. One was an obvious button that was visible but didn't do anything when pushed, and the other was a hidden button to activate it. The researcher pushed the hidden button prior to giving it to the child so the children could see that it was a toy that worked but they didn't know how they could make it sing.

For the analysis, the researchers then looked at how many times the toddler pressed the inactive button, a measure of persistence, before two minutes was up, they handed off the toy, or they threw the toy on the ground. In the end, the toddlers who saw adults work through the tasks made more attempts to achieve the goal with their own task compared to children who either saw the adult easily perform the tasks or did not see any modeling. The authors note the value in having children "see you sweat" and conclude that "showing children that hard work works might encourage them to work hard too."[16]

This experiment does not stand alone, as researchers showed similar results in a different study with four- and five-year-olds. Through a series of four experiments with more than five hundred children, preschoolers observed adults performing a task and either succeeding or failing, as well as trying hard or not. The children then tried their own task. It was shown that persistence was strongly linked to the combination of seeing the adult both succeed and work hard. In one of the parts of this study, another important aspect of mentoring was highlighted: setting honest expectations. In this portion, children were given a puzzle box that was designed to be completed by adults. They were also shown an activity board designed for their age so they could see the differences in difficulty of each task. They were explicitly told, "Some of the toys are made for grown-ups; they can be hard for kids." They were again reminded of this just before they started to work on the puzzle. Here, the researchers found children were able to calibrate their persistence and they tried harder when their expectations were set ahead of time. Again, seeing the adult succeed at the task was key here as well, and the combination of seeing an adult succeed and setting expectations around the difficulty of the task led to the highest level of persistence.[17]

Seeing our mentors and role models persist is important for motivation at all ages. In a study published in 2020, researchers at Pennsylvania State University recruited more than six hundred adult participants online. In a series of three experiments, they exposed participants to identical struggle stories about Albert Einstein, Thomas Edison, and a non-famous scientist. They then asked participants questions about their beliefs regarding these scientists and had them perform actual mathematical tasks. Like toddlers, adults also demonstrated that their motivation and persistence on tasks increased when they understood the challenges a role model went through to attain their success. Einstein is generally viewed as a genius, whereas Edison is seen as a hard worker. So, despite identical stories, participants performed better in the mathematical tasks when they viewed someone as hardworking, like Edison.[18] Lead author Danfei Hu commented, "If we can send the message that struggling for success is normal, that could be incredibly beneficial."[19]

Choosing a mentor who is open and honest about sharing the struggles they went through to get to where they are today is extremely helpful. Hearing about this, coupled with anecdotes of how they continue to overcome obstacles to be successful, can motivate you to be more persistent. And, if you are in the mentor role, as you meet with your mentees keep this in mind as one of the most helpful aspects of what you can share.

A Mentor Is There to Encourage You

While it is helpful to have guidance on the right project and an exemplar of persistence, sometimes all we need is a little encouragement, kind words, or even a high five to help us get through the next big step. Toddlers and adults are highly responsive to encouragement, and a mentor who can do this at the right time is what we all need.

First, let's go back to the study we discussed in the last section in which seeing success with adult effort and setting honest expectations increased child persistence when working on a puzzle box. This study had two additional parts to it that are relevant to our current discussion. One was called the Pep Talk condition and the other was the Statement of Values condition. Keep in mind that the task the children were asked to do was impossible, so researchers were really seeing how long they would try before giving up. In the Pep Talk condition, children were told, "I think you will do a great job playing with this toy! I have a lot of confidence in you! You got this!" And in the Statement of Values condition, a longer script was used that still provided encouragement but did so in a way that focused on the importance of hard work:

> Lots of things are really hard, aren't they? Well, we are going to play with some toys today, and sometimes, new toys are tricky. But you know what the best thing to do is when something is tricky? To try your best and not give up. Do you agree? So, what do you think the best thing to do is when something is tricky? (Let child answer) Yeah, it's just really important to try our best and not give up.[20]

For these two conditions, what was important was the length of time spent trying to complete an impossible task. The maximum time allowable in the experiment was a little over four minutes, a very long time for anyone to persist with an impossible but seemingly simple task. Compared to the conditions where children had honest expectations set, or only observed the effort an adult put into the task, more children persisted all the way to the end of the experiment in the Pep Talk condition (38 percent) and the Statement of Values condition (50 percent). This is called the "ceiling" of the study. In other words, these preschoolers had to be told to stop even though they were still working through the impossible puzzle box. Simply put by the authors, referring to the researcher, "Words she said to the child mattered." There was an enhancing effect when the child not only saw the adult succeed and work hard to achieve that success but was also "endorsing the value of hard work."[21] This is what led to maximal performance.

Encouragement and pep talks can be experienced everywhere, from sports teams to military operations to the workplace. And there's a reason for this: They work. In adults, two researchers stand out as having demonstrated the power of motivational language over the last three decades. Jacqueline and Milton Mayfield are professors at Texas A&M International University and focus on three aspects of motivational language that have a wide range of benefits. The first is direction giving, or in other words being clear on what the person should be doing, with specific goals. The second is using empathic language, like we see with the toddler-directed speech we discussed. This builds interpersonal bonds and lets the person on the receiving end know that they are valued. And finally, the third aspect is meaning making. This is a way of explaining why the task is important and can connect to the values of the leader or organization, similar to the statement of values we discussed earlier.[22,23]

Through studies done by the Mayfields and others, motivational language has shown links to several important aspects of working life in adults. Specifically, motivational language is positively related to innovation, creative idea generation in teams, employee self-efficacy, worker performance, and job satisfaction. It has also been shown to be protective against employee withdrawal behaviors such as absenteeism.[24] And while the greatest benefits are had when you hear all three parts of motivational language from a mentor, even one part can be helpful. In a study published by the global nonprofit Catalyst in 2021, nearly nine hundred American employees were surveyed across different types of industries. When compared to having a manager or leader with low empathy, employees who had a leader with high empathy reported they were more often innovative and engaged at work.[25]

No matter how they do it specifically, the most important thing a mentor can give you is the encouragement you need to be persistent. Persisting through tasks that are challenging and not necessarily enjoyable is what can help us reach our long-term goals.[26] For toddlers, the least enjoyable task you could possibly ask them to do is brush their teeth, and there is a study that shows children brush longer on days when they receive praise.[27] Also for young children, verbal praise is great, but a thumbs-up or a high five work equally well, if not better.[28]

Finally, while it's important for mentors to offer consistent encouragement, it's critical they do so only with words or gestures and not take over your work. This is especially true if you are in the mentor role and see one of your mentees working slowly through a task. Our tendency is to jump in and help because the task can get done faster, but this is counterproductive as it decreases the mentee's own persistence and motivation. In a study published in 2021, four- and five-year-olds were tested on their persistence on a new task if initially they were left alone, had some teaching, or had an adult who took over the first task. The preschoolers' job was to open a wooden box with a toy inside, but the box had been cruelly glued shut. Prior to this task, sixty children built a puzzle with an adult. With half the children, after ten seconds, the adult said, "Hmm . . . this is hard, why don't I just do it for you?" and completed the puzzle. With the other thirty children, the adult helped them along with instructions and praise. Thirty different children went straight to the wooden box test. In the end, the children that persisted most with the impossible task were those who were guided along by the adult initially, followed by those who did not participate in the puzzle task. Both of these groups persisted twice as long as the children who had the puzzle completed for them.[29] For adults, as well, taking over a task from someone can have real consequences. Aside from potentially making them feel inadequate and decreasing motivation, this type of behavior has been shown to hinder team performance.[30]

It's truly incredible how much toddlers encourage one another, besides all the encouragement toddlers get from the wonderful early childhood educators who are with them most days. It's difficult to go more than ten minutes without an entire day care class raising their arms up and shouting, "Hooray," for something that was done well either in person or by a character in a book. Clapping and cheering are well deserved for almost everything, including getting your shoe on the right foot. If given the opportunity, toddlers could go around a room full of people continually giving high fives for an hour. What they also understand is that sometimes you just need to encourage yourself. Giving yourself a high five in the mirror or a big "hooray" when nobody is around is perfectly acceptable, and helpful.

Asking for Help

As we discussed in Chapter 2 on kindness, helping others can make us feel incredibly good, and toddlers spend much of their day looking for ways to be helpful. What is also unique about toddlers is that it is easy for them to ask for help, unlike adults. Among adults, nobody understands these things better than people who are lucky enough to spend their time interacting with young children. In her TED Talk from 2020, former kindergarten teacher YeYoon Kim summarizes it best when she describes how she felt helping five-year-old Sam. "Being asked for help is a privilege—a gift for you to do something for someone, especially when it's coming from their place of vulnerability." She then goes on to discuss some of her own personal struggles and how hard it was to ask for help from others. "And if you think about it, isn't it so weird we spend all of childhood being so good at asking for help and are expected to grow up to be these self-reliant human beings? And we get so good at it that we have to be reminded that it's okay to ask for help?"[31]

You could have the best mentor available, but if you don't utilize them by asking for help when you need it, then you won't benefit. It's hard for adults to ask for help. There is a fear that the person will say no or that we will inconvenience them too much. These beliefs, however, are overly exaggerated in our minds. In 2022, researchers at Stanford University and the University of Chicago conducted a series of six experiments with more than two thousand adults. Scenarios were set up both online and in person where participants had to imagine asking for help, recall events where they asked for help, or actually ask for help in person. For example, one task had participants ask another person to take their photo at a garden and another had them imagine what it would be like to ask someone else to use their phone. Overall, the researchers found that adult viewpoints were completely misguided. Consistently throughout the experiments, participants underestimated another person's willingness to help and how positive it would make the other person feel. They also overestimated any inconvenience felt by the giver. What we often fail to appreciate is that both the giver and receiver feel good from this type of interaction, and adults would benefit from asking for help more regularly.[32]

As we have seen in previous chapters, and what we will talk much more about in Chapter 10 on taking risks, toddlers don't have the same mental barriers adults do. Nothing embarrasses them, from public displays of failure as they try to achieve new goals to walking around all day with a booger or food on their face. Compared to those scenarios, asking for help is easy! Despite common false beliefs many people have about toddlers, they "are not erratic, impulsive, and unpredictable in their pursuit of goals" as the researchers that we will discuss in the next study write. Toddlers can work as hard as anyone on tasks, but they are also rational and know when it would be more efficient or beneficial to ask for help.

To demonstrate toddler help-seeking behavior, researchers at the University of Washington conducted a study with nearly one hundred one-year-olds. They were initially split into three groups in which they simply observed an adult pull a rope attached to a box that had a toy inside. One group saw that the adult found it very easy; the next group saw the adult was challenged but could do it; and the last group saw that it was impossible for the adult to do. They then tested toddler persistence, but this time they glued the box to the table so it would be impossible. First, in line with our discussion on leading by example, the toddlers who saw the adult struggle but succeed put increasing effort in each time they tried to pull the rope. But here, importantly, toddler help-seeking behavior was examined. The toddlers asked for help the most when they saw it was easy for the adult. That is, they recognized expertise and sought this out. Also, after the initial phase, the box was unglued, and toddlers could do the task. The researchers then found a decrease in help-seeking behavior if they saw the task was either easy or hard but possible. When they saw it was impossible, their help-seeking behavior remained low because they knew it was impossible for everyone. The authors concluded that toddlers seek help when "(1) they actually need it and (2) their social partner's competence at the task exceeds their own."[33] This is an ideal mentor-mentee relationship we can all learn from.

Find Your Batman

At this point, we now have a good idea of what an ideal mentor looks like. They are someone who guides you to challenging yet not impossible tasks, demonstrates their struggles and successes, gives you frequent encouragement, and is responsive to your requests for help. It would be difficult to find a person who can exhibit all these qualities well, and even if you are lucky enough to have such a great mentor, they may not be available to you all the time. In those moments or times when you don't have a mentor at all, the only person left to turn to is a superhero.

By far one of the hardest things physicians have to do in the pediatric ER is make a new cancer diagnosis. Usually, we know from the first conversation. The child has been tired for a month or more, has lost weight, has bone or joint pain, and now has a new rash consisting of tiny red dots. These are called petechiae and are a sign of bleeding. We patiently wait for the blood work, hoping it will be a benign blood disorder, but not uncommonly, it's leukemia. This is the most common cancer in childhood, and all children with this diagnosis bravely endure years of treatment. Fortunately, most children do well and can beat the cancer, but the frequent hospital visits, blood draws, and chemotherapy take their toll on kids and their families.

Thankfully the most amazing charity exists to bring hope and joy to these children at the most difficult time. It's called Make-A-Wish and allows children with a critical illness to have one of their wishes come true. Make-A-Wish was started in 1980 in Phoenix, Arizona, with one little boy, and now has grown to serve hundreds of thousands of children in more than fifty countries.[34] In a 2018 study from Nationwide Children's Hospital in Columbus, Ohio, researchers demonstrated that children who were granted a wish had fewer ER visits and unplanned hospital admissions.[35]

Perhaps the most famous leukemia survivor and Make-A-Wish recipient is Miles Scott. Miles is from California and, as a toddler, was diagnosed with leukemia at just eighteen months of age. He underwent three years of chemotherapy and beat his cancer. As something to look forward to, and as a celebration of his final treatment, Miles finally got his wish when he was five years old. Of all things, Miles wanted to be Batman's sidekick, Batkid. On a spectacular fall day in 2013, during which more than ten thousand people participated, Miles was transformed into Batkid, and he and Batman fought crime as San Francisco was turned into Gotham City by the Bay. After receiving a call for help from the mayor, Batkid and Batman traveled in the Batmobile, saved a woman from a bomb, stopped a bank robbery, and rescued the San Francisco Giants mascot from the Penguin. The day ended with Miles receiving the key to the city, and November 15, 2013, was declared Batkid Day.[36] In 2015, a documentary was released about that day called *Batkid Begins*.[37]

Superheroes like Miles Scott and Batman represent someone aspirational and act in a manner we think our ideal selves would behave. In that way, they can have a profound effect on both children's and adults' motivation. When we think like these types of people or characters and remove ourselves from whatever we are working on, we are utilizing a type of self-control strategy called self-distancing.

This method was best demonstrated in young children in a paper published in 2017 called "The 'Batman Effect': Improving

Perseverance in Young Children." One of the coauthors of this study was Angela Duckworth, author of the well-known book *Grit: The Power of Passion and Perseverance*.[38] In the study, four- and six-year-olds were tested to see how long they could perform a boring task. This task, which they were told "is a very important activity and it would be helpful if you worked hard on this for as long as you could," consisted of pressing the space bar when they saw a piece of cheese on a screen and doing nothing if they saw a cat. The children also had the option of pressing the "break" button on the keyboard and then playing a much more fun game on an iPad.

Before testing, the children were split up into three groups. In the first group, children were instructed to think about themselves and ask, "Am I working hard?" In the second group, they were instructed to think from a third-person perspective and ask themselves, "Is [child's name] working hard?" And finally, in the last group they could choose to be either Batman, Bob the Builder, Rapunzel, or Dora the Explorer. Of course, to be that person they were also given a prop that could transform them. In the case of Batman, his cape. And, while working on the task, a sticker was placed on the computer and iPad that either had the letter "I," the child's name, or an image of the character they chose, depending on the group they were in. In the final analysis, the "Batman Effect" was proven to be real. Regardless of age, children worked longer on the boring task if they became a different character.[39]

The "Batman Effect" is not limited to Batman or persistence. Researchers at Tel Aviv University tested how toddlers ages three to five were able to delay gratification and wait for larger rewards if they became Superman. In their experiments, simply putting on a red cape immediately transformed toddler behavior. Even though they had to remain seated, they spread their hands out in front to fly and repeatedly touched the cape. The red cape alone, even without describing Superman's abilities, significantly increased their ability to wait for rewards.[40]

The idea of behavior changing after watching someone we admire but have no direct contact with is not limited to toddlers. Adults can benefit too. Just like the "Batman Effect," an "Obama Effect" has also been demonstrated. In 2008, researchers at San Diego State University, Northwestern University, and Vanderbilt University recruited nearly five hundred Black and white Americans. The researchers controlled for education level to ensure this would not influence their results and then administered a verbal exam at four different time points over a three-month period. This included the time before Barack Obama accepted the Democratic Party's nomination to the time he was elected president. The researchers found that when President Obama had significant accomplishments, after his convention speech and after being elected president, Black American exam performance improved while white American exam performance remained constant. These were people in a random sample, completely removed from direct contact with the president, yet he still had a powerful effect on them.[41]

The superhero effect can also be felt more directly, and there are steps you can take to benefit from it. Unfortunately, there are no studies that had adults wear capes, although I have no doubt this would help everyone. There is, however, one fantastic study published in 2018 that used superhero imagery and posters with adults. Researchers at Hope College and Virginia Commonwealth University conducted two studies, one online and one in person, to assess how adults potentially change their behavior when presented with superheroes. In the first study conducted online, 246 adults were randomly assigned to the superhero condition or the neutral condition. In both groups they had to look at four everyday items, two desks, a bedroom, and a garage. In the superhero condition, however, the images were edited to contain Superman and Spider-Man logos. Participants were then asked a series of questions about how likely they were to help someone in scenarios such as shoveling snow for an elderly neighbor, finding a lost dog, and donating to charity. Interestingly, participants who had been shown the edited superhero images reported greater intentions to help others.

Intentionality is one thing, but can this change actual behavior? This next question was answered in the second experiment, in which they tested 123 adults to see their willingness to do a boring task. In this part, they split the participants into two groups and brought them into a testing room. Both rooms were identical except for the poster hanging on the wall. One group had a bicycle poster, and the other had a Superman poster. After completing some paper materials, the participants were told that the experiment was complete but that they could help with a different pilot study rating geometrical shapes. This is not exciting work; however, more than 90 percent of participants who were in the room with the Superman poster did the task whereas only 75 percent of the participants in the room with the bicycle poster participated.[42]

Superheroes are important to all of us because when we act like them, we can improve our own lives, whether that means being nicer, being able to wait for bigger rewards, or doing boring tasks that may eventually lead to higher achievements. In the end, we just might be able to keep these powers. Going back to the study from Tel Aviv University, one little girl took off her cape during the experiment. The experimenters were curious as to why she did that, and when they asked about it later, she summarized it best by saying, "I didn't need it anymore; I said goodbye to Superman and took his powers for myself."[43]

Toddler Teachings
Go out and find a mentor or mentee. This can be challenging at first, but many great things can happen.
Observing and hearing about hard work are inspiring!
Show and receive encouragement whenever you can. A loud "hooray!" or a high five, even to yourself, is motivating.
Never be afraid to ask for help. This is often the most efficient way of getting something done, and helping you will most likely make the other person feel good. Everybody wins.
Be your favorite superhero or someone you admire. Putting on a cape works best, but a picture by your workspace is also great. This can help you self-distance and increase persistence.

Chapter 8:

Self-Talk

Encourage and guide yourself to success!

Toddlers don't get all the recognition they deserve for being the amazing people they are, but occasionally, someone will capture something that shows their true nature and inspires all of us. Perhaps the most famous example is when two-year-olds Maxwell and Finnegan ran toward each other for the biggest hug ever seen on a New York sidewalk. This video got more than 100 million views and earned them guest appearances on CNN and *The Ellen DeGeneres Show*.[1] While this was a wonderful example of normal toddler behavior that we could all see and admire, what we can easily miss are the inspiring things toddlers do when they are alone.

In early 2022, it was Aubrin Sage's turn to shine. At the time, Aubrin was four years old and lived in Yakima, Washington, where she was a regular snowboarder. Aubrin's dad wanted to better understand her thought process as she was going down the slopes, so he decided to put a mic on her so he could capture everything she was saying. At the same time, he followed and filmed her. In an adorable video that got international attention, Aubrin is seen dressed in a full green dinosaur outfit as she makes her way down a ski hill. As if that isn't cute enough, she starts singing, "Let's go down this big ol' hill," and sometime later she wants to "go in that secret path," planning a side trail she wants to take. Once she finds it and enters near some trees, she knows she needs to slow down and announces, "Heel slip," as she puts back pressure on her feet, grinding the powdery snow and slowing herself. In the next tricky part, which is steeper and narrower, she says to herself, "I won't fall, maybe I will, that's okay, 'cause we all fall." In between there are a lot of "Weewoo!" sounds, and indiscernible chatter.[2]

What Aubrin is doing here, and something all toddlers do much of the time, is called private speech. This is when we talk to ourselves out loud. Toddlers do this as they intuitively know there is a benefit, and for them, research has shown that it assists with problem-solving tasks.[3] This is important because there are wide-ranging benefits for adults as well, including learning,[4] emotional regulation,[5] and even scoring more shots in basketball.[6] In this chapter we'll start with discussing how we talk to ourselves when we are young and how this changes over time. We will then get into specific ways toddlers use self-talk to their advantage and how these can translate to adults. As long as we can get over the shyness we might have of other people hearing us talk to ourselves, this is an incredibly easy and powerful way to self-motivate. But even if we keep it all to ourselves, as inner speech, it will still help if done in a deliberate way.

From Outside to Inside

We don't actively think about it very much, but everyone talks to themselves in some way. Sometimes we do it to help ourselves, such as giving ourselves a boost of motivation, while at other times it can make us feel worse, like when we get angry with ourselves for not getting something done. Most of this, for adults, happens silently in our head and only occasionally do we speak out loud. Toddlers, on the other hand, are more than happy to say everything out loud. They like announcing what they are doing and guiding themselves, and often naturally refer to themselves in the third person. Walking down the day care hallway at pick-up time, I often hear things such as "Julie can do it!" as little Julie squeezes her hand into a mitten, or "Colton made a mistake" as Colton looks down and sees that he's put his boots on the wrong feet. As we will see later, this simple change in how we refer to ourselves can have an enormous benefit.

The fact that we hear toddlers often talking to themselves out loud while we don't hear the same thing with adults is part of our natural development. Toddlers can say their first words around the age of one, and what starts with social communication then turns into self-talk. For toddlers this is called private speech, which is self-directed speech, out loud, both comprehensible and incomprehensible to others. It increases in toddlerhood and peaks around the ages of four to six. That's the point when inner speech first starts to develop.[7] After toddlerhood, private speech decreases but transforms into other forms of self-talk. At first it becomes whispers and more muttering and then finally silent inner speech takes over as the dominant form that we as adults experience.[8]

Our brains are always looking for ways to be more efficient, and this transition from private spoken speech to inner silent speech is one of these proposed pathways. When we speak out loud, our brain has to process the structure of what we are saying with proper syntax. This is not the case with inner speech and allows for a re-duced load for our brain to process.[9] When we need to, however, we also have the power to unpack this condensed speech and have full conversations with ourselves.

In a review article published in 2022, researchers at the University of Osnabrück in Germany and the University of Vienna in Austria point to two examples of how this unpacking assists our thinking. The first is in problem-solving when we say things "experimentally" to ourselves. These are hypothetical inner speech scenarios that allow us to better understand a particular situation. For a difficult problem we may propose a solution that might not be the actual an-swer but helps us think in a different way. The second example is what is called "deliberative mastication." In the example from the article, someone has been invited to a dinner party. This triggers an inner dialogue of whether the person wants to go, what the party will be like, who will be there, and what they will talk about. By having these conversations with ourselves, we can then see how we might feel in those hypothetical situations and "make explicit the steps in a decision process."[10]

While the progression from out loud private speech to silent inner speech is happening to us, our brains still take those signals and pro-cess them in similar ways. Brain wave studies in adults demonstrate similar patterns whether we hear something or produce it as inner speech.[11] There is also an important distinction made in adult fMRI studies in the way in which we talk to ourselves as active (willful) or passive. This distinction is seen by different areas of our brains being engaged while we are listening or talking to ourselves in our heads.[12]

Whether they are simply single words we say to ourselves or full conversations, the power of self-talk is real. For the rest of this chapter, we will go through the main benefits of talking to yourself and hopefully convince you that we should all be doing it more. And of all the things we have discussed in this book so far, this is probably the easiest to implement. For toddlers, our focus will be on private speech as they have not fully developed the capacity for inner speech. For adults, we'll talk about both private speech and inner speech. We should also note that there is unconscious speech that happens as we think about things, but this chapter will focus on speech that is willful, whether that be aloud or silent.

Talk to Yourself to Be a Better Problem Solver

Keeping up with Arya on a weekend day can sometimes be challenging with all the running around, playing, and answering questions. So we usually try to do some alone time when she can play by herself and I can rest for a few minutes. Right now, her favorite activity to do alone is make puzzles and, even though she is in another room, I can still hear her speaking aloud to herself. "Turn it around," "not like this," and "that fits!" are some of the things I hear as she recreates the image of a snugly koala bear and her baby.

Like a toddler solving a puzzle, challenges that we can overcome make our own work more enjoyable. Without challenges, jobs are boring. At the same time, staying motivated to achieve our goals can be difficult, but there are scientifically proven ways we can improve motivation. Seeing our progress over time, as we discussed in the last chapter, helps us stay persistent.[13] And one of the simplest ways we can work through new problems and improve is through self-talk.

Toddlers, in their quest to learn new things and achieve mastery, are prime examples of people who have perfected the art of self-talk. With the amount of time they spend talking to themselves, it's helpful to see what actually works for them. A study published in 2021 from the University of Queensland took a deeper dive into all the ways toddlers used private speech when doing a task. In this study, seventy-one three- to five-year-olds had to replicate either a house or a garden using LEGO sets. The researchers recorded everything the subjects were saying to themselves and noted how the toddlers used self-talk differently at different times. Initially they would plan out loud what they were going to do and self-motivate themselves saying things such as, "Okay, I've got this." Next, they would talk about their own performance as they worked on their task, for example, "I'm not getting this right." And finally, they would reflect, saying, "Hurray, I did it!" or "Can't do it." And as is the case with all of us, irrelevant speech came up as well, and this was captured. For toddlers, these were things such as saying "choo choo choo" while constructing the house or garden.

When the spoken words were analyzed, the researchers found that all of the toddlers used private speech in some way. And they talked to themselves a lot! By far the most common use was performance feedback. On average, toddlers said something to themselves related to how they were executing a task more than two times per minute, and some toddlers were above seven times per minute. When their words were compared to the accuracy of what they had built, the research team found that toddlers who verbalized a plan did better. This included "task analysis, task goals, [and] planning or motivational statements." Furthermore, children who had more task-irrelevant things to say performed worse, which lends further support to the importance of relevant private speech.[14]

Talking to ourselves about the tasks we are doing can help us plan and execute next steps. As long as our self-talk is relevant to the task, it focuses our attention and can gently speed up the process of improving. And for an even bigger boost in performance, mastery, and motivation, there is also an important relationship among kindness, discussed in Chapter 2, play, discussed in Chapter 5, and self-talk. In 2016, developmental and educational psychologist Jeremy Sawyer at the City University of New York conducted an experiment with thirty-eight children ages three to five. This task was a fishing game in which the children used a toy rod with a magnet to catch metal fish from a pond demarcated by a Hula-Hoop. Some fish were easy to catch, others difficult but possible, and one fish was made impossible—it would slide off the rod every time it was lifted. The toddlers were then put into two groups, a playful condition, and a non-playful condition. In the playful condition the children were introduced to a family of toy figurines. They were told that a family was hungry, and they had to catch fish so everyone could eat together. In the non-playful condition, the game was framed as work and stickers were provided to motivate the children. All their private speech was recorded.

In the analysis, mastery motivation was specifically examined as a combination of children's performance and persistence, and it was found that children in the play condition had higher scores. When it came to catching the easy and medium difficulty fish, children in both conditions used private speech about equally; however, when it came to the impossible fish, children in the play condition used it twice as frequently. These children were more motivated to catch the fish and thus used private speech more. And although catching fish for the family was related to play in the study, this also goes back to children's natural kindness. You can hear it in their voices. "I'll catch these fish so the family won't be hungry."[15]

Let's now turn to adults and see how self-talk can help us learn and solve problems. First, we need to understand that talking to ourselves is normal and we might even be doing this out loud without knowing it. This is especially true when, like children, we have a new or challenging task. In a study from St. Francis Xavier University and the University of Waterloo, fifty-three undergraduates were given computer tasks of various difficulty. They were recorded while they were working through these tasks, and in the analysis, every single participant was found to have used private speech during the experiment. However, when participants were asked if they had talked out loud during the experiment, 40 percent said they hadn't. Of note, the researchers also found that in general, there was more self-verbalization when tasks were difficult, lending support to the idea that this could be particularly helpful for learning and accomplishing harder tasks.[16]

The next study we will look at examined this idea of the importance of self-talk for harder tasks in more detail. It was conducted in Spain, where researchers enrolled 126 adults who were taking part in a literacy program. Each participant was asked to perform a card-sorting task, which was challenging given their level of literacy. Although they knew they were being recorded, they were told a cover story as to the purpose of the camera in the room, and not that the intent of the recording was to capture what they were saying to themselves. Also of note, there were other adults around, so they were not alone. Interestingly, these adults said to themselves some of the same types of things that toddlers said when they were studied, things relevant to their task such as "This one over there," and motivational speech such as "I am doing well!" There was even irrelevant speech such as "I took a bus today." Researchers were also able to capture more subtle instances when the participants were talking to themselves but not overtly, classified as partially internalized private speech. In the analysis, the researchers found that people who engaged in internalized private speech, self-regulatory private speech, or private speech preceding an action performed better with the given tasks, and they completed them in less time.[17]

And even if it's not the most difficult task that you are working on, private speech can still help. Sometimes the most stressful part of our day can be when we misplace something, especially if it is our keys and we are running late. Well, some more good news here: Talking to yourself can help with visual searches. In a series of experiments led by cognitive scientist and psychology professor Gary Lupyan at the University of Wisconsin-Madison, between twelve and twenty-six adults were asked to find various objects presented as images. There were also distractor images, often similar to the target, to make this more challenging. Sometimes the participants were given written instructions of what to find, and other times they were told to search for the object while saying the word to themselves. The people who said the word to themselves found objects faster. As the researchers write, "Actually hearing 'chair' compared to simply thinking about a chair can temporarily make the visual system a better 'chair detector.'"[18]

Whether we do it out loud (as private speech) or silently (as inner speech), these types of deliberate self-talk can help us learn and complete tasks, especially the most challenging ones. Toddlers aren't shy about self-talk, and neither should you be.

Managing Big Emotions

Toddlers are often defined by what are referred to as "big emotions." They are extreme in almost every way. Unfortunately, what is often seen by others are tantrums. And while I agree these brief periods of anger and frustration are intense, most of their lives are immersed in positive big emotions. Nobody else can achieve the happiness of a toddler watching a butterfly, show such deep love for a pet, and always demonstrate enthusiasm when learning. As toddlers develop, they learn to moderate their behavior in positive ways, and self-talk can help with this. And while it's good that toddlers eventually become less expressive with their anger, it's sad at the same time that some of those positive big emotions also get less intense. As adults, it is more challenging to give a massive, loving hug or a passionate high five to every person we see, something that came so naturally when we were two. Nevertheless, we could all benefit from behavioral moderation at times, and the adult data and techniques we'll talk about here with self-talk are incredibly powerful.

In the last section, we discussed specific aspects of toddler private speech that help with accomplishing tasks and learning, namely task planning, goal setting, and motivational talk. We also saw that there was a difference between task-relevant and task-irrelevant speech. This distinction has been formally classified as mature, if it is relevant, and immature, if it is irrelevant to the task. Mature private speech specifically focuses on the activity, goal, or feelings about the task while immature private speech is simply making sounds, repeating words, or completely off topic. Using this framework, researchers from four American universities conducted a study with 160 three-year-olds and followed them over six years, until age nine. Initially, at age three, the researchers were interested in measuring private speech as the toddlers completed a puzzle task. They were then brought back at age four, this time to measure their inhibitory control. This was measured through a series of three tasks, one of which was called "gift delay," as an example. In this activity, the child had to sit facing a wall while the experimenter wrapped a gift and then left the room. The child was tested on how long they could wait before touching the gift. Finally, at age nine, the same children were tested on their emotional regulation. This was done through a survey given to their mothers to fill out, as well as through a rigged game in which they were told they could win ten dollars, but that was impossible.

As predicted by the researchers, those toddlers who showed more mature private speech at age three had better inhibitory control at age four and better emotional regulation at age nine. What was also interesting was at baseline, when the children were three, their mothers were asked about their anger reactivity. When this was put into the analysis, it was discovered that children with higher levels of anger had a stronger effect of private speech helping to regulate their emotions later in life. This points to the fact that, similar to a previous case in which we saw private speech having the biggest effect in the most difficult situations, private speech has the largest impact when emotions are more extreme.[19]

Emotional regulation using self-talk in a variety of ways has been well studied in adults. The most well-known researcher in this field is Ethan Kross, professor and director of the Emotion & Self Control Lab at the University of Michigan. He is also the author of the fascinating book *Chatter: The Voice in Our Head, Why It Matters, and How to Harness It*.[20] Kross and his team have demonstrated the changes that happen inside our brains when we talk to ourselves and how we can utilize this information for our benefit. These techniques are especially useful if we do so in the second or third person so we can self-distance. This is the same strategy we discussed in the last chapter when we talked about how we can become superheroes. But before we look at some practical ways self-talk can help us at work, let's start this discussion with two important neuroimaging studies to demonstrate how our brains process self-talk differently.

In the first study, Kross and his team used fMRI and event-related potentials (ERPs), which are brain waves, to look at how talking to ourselves in the third person affects our brain activity when we are experiencing negative emotions. The participants were twenty-nine undergraduate students who were assigned to either the first-person condition or the third-person condition. First, they were shown aversive images designed to elicit emotional responses. For example, a fierce-looking dog baring its teeth to elicit fear.[21] Then they asked themselves two different questions depending on the condition to which they were assigned: "What am I feeling right now?" for the first condition or "What is [participant's name] feeling right now?" for the second condition. When the researchers looked at the brain wave responses, they found a reduced marker of emotional reactivity when the question was asked in the third person. The researchers

then conducted a related experiment in which they had participants recall negative events that happened to them. Using a similar
procedure as in the first experiment, they found similar results and
concluded that "third-person self-talk may constitute a relatively
effortless form of self-control."[22] In other words, when we talk to
ourselves from the third-person perspective, we can tone down big
emotions we might have and be more in control of them.

The second study examined how we give and process criticism.
In this study fifty-five adult participants were told that they were in a
mentorship role, and it was their job to give feedback on a mentee's
speech. The participants were told to either use their own name and
the pronoun *you* when reflecting on their emotions and the evaluation, or to use the pronouns *I* and *my*. They then wore an electroen-
cephalogram (EEG) cap to measure brain wave activity, and while
watching the speeches, they had to press a thumbs-up or thumbs-
down button at different points in the speech. Finally, they gave
verbal feedback to the mentee, and this was recorded. Later, these
videos were scored by independent raters for positivity, warmth,
and helpfulness. Similarly to the previous study, there was decreased
brain wave activity in regions responsible for self-referential processing for those participants that used their name or *you*. More importantly, this self-distancing technique resulted in giving feedback
that was more positive, warm, and helpful.[23]

These studies are important to understand because thinking about
negative experiences can take up a lot of space in our minds. For instance, *Why did my coworker say that? Why did I not get that pro-
motion?* We can lessen the burden of this if we simply think of these
things, and talk ourselves through, in the second or third person.

Similarly, giving or receiving feedback is something we often have to do at work, and this simple reframe can make us better at both.

Now that we have seen that this change in perspective can alter our brain wave activity, let's look at a larger study to see additional examples of how powerful this effect can be when participants are not hooked up to electrodes or in an MRI machine. In a study published by Kross in 2014, his team examined how we could potentially manage social stress better, including worrying about future events. This project included nearly six hundred adults over seven different studies. Again, they were looking at differences in using first-person pronouns compared to non-first-person pronouns (second or third person). These studies were fascinating because they brought out situations we face in daily life that are potentially stressful. In one study they looked at people making first impressions while meeting someone new, and in another it was public speaking. Take a look at these examples from essays participants wrote after the challenge that highlight how they felt differently when asked to give a speech.

Essay sample after completing first-person condition:

I can't prepare an oral speech in three minutes. It takes days for me to examine my strengths, weaknesses, etc. I need to have my oral speech written down and perfected, and therefore, this is not going to work out.

Essay sample after completing non-first-person condition:

First, I asked myself what was I nervous about? It's not like this will be the first interview or speech I've ever had to give. And even if it doesn't go perfectly, it won't be the end of the world. I mostly think reassuring and comforting thoughts to motivate and encourage myself.

Across these studies the authors found that simple, "small shifts" in language influenced a person's ability to regulate their thoughts, feelings, and behavior in social situations. Importantly, in these studies they also looked at whether people had social anxiety and found that regardless of people scoring high or low for social anxiety, they benefited similarly.[24]

Second- or third-person self-talk is the easiest way to help you through anxiety-provoking situations. You can do it out loud or as silent inner speech, as long as you are deliberate and avoid using first-person pronouns. There are several other strategies to decrease anxiety, and we will talk about those at the end of the chapter.

How Self-Talk Can Improve Diet, Sleep, and Exercise

So far in this chapter we have discussed how self-talk can be helpful in your daily work by enhancing your problem-solving skills as well as decreasing anxiety related to things such as giving a presentation in front of a large group of people. But the benefits of self-talk don't stop there. Because it is such an easy thing to implement, it has been studied in a wide range of other scenarios with positive results. We started this book with the foundation of better health and wellness including eating right, exercise, and sleeping well. So let's go back to Chapter 1 for a moment and discuss how self-talk can enhance all these.

In Chapter 1 we discussed toddlers' remarkable ability to stop eating when they are full and resist high-calorie foods as long as they

weren't restricted. But because we are so far away from these practices, we might need a little boost to get us back to the toddler path
of eating healthy. The ability to make healthier choices using self-
talk was tested in a study published in 2020 by Kross's team in collaboration with the Department of Psychology at the University of
Minnesota. The researchers were interested in seeing which food an
adult would choose between an unhealthy and a healthy option. Before the test, they also assessed whether participants were currently
dieting. At the time of the decision, they were instructed to engage
in self-talk in either asking themselves, "What do I want?" or "What
does [participant's name] want?" In addition to this, they had half
of the participants watch a health-promoting advertisement and the
other half a home improvement video as the control. Over two hundred adults were included, and interestingly, dieters benefited the
most from the combination of distanced self-talk and watching the
health video. Non-dieters, however, made healthier decisions using
distanced self-talk regardless of whether they watched the health
video.[25]

Next, let's talk about exercise. There is an incredible body of literature showing how self-talk can assist in higher performance in
sports whether you are alone or are playing a team sport. Researchers
from Greece published a fascinating study with sixty young adult
men taking basketball shots. They were split into three groups with
the goal of getting as many basketballs in the hoop in three minutes
as possible from designated spots on the court. One group received
no additional instruction, a second group was told to repeat the word
relax before each shot, and the third group was told to repeat the
word *fast* before each shot. The group that said *relax* demonstrated

improved performance over the control group while the group that said *fast* did not. Even these single self-talk words, said in the right context, can help. And what's nice about this is you can experiment with different words and see what works for you.

While many studies show similar effects in a wide range of sports including tennis[26] and rugby,[27] it's helpful to look at the meta-analysis data that combines multiple studies. In one such study, from the University of Thessaly in Greece, thirty-two studies were pooled together. These studies all incorporated self-talk in sports. Given the number of studies, the authors were able to break down the data further and look at skills that required fine motor abilities such as throwing darts and golf putting, as well as skills that required more strength and power such as cycling and long-distance running (gross motor skills). They also were able to analyze the type of self-talk: motivational or instructional. Motivational self-talk aims to create a positive mood and build confidence and includes things such as saying, "Let's go!" and "I can do it!" Instructional self-talk focuses your attention on a specific task or strategy. These can be things such as saying, "See the target" and "High elbow." The participants included beginners to experienced athletes, so the results are applicable no matter what level you are at. Overall, self-talk in general was shown to have a positive effect on all types of sports taking all participants together. Specifically, self-talk was shown to be more effective for fine motor tasks compared to gross motor tasks and for relatively new tasks compared to those that were well learned. Even the type of self-talk made a difference for fine motor skills: instructional self-talk was shown to be more effective than motivational self-talk.[28]

In sports and exercise in general, self-talk is the simplest method you can employ to improve. This is especially true for new skills, so if you've ever wanted to try a new sport, self-talk may help. And while this won't make your amateur skills reach those of a professional,[29] it can continue the cycle of improvement and motivation, helping you to enjoy the sport more, and improve your physical health through exercise.

Finally, let's turn to sleep and some specific self-talk strategies if your thoughts are keeping you from sleeping. You may have noticed this yourself, but sometimes it might be hard to sleep because you feel anxious. This can either be because of worry about a future event or rumination. Rumination is repeatedly thinking about problems or events that have already happened and you likely had no control over. When these two factors were studied in nearly five hundred adults, they both separately predicted sleep impairment.[30]

Worry and rumination can be debilitating for some and can lead to problems extending far beyond sleep disturbance. Ethan Kross, in his book *Chatter*, offers some practical solutions if you are having difficulty with worry and rumination. Keep in mind that these can be applied to any scenario but may be particularly helpful with sleep, as worry and rumination are known causes of insomnia. First you can imagine advising a friend. Pretend that a friend has the same problem as you and think about the advice you would give that person. Next, you can try to reframe the experience as a challenge. You might be able to tell yourself how you've previously succeeded in a similar situation. And third, as we've discussed in several examples, you can use distanced self-talk. Talking to yourself using the second person, "you," or third person, using your own name, leads to less activation of the parts of the brain associated with rumination.[31]

Toddlers are incredibly smart and in tune with how their minds work. They know that if they talk to themselves, they will perform better, so they do this all the time. It doesn't matter to them whether other people can hear them, and in fact there is even data that certain types of private speech are increased when others are around.[32] In one study, when specifically asked about their own use of private speech, three- to five-year-olds rate it as being helpful, making the task easier, and making the task go faster.[33] They utilize self-talk strategically, when problems are more difficult and when they are learning new things, and dial it down when they don't need it as much, for example, when they are engaged in play.[34] Unlike adults, they also don't get down on themselves or engage in as much negative self-talk. When a task is difficult and they can't find a solution, adult self-talk focuses on their own incompetence or on the difficulty of the task itself. Not toddlers. They simply express negative feelings in a neutral and nonspecific way without assigning blame. "Oh no! What a bummer" is all that is required before moving on.[35]

Similarly, self-talk is incredibly powerful for adults too. It helps with memory, confidence, motivation, problem-solving, and decreasing negative emotions.[36,37] If we utilize a second- or third-person perspective, it reframes situations and makes it easier for us to see situations from an objective perspective rather than being infused with the emotional bias we always carry.[38] And beyond problem-solving and emotional regulation, self-talk can move us toward achieving more foundational wellness goals such as eating better. When we were young, this came easy to all of us. Now, it seems perhaps a bit awkward. But if we can push ourselves to utilize more self-talk, it can benefit just about every aspect of our lives.

Toddler Teachings

Talking to yourself is completely normal, and you are likely doing it sometimes without noticing. Make it more deliberate.

For the most difficult problems, focus on talking yourself through your goals and what you need to do next to help you execute. Some self-encouragement along the way never hurts.

Try to focus on task-relevant self-talk rather than the irrelevant, such as the "choo choo choo" that might be happening in your mind.

If you are experiencing negative big emotions, use distanced second- or third-person self-talk to gain an objective perspective and help you regain control. Positive big emotions are always okay.

Use self-talk to help nudge you toward achieving the foundational goals of wellness, which include healthier eating, better sleep, and more exercise.

Chapter 9:

Asking Questions and Saying "No!"

"No, I don't wanna . . ."

In the last chapter, we talked about what we could learn from toddler self-talk. It turns out, there are equally valuable lessons when we listen to what toddlers have to say to others. While it's true that they do say the cutest things, they also say important things. Their sincerity allows them to say precisely what they are thinking and feeling without the filter we insert as adults. This helps them in a variety of ways, most notably with learning and autonomy. Wouldn't we all like to understand things better and have more control of our lives? Toddlers have this figured out and can help all of us with their example.

A conversation with a toddler is quite different from one with an adult and generally more fun. Besides the jokes and silliness, you will always get asked to do some sort of activity. Toddlers are not the type to sit and have a long conversation. As we discussed earlier, they like to keep busy and would prefer to be engaged in either physical activity or a form of play. Next, no matter what you are doing or where you are, you will be bombarded with questions. In their never-ending quest to learn new things, they are more than happy to ask rapid-fire questions of someone who knows so much more about the world and can explain it to them. And they are not just simple questions. Once those are answered, they will go deeper and deeper with "why" until you begin to question those things yourself.

And when the questions come back to them about how things work, one of two things will happen. Either they will have a genuine explanation that involves a unicorn or some other animal, or they will readily say, "I don't know." They understand when they don't know something and have no shame in telling you. And they respect adults who admit they don't know a particular piece of information. Research has shown that four-year-olds can distinguish between someone who is generally knowledgeable but admits to not knowing something and others who are unreliable because they said something untrue. They respect the "I don't know" and will still go back to that person in the future.[1]

The conversation with questions and answers can generally flow happily until you ask them to do something they don't want to do. Wow. That can be a conversation killer. Toddlers have rightfully gained the reputation of having the strongest, most powerful "No!" Somehow, when asked to do something as harmless as take a bath or put on some pants, they can look you right in the eye and as firmly as anyone could ever do it, bellow "No!" And while this can be a problem for the adult in their life who needs them to do certain things, it's also admirable. Over time, many of us have lost this ability, which can lead to overcommitment and stress.

In this chapter we will discuss these two important conversational abilities that all toddlers possess: asking questions and saying no. For each of these, we'll start by discussing why toddlers do them and what they gain. Next, we will discuss why we as adults underutilize these in conversation and explain how we are losing out in the process. In this discussion we will see how simple things such as small talk and substituting "don't" for "can't" can make a big difference in improving our well-being.

Little Socrates

Once they are able to speak and form words and sentences, the questions posed by toddlers are endless. Being on the receiving end of these questions is both fascinating and humorous as we gain some insight into their small but powerful minds. They have the ability to make us think in ways usually only highly trained educational professionals or psychotherapists can, demonstrating their wisdom well beyond their years. For decades, ever since early childhood was studied formally, these questions have been recorded and analyzed in order to understand toddlers better. In the late nineteenth century, psychology professor James Sully at the University of London published a book titled *Studies of Childhood.* As part of his book, he included extracts of a father's diary as he watched his son grow, and as we would expect, it contains a wealth of questions. For example, at age four the little boy asked, "Where was I before I was born?" At age five, "How is it, Papa, that when we put our hand into the water we don't make a hole in it?" This child was constantly trying to get to the truth and questioning his father. He would consistently use logic and a series of follow-up questions that challenged his father and made him think more. As Sully put it, the way in which this young boy asked questions was "very much after the manner of the astute Socrates."[2]

More recently, to gain a better understanding of toddler questions, researchers have focused on the Child Language Data Exchange System (CHILDES). Started in 1984, it contains transcripts of children's conversations from as early as 1960, now with data in twenty-six different languages. It is currently maintained at Carnegie Mellon University and is publicly available.[3] Using this data, one team of researchers chose four children ages one to five, and analyzed their audio recordings. These audio files were recorded over several years at the children's homes, providing an incredibly rich dataset. The analysis included over two hundred hours of conversation, and during this time, the toddlers asked an astonishing 24,741 questions! This worked out to an average of 107 questions asked by each child per hour while children were speaking to an adult.

The researchers then dug deeper and investigated the types of questions the toddlers asked. Contrary to another misconception about toddlers that they are attention seeking, only 6 percent of their questions were for this reason. An overwhelming majority, 80 percent, were either information-seeking or clarification questions. They asked about other things as well, such as play or permission to do something, but their central goal was clearly on learning. Interestingly, 4 percent of the questions stumped the researchers and could not be categorized, and 1 percent were directed to another child or an animal, pointing to the fact that they do know their dog or sibling likely won't be able to explain how the sun works. Still, once in a while it's important to ask your pet questions. Unlike adults, who often engage in chitchat (not that that's a bad thing as we will discuss later), toddlers utilize the majority of their questions for information gathering and learning.

To be absolutely sure the children were not attention seeking or simply enjoyed being in a conversation, the researchers then went a step further and analyzed what the children did with the information they received. Simply put, the children either received the target information they were seeking or they did not. If they did not, then they were significantly more likely to repeat their question. And while this constant repetition of questions can be exhausting for the receiver, this study showed that when children received the information they were looking for, they stopped.[4]

While asking questions primarily serves the role of gathering information for toddlers, it is also critical for social and language development. We see this in children with autism who have difficulties with social initiation and generally don't ask questions in social situations. However, research has shown that if we teach autistic children to ask more questions, then their language abilities improve.[5]

At 107 questions per hour, it's clear that toddlers love to ask questions. As we have seen throughout the book, they are often motivated by learning, and if it's going to take that many questions to learn, they will do it. And again, their persistence shines here. They will go on and on, repeating a question until they get the answer they need. Asking questions is an important skill and something adults often hesitate to do. Questions are both important for getting the right information but also for relationship building, and in the next few sections, we'll see how asking more questions can both improve knowledge and relationships.

We Are Question Shy

After decades of lived experience, it somewhat makes sense that we ask less than a hundred questions per hour as adults, although we all still have a lot to learn. The problem is not that we can't easily generate this number of questions, it's our hesitation to ask them. We know the benefits of asking questions, especially to gain a piece of knowledge we need or to get assistance, but many of us still hesitate while toddlers don't. This can be particularly true in the workplace, where we may have self-doubt in our abilities despite objective success, a phenomenon called imposter syndrome. Imposter syndrome is common across a wide range of ages and settings including high school, college, working professionals, academics, and physicians. Ethnic minorities have higher rates of imposter syndrome, and it is associated with impaired job performance and burnout.[6]

Because we may doubt our abilities or we are worried about how our peers may perceive us when we ask certain questions, we ask less of them. In 2020, two researchers from the UK and France studied 281 alumni of a top-ranked business school and asked them how they utilize questions at work. Although more than 80 percent said questions were a better way to get input from subordinates and show humility, only 29 percent said they asked questions at every opportunity.[7]

This hesitation to ask questions because of how we will be viewed is exaggerated in our minds. The researchers of the same study went on to recruit hundreds of American adults for a series of four additional experiments. They were given scenarios to read online in which a fictional CEO or VP sent an e-mail with questions. Different manipulations were done to the text when describing the business leader, for example, giving the person higher or lower credentials, having them explicitly state they did not know the answer, and changing their reputation as someone who was or wasn't willing to admit mistakes. Across these studies, the researchers found there was some amount of being perceived as less competent only when the leader was given low credentials but not in any of the other scenarios. More importantly, these competence penalties were buffered by humility premiums. Asking questions but also being humble by being considerate, being a good listener, willing to admit mistakes, and showing care demonstrates humility. This not only decreased any questions of competence, but it was also shown to have positive effects on trust and helping intentions, beyond simply getting the answers to the questions.[8]

Another issue that contributes to our lack of questioning is that most of us feel that some questions are too sensitive. While this can be true, and nobody should ever be asked if they are pregnant outside a medical setting, for example,[9] we generally overestimate negative perceptions some sensitive questions may create. In a fascinating study published in 2021, researchers had participants ask strangers and acquaintances sensitive questions. They wanted to see first, if the participants would do it, and second, how each party felt about these questions. They recruited more than one hundred adults and paired them either with a friend they came into the lab with or with a random stranger who arrived separately. Before the conversations, each person was asked a series of questions including how they predicted the other person would feel about them. After the conversation, they were asked how they actually felt. Half the group was assigned to be "askers" and were given a list of five sensitive questions, for example: "Have you tried to gain access to someone else's e-mail account or text messages?" and five nonsensitive questions such as "Do you drink coffee?" The most important takeaway from this study was that whether the asker was paired with a friend or a stranger, they significantly overestimated any harmful effects of asking sensitive questions. They were a bit better at getting closer to the truth with people they knew but were still off. The authors of the study conclude, "People do not mind answering sensitive questions nearly as much as those contemplating asking the sensitive questions anticipate."[10]

In summary, adults, unlike toddlers, hesitate to ask questions for a variety of reasons. While we know how important questions are, we don't ask them as much as we know we should, even when we recognize the potential benefits go beyond simply knowledge acquisition. We are overly worried about what people will think of us and how it will affect them. Questions, when asked in the right way, can build trust and, as we will see later in this chapter, are key to building relationships.

Asking Questions Can Accelerate Learning

We have all been in situations with a painfully awkward silence at the end of a presentation. Sometimes after the speaker asks, "Are there any questions?," there simply aren't any. This can be hard for a speaker after preparing all the material. Was it that the material was explained very well, or was the talk boring? This situation, however, does not exist when presenting to a group of toddlers. Whether they are learning about nature, reading a book together, or simply discussing the plan for the day, you cannot keep their hands from constantly shooting up; they want to ask questions repeatedly.

Given the high proportion of information-seeking questions toddlers have, it's clear their goal is learning. And for adults, while it may seem obvious that asking people questions will lead to a greater understanding of a given issue, let's connect questioning to both reading, discussed in Chapter 4, and self-talk, discussed in Chapter 8, to see how asking more questions can help in our learning.

So far, we have established that for adults, unlike toddlers, we often ask fewer questions because of largely unfounded worries about how it will make us look and how others might feel. So let's start with something easier that you can do: Ask yourself questions. As we discussed earlier, reading has a multitude of benefits. And while it would be great if we could remember everything we read, our minds, unfortunately, are not designed for that.

Self-questioning, however, is one strategy that can help. In a study from Washington University in St. Louis, researchers tested different learning strategies in a population of nearly fifty undergraduates. The exercise consisted of reading four passages and then completing a twenty-four-question test. Before the test, the participants were split up into three groups. The first was told to reread each passage, the second was instructed to generate three conceptual questions and answers for each passage, and the last group was asked to generate three detailed questions and answers for the passages. The authors found that generating conceptual questions and answers was superior to both rereading and generating detailed questions. And while there was no difference in performance when generating detailed questions compared with rereading in this study, we will discuss another strategy to better remember details next.[11] For now, it's simply important to know that for the main ideas and concepts, which is most of what we want to take away from a book or article, for example, generating your own conceptual questions and answers is an easy way to improve your recall.

Beyond recalling larger concepts, however, sometimes remembering the details is important in your work or if you are a student studying for a test. In that case, going a step further and generating flashcards of your questions can improve your recall of information. In a study published in 2022, researchers examined three hundred adults in a series of experiments testing them on what they had learned from reading two passages. These passages were not easy. They were on the topics of expressionist art and ancient Rome and, using an objective measure of readability, were scored to be "very difficult" and at the level of a college graduate. The participants were split up into two groups. After reading the passages, one group had to generate their own flashcards and then practice with those while the other group was given premade flashcards. They were then tested on the material forty-eight hours later. Overall, across all studies, users who generated their own flashcards scored higher on detail-oriented questions, as well as on application questions measuring whether they could transfer their learning more broadly.[12]

While simply starting to ask more questions at work or in social situations might be awkward or challenging, self-questioning is an easy way to gradually increase asking. Self-generated questions and flashcards can help you remember better what you have read and learned. In the next section we will talk about how bringing more of those questions out into social situations, as toddlers do, can help us build and strengthen relationships.

Get That Second Date

Toddlers have the unique ability to build relationships quickly, much faster than anyone else. Through smiling, laughter, play, and a genuine desire to be kind and helpful to people, making friends is easy. And although their goal in asking as many questions as they do is not specifically to build relationships, questions do offer a powerful way to strengthen personal bonds. For adults, this can translate beyond friendship to romantic relationships.

While it's not something we think about very much, we do ask a number of questions in social situations but more because of social norms. When we make small talk and ask the simple "How are you?," we are making that social connection and communicating in a more polite manner.[13] But we could do much better, and in this section, we'll talk about a few ways that questions in social situations can help us improve our relationships.

Since we are on the topic of small talk, let's start with office chitchat. Before the COVID-19 pandemic, when there were fewer remote workers, a 2019 survey of office workers found that three quarters of respondents saw water cooler discussions as a means to break up the workday. By far the most likely topics discussed were the weather and weekend plans, followed by sports.[14]

These types of discussions were studied in more detail by research led at Rutgers University. The study included one hundred American employees who worked outside the home and on a traditional nine-to-five schedule. For fifteen consecutive workdays, the employees were sent surveys that had questions measuring small talk, work engagement, and emotions. Sleep was also controlled for, as this could have an impact on emotional well-being. As one might expect, small talk was found to be distracting, but more interestingly, it enhanced positive social emotions at work. And getting back to our previous point, that we ask fewer questions in general, the authors point out that "the scripted nature of small talk can alleviate some uncertainty around successful small talk rituals by helping to prepare individuals with content in which they can ground a conversation."[15] Small talk is both easier for us to start and continue and is a good foundation for social connections, using questions in a way in which we can feel more comfortable.

Small talk is helpful, and everyone needs a boost at work, but questions have the power to do much more. Let's end this section with a discussion on more personal relationships and talk about how questioning might help with dating. In a widely cited study published in 2017, researchers at Harvard University sought to understand how asking questions makes us more likable. To test this, they organized a speed dating session with 110 adults. Each person went on between fifteen and nineteen four-minute dates. At the end of each one, they were asked to fill out a brief survey with the primary question being if they wanted to go on a second date. The analysis included looking at more than 4200 conversational turns and drilled down on the types of questions that were asked. The authors found that those people who asked more follow-up questions had a higher rate of success. And these types of questions were not difficult to ask; they simply responded to what their partner was saying. The example in the article is Partner A says, "I'm planning a trip to Canada," and the follow-up question from Partner B is "Oh, cool. Have you ever been there before?" This perceived responsiveness is what the authors point to as the mechanism by which follow-up questions lead to increasing liking.[16]

In trying to make a good impression, people naturally talk about themselves. But, as the authors of the speed dating study point out, people are "largely unaware that asking questions has social benefits."[17] Asking questions is what makes your partner feel you are more responsive and, therefore, a more likable person.

Now that we have talked about the benefits of asking more questions, as toddlers do, let's examine something else they do multiple times per hour: say no. In the rest of this chapter we will examine why, similar to asking questions, adults struggle while toddlers shine. Simply yelling "No!" like a toddler might not work for adults in most situations, but we will talk about other specific strategies that may help clear up your cluttered schedule and your mind so you can focus on the things you both want to do and are the most important.

They Don't Always Say No

As we touched on earlier, the toddler stage is marked by rapid development in language. Starting with a few words at age one, by age two they can say fifty words and ask two-word questions. This is followed by a period of exponential growth, and by age five they have a vocabulary of more than two thousand words.[18] Still, some of the most important words come before their second birthday. It is then they learn to say yes and no and start to discover the power that comes with those words.

Because of what we see on the Internet and experiences we may have had overhearing the mighty toddler "No!," we might think that they have a tendency to say this to everything. Surprisingly, this is not true,[19] and they are quite selective with how they use it. In a series of experiments with young children, developmental psychologist Mako Okanda at Otemon Gakuin University in Japan demonstrated that toddlers have a "Yes" bias when asked yes-or-no questions about both familiar and unfamiliar objects. For example, when presented with a shoehorn (unfamiliar object) and asked, "Is this worn on the head?," toddlers have a tendency to say yes. Over time this changes, and when they reach four- to five-years-old, they lose this bias. By age six, they have a tendency to say no. Interestingly, the youngest toddlers also have the shortest response latency, meaning they answer very quickly.[20]

So if toddlers don't have a natural tendency to say no, where does this tendency come from? Well imagine that instead of being an infant with an adult schlepping you around, spoon-feeding you, and dictating exactly what you should be doing every minute of the day, you suddenly had freedom. In the toddler years, you learn to walk, then run, climb stairs, and jump! You go from cooing to words to asking questions and making requests. You can explore all by yourself, in cupboards, behind the couch, and even with electrical outlets. Now that you are the boss, you want to make all the decisions, and saying no represents the ultimate form of autonomy.

Nooooo!

While toddlers don't use "no" all the time, they certainly use it emphatically when they want to exert their control, which is often. When they are with their caregivers, toddlers have many conflicts. And this isn't a bad thing. They are learning how to set boundaries for themselves and what others expect from them. They are also learning how to resolve conflicts.

To examine this in greater detail, researchers from Lehigh University and the University of California, Davis, performed an experiment with sixty-four mother-child pairs. They were recorded both in the laboratory setting, at age two, and at home, at age three. All types of conflicts and disagreements were recorded in both settings, including those around rules, respecting personal space, and disputing facts. Overall, the researchers found that toddlers had between twenty and twenty-five conflicts per hour, often involving the toddler saying an emphatic "No!" Here is one example from the study (I've edited the conversation for the sake of space):

Mother: Do you want to play with the puzzle?

Child: No, the toys.

Mother: Well, honey, those are her special toys. We can't play with those toys, remember.

Child: I know. I want.

Mother: I know you want to, but you can't.

Child: I want my other shoes.

Mother: You don't need your other shoes. You wear your Pooh sandals when we go for a walk.

Child: Nooooooo.

Mother: No, you don't need your other shoes. You wear your Pooh sandals when we go for a walk.

Child: Ahhhhh! Want pretty dress.

Mother: Your pretty dress?

Child: Yeah.

Mother: You can wear them some other day.

Child: Nooooooo!

Mother: Now here, maybe you can wear them on Sunday, when you go to Sunday school. You can wear your pink dress and Pooh sandals, okay?

Child: Nooooo!

Just in this short conversation that somehow went from puzzles to clothing to shoes, the toddler said no four times.[21] She really wanted her other shoes and the pretty dress that day, and why not? As we previously discussed, engaging in conflict is not how toddlers spend most of their time. They would much rather be exercising, playing, and making jokes. But the point is, they are not afraid to say no.

The autonomy that comes with saying no cannot be overstated because in our own lives many of us have lost this power. It's something we are often shy to do while toddlers do it multiple times per hour. Losing this ability feeds into losing control of our time, our schedule, and eventually feeling overwhelmed and burned out. René Spitz, a renowned Austrian American psychiatrist famous for his work on the importance of attachment in infancy,[22] wrote that the moment a toddler is able to say no to her caregiver is "beyond doubt the most spectacular intellectual and semantic achievement during early childhood."[23] Arguably, regaining this ability as an adult is equally an important achievement, and in the next sections, we will discuss why we have lost this ability and some strategies to gain it back.

Being an Adult Puts You in a Pickle

Unfortunately for adults, saying no does not come as easily for two reasons. First, like toddlers, we also have a yes bias, but instead of saying yes to questions about unfamiliar objects, we tend to say yes to tasks others ask us to do. And secondly, we are notoriously inaccurate in estimating how much time a given task will take. These two things together work against us when we want to say no, but understanding them and the reasons why we say yes may help in being able to say no more often.

Since we were toddlers ourselves, exploring the world and making messes everywhere, the word *no* has come to signal something negative, a word to stop. At the same time, *yes* has been used in a positive and more often encouraging way, so we have developed to understand "yes" as having a positive emotional valence while "no" has a negative emotional valence. When studying adults using fMRI, neuroscientists have confirmed that hearing these words sends either a positive or negative signal to the part of our brain responsible for assigning an affective value, depending on whether we hear "yes" or "no."[24]

Humans are social people, and we naturally want to help others. We saw how strong this was in Chapter 6 when we discussed teamwork, and this drive stays with us because it is how we have evolved. And in Chapter 7, we looked at one example of how people asking strangers for help were more likely to get a yes than they predicted.[25] In addition to our natural tendency to cooperate and help others, we are also fighting against something called harshness bias. This means that we believe if we say no, we will be judged more negatively than we actually are.[26] When we get requests, we naturally feel a social pressure to say yes. And this drive to say yes, unfortunately for us, is not limited to requests we receive for help; it extends to other asks, even if we truly don't want to do them.

The best example of this is perhaps from a Canadian library book vandalism study from the University of Waterloo. In this study, researchers recruited twenty-five undergraduate students. They were each given a hardcover book with a library reference number on the spine (to make it more believable) and a pen. Their task was to approach other students and say: "Hi, I'm trying to play a prank on someone, but they know my handwriting. Will you just quickly write the word 'pickle' on this page of this library book?" The researchers were specifically looking at how many students would need to be approached before three said yes. The students doing the asking predicted that it would be between ten and eleven, but in reality, it was only between four and five. Most people were willing to be vandals. The responses received from the students being asked to vandalize are quite telling, whether they wrote the word or not. Some of the remarks include, "I gotta vandalize this pretty book?" "Are you sure? Um, okay . . .," and "I don't write on library books. Sorry about that." This last statement is important, and we will get back to the importance of saying, "I don't" in the next section. Overall, it's difficult for us to say no to tasks we genuinely don't want to do or even think are right. As the authors put it, being on the receiving end of this type of request can be awkward, and the social pressure to say yes is "remarkably powerful."[27]

The second major problem of why we tend to say yes is because of something called the planning fallacy. This concept was first introduced in 1977 by Israeli psychologists Daniel Kahneman and Amos Tversky. The planning fallacy is our inability to properly estimate the amount of time a task in the future will take, despite previous experience of a similar task taking longer than expected.[28] And we see this in a wide range of areas, from academia[29] to surgery[30] and even holiday shopping.[31] You probably have examples from your own life, as well, as it is something we all do. Many people consistently underestimate the time it will take to drive somewhere, or the time it will take to complete a report at work. For me, despite more than a year of experience, I regularly underestimate the time it takes to get a toddler ready in the morning. One day we must have a deeper discussion on which stick-on earrings will match a particular dress, and another day we have to decide whether to brush teeth from outside to inside, or vice versa. At least once a week, we should review the pros and cons of walking to day care with an umbrella on a sunny day.

For larger projects, our time and cost estimates are even worse. One of the most famous examples is the construction of the iconic Sydney Opera House. When originally planned, it was expected to take four years to build and cost $7 million. In reality, it took fourteen years to construct, at a cost of more than a $100 million dollars.[32] And while it's impossible to completely get away from the planning fallacy, there are a few things you can do to understand your commitments better and say no to more tasks. We will discuss these in more detail in the next sections.

There are many reasons we say yes, but social pressure because of how we have evolved and the planning fallacy are two of the most important. Understanding them can help us better implement the strategies we discuss next. Before we do that, however, it's important to acknowledge two critical issues in this discussion. First, saying no is much easier in theory than in practice, and there are structural and systemic issues in the workplace that make this even harder for women and minorities.[33] And second, there are many people who are not knowledge workers and have much less choice in what they are able to say yes and no to. Getting overwhelmed with tasks at work is often a workplace issue and not a personal issue.[34]

Overall, despite our best efforts, our natural adult "yes" most often overpowers our inner toddler "no." In the next section we will talk about some specific strategies to get back to being able to say no more easily, as toddlers do.

The Overly Ambitious Adult Plan

Now that we have discussed the reasons why we so readily say yes, let's talk about some ways we can get back to our toddler selves and say no more often. We don't want to be as extreme as they are, with multiple conflicts per hour and raising our voices when we say no, but having an overfilled calendar with an eternally unfinished to-do list is not perfect either. A more polite middle ground would be ideal, and in this section, we will review specific strategies to say no that you can try.

Let's start with the planning fallacy and some ways to get around it. In an article published in *Big Think,* Kevin Dickinson discusses a scenario we can all relate to. It's Monday morning, and his plan is to "crush it." He wants to get up early, exercise, respond to all his e-mails, and write an article. After work, he will cook dinner, help his kid with homework, and do some reading. Despite every intention to complete these tasks, he ends up sleeping in and missing the workout, pushing several work tasks to Tuesday, and ordering a pizza in the evening.[35] This sounds familiar because it happens to everyone. There are, however, some useful strategies we can implement to help us get around the planning fallacy.

First, you could experiment with what is called unpacking, or task segmentation.[36,37] This is especially useful for larger, more complex tasks, and what it involves is instead of making one estimate of the total time it will take for the task, you break down the task into individual parts and assign a time value to each of those parts. Using this method, researchers from the University of Illinois

Urbana-Champaign demonstrated less biased time predictions with tasks that had some complexity such as formatting a document given specific instructions. In the experiment, it took participants more than twice as long to complete a task compared to the amount of time they predicted it would take. When the task was unpacked into its individual steps, however, it only took them 34 percent longer to complete, compared to 129 percent longer in the packed condition. This research group completed a series of other experiments as well and found that the more complex the task, the more unpacking can help make better time predictions.[38]

Another strategy to mitigate the planning fallacy is to have what is called an implementation intention. This is best explained by a study conducted at the Radboud University Nijmegen, the Netherlands. In this study, which included more than a hundred adults, participants were asked to write a report on their leisure time and hand it back in one week. All participants were asked to predict the days on which they would start and finish their report. Then half the participants were asked to choose a specific time and place that they would write their report, put it in writing, and then visualize this while thinking, "I intend to write the report in situation X." The participants who did this, compared to the ones who didn't, were shown not to be overly optimistic about whether they would complete the task. Not only that, but they also had a higher level of task completion.[39]

Finally, another closely related tip that may be helpful with planning in general is to use a paper calendar and ditch your mobile device. In a study published in 2022, researchers found that adults who used a paper planner (that showed a two-week view) were able to develop higher-quality plans and had a higher likelihood of completing their plans compared to those who used their phone calendars. Of note, users who changed the default mode of their phone calendars to take a broader view of their schedule were also able to develop better plans, but people who used the paper calendar still outperformed them in terms of plan completion.[40]

On a related note to the planning fallacy, sometimes the issue is that we say yes too quickly. For most larger asks, and even smaller ones, one suggestion would be to wait at least twenty-four hours before giving a response.[41] This gives you the time to process the request, better map out how much time it will take you, and figure out if this is something you want to prioritize. At least for e-mail, where many of our requests are coming from, research conducted in the workplace setting in Spain has shown that we overestimate how quickly we think the sender needs a response with nonurgent e-mails sent outside work hours.[42]

Sorry, I Don't Do That

Now that we have discussed scheduling in detail, let's go into an even easier strategy that, if aligned with your goals, might have a dramatic effect on both what you say no to and how effortless it can be. In the last chapter on self-talk, you will recall we discussed straightforward strategies that help us reframe how we motivate ourselves. Simply referring to ourselves in the second- or third-person, instead of using "I," can make a meaningful difference. Luckily, there is a similar strategy you can use to say no that only involves a simple word change for your response.

In 2012, researchers from the University of Houston and Boston College published a study that examined how well adults were able to say no using two different methods. They performed four different experiments, and we will focus on two of them here. In the first experiment, they recruited 120 adults and told them the study was to test a new healthy eating strategy. First, they were asked about healthy eating and if this was one of their goals. They were put into two groups in which one group was to rehearse a strategy of telling themselves, "I don't do X," while the other group was to say "I can't do X." Before the end of the study, the participants completed some unrelated work, and as they exited, they were told that as a token of appreciation they could choose one snack. One bowl contained chocolate candy bars while the other had granola bars. As they made their choice, the experimenter discreetly noted this on the questionnaire. The authors found that for people who said healthy eating was important, the "I don't" strategy was more effective than the "I can't" strategy for avoiding the candy bar.

In the next experiment, the researchers wanted to see what would happen outside the research lab setting. First, they organized a health and wellness seminar in which thirty women ages twenty-two to fifty-three participated. They were divided into three equal groups, and each group was given different instructions on what to do if they were tempted by something that may make them lapse, such as someone offering a chocolate bar. One group was instructed to use the "I can't" strategy, the second group was instructed to use the "I don't" strategy, and the final group was told they should simply refuse. For the next ten days, each participant received a daily check-in e-mail asking them whether the strategy worked that day. At the end of this study, eight out of ten participants in the "I don't" group reported that the strategy worked all ten days. Compare this to one and three days in the "I can't" and refusal group, respectively.

Although this is a smaller study with a short time frame for the follow-up, this strategy is worth a try. As the authors point out, using "I don't" is more psychologically empowering, speaks to your identity of the type of person you are rather than a temporary situation, and therefore has a greater chance of working.[43]

A good example of how this simple change in language better defines who you are, rather than a choice, is veganism. In an article published in *Medium*, author Amanda Connor explains that when it comes to meat, it's not that she can't eat it; she actually could. The issue is that she has chosen to exclude certain foods from her diet because of her beliefs and, therefore, doesn't eat meat.[44] This simple change in language works because it gets to your principles and is not related to a temporary situation.

When a toddler says no, they are doing much more than stating a preference: They are making a statement that they are independent people capable of their own decisions. And while they may not make the best decisions and need time to make mistakes and learn, the idea of taking control of how they spend their time is important. It's something we as adults don't naturally do, but we can learn from our toddler friends and, with this strategy, free up some much-needed time for the people and projects that are the most important to us.

Toddler Teachings

Don't be shy when asking questions. They won't make you look bad and can often have the opposite effect.

Small talk can be a nice break and can give you a mental boost at work. "How is your day?"

Follow-up questions can make you more likable and increase your chances of dating success.

Saying "Nooooo," but in a polite way, is an expression of your autonomy.

When a request comes in, break down the task into individual parts and fit those onto your calendar before you decide to say yes. Try this with a paper calendar.

Using "I don't" can help you avoid awkward social pressure and stay focused on your goals.

Chapter 10:

Risk-Taking and Confidence

Jumping out of this tree house is the
only way I will learn if I can do it . . .
and I can probably fly anyway.

Adults live in a world of limitations. There are limitations imposed upon us by others, but often even more powerful are the perceived cognitive and physical limitations we see in ourselves. These can hold us back from something as simple as asking a question, as we discussed in the previous chapter, or can be more detrimental such as when we don't apply for a job because we feel we aren't qualified. We may decide that a new physical activity is not right for us because we feel we are not "in shape." Toddlers, on the other hand, don't live in this type of world. In their world, truly, anything is possible.

I once had a discussion with a three-year-old named Olive, who was in the hospital visiting her older sibling, who was ill. Olive was telling me that after this visit, she wanted to visit her aunt in a city about an hour's drive away. When I asked more about this, specifically how she would get there, she thought for a moment and said, "I will ride a bike." It didn't even cross her mind that she would not have the physical strength to ride a bike that far, would not know which direction to go in, that it would not be safe in any way, and perhaps most importantly, that she does not know how to ride a bike. In Olive's mind, there was a simple solution to my question, and I'm sure if her parents were to say "Okay," she would follow the next most logical steps of finding a bike and jumping on it to see how far she would get.

What Olive, and every other toddler, can teach us is that we should not be afraid to take risks and be confident in our abilities. This is how they learn new skills and continue to improve, and so can we if we behave more like them. In this final chapter we will talk about these two wonderful toddler traits in more detail and see how applying them to our own lives can get us closer to fulfilling our greatest aspirations.

"Scaryfunny"

After treating thousands of toddlers for injuries in the pediatric ER, two conclusions can be made. First, toddlers enjoy taking risks, and second, they are highly confident in their limited abilities. As part of their active lifestyle, they routinely jump off couches, slide down stairs, and can easily spend an hour trying to open a child-proof medication container. They are thrill seekers, craving new experiences in which they may get injured. And injuries don't stop them. After putting on a cast for an older child or teenager, we give them detailed instructions from the ER, including a restriction from playing sports and to rest the injured limb. With toddlers, the best advice is often "Good luck!" They will never take it easy and can't wait to run around as soon as the cast is on. Often, they must come back to the ER a few days later to get a new cast because they either broke their old cast or wiggled their way out of it.

Risk-taking is important for toddlers because it is how they learn to do almost anything. From their very first steps, they push through anxiety and the failure of countless falls so that they may achieve bigger goals. This is at the heart of what risk-taking is about for toddlers. It allows them to learn, improve, gain self-confidence, and eventually, achieve mastery. There is uncertainty of success or failure, but that doesn't matter to them for two main reasons. First, they know that if they don't take risks and try a given task, then there is no chance they will ever be able to do it, and second, minor setbacks are a natural, necessary part of the process on the path to success. As we have seen now from many examples in this book, toddlers are persistent, and there is no exception with risk-taking.

Although toddlers take risks in every setting, we can see this behavior most clearly in outdoor, unstructured environments. And this has been studied extensively for more than a decade by Ellen Sandseter, professor at Queen Maud University College in Trondheim, Norway. In one study from 2007, Sandseter observed thirty-eight children, ages three to five, at two preschools. The study included indoor and outdoor observations, as well as interviews with the children and staff. With this data, Sandseter found that toddlers have a "strong interest" in risky behavior. And it wasn't as though the children didn't understand the risks they were taking and were doing these things because of inexperience. In fact, it was the opposite. They clearly expressed in the interviews how they might get hurt by these activities. They also knew there were rules against certain things and even found the activities scary. However, they still went ahead and did them. One of the best examples was a climbing tower the kids had access to. The instructions, per the manufacturer and the children's teachers, were to climb to a clearly marked spot on the tower and jump down. These toddlers, however, took greater risks by climbing on top of the roof of the tower. This was expressly against the rules, and despite knowing this and being scared, the children still did it. One five-year-old remarked, "Yes, it's a little bit scary, but it's great fun—I often land on my bottom, and that hurts a bit—but it's great fun anyway!"[1]

This idea that activities can be both scary and fun at the same time led Sandseter to do a follow-up study to look at how young children experience risky activities. This study included twenty-nine four- and five-year-olds in two Norwegian preschools. They were filmed over nine days as they participated in outdoor activities at their preschool and also while hiking. In order to understand what the children were experiencing, the researchers analyzed their body language, facial expressions, and the words they used. The researchers found that two dominant emotions were present: exhilaration and fear. The preschoolers sought exhilaration through risky play by moving higher (balancing on big rocks and climbing) as well as by increasing their speed (swinging on ropes or sliding down hills). Fear was manifested by worried facial expressions and asking things such as "Is this dangerous?" Occasionally fear did take over, and the child backed off. This feeling is what Sandseter calls "scaryfunny." What the children were doing through risky play was to keep "exhilaration bordering on the feeling of pure fear" without going into complete fear, which would make them stop. In order to get to mastery and push themselves further, young children need to experience exhilaration mixed with the right amount of fear. This is how they challenge themselves and progress further.[2] Sandseter describes the chance of being afraid and potential harm as the price that must be paid to "master something one would not ordinarily dare to do."[3]

Unfortunately, as we have seen in several examples so far, we lose some of these traits as we age. We'll talk about this more later, but for now, let's briefly discuss how adult fear manifests into limiting toddler risks. In an article titled "Ten Ways to Restrict Children's Freedom to Play: The Problem of Surplus Safety," Sandseter and colleagues argue that placing limits on children's risky behavior can be detrimental. Of course, there are times when this is necessary, such as having fences around pools to prevent drowning, but oftentimes adults are overly worried and overly protective of toddlers' risky behavior. One of the primary mistakes we make is that adults "cast the net widely and capture many positive play activities involving risk in order to eliminate some isolated problems." The authors go on to discuss how taking risks while playing is part of normal development and a known but acceptable consequence is injury. On playgrounds, for example, there is a very low risk of injury given how much children use them, and adult fears and concern can sometimes lead to "a situation of surplus safety." This, unfortunately, can be limiting for young children who are smart, are constantly learning from their experiences, and can gauge when an activity may be too risky for them.[4] In Norway, for example, kindergarteners are regularly exposed to outdoor, natural play areas without playgrounds and fences, and there is a widely held view that children have a right to play and challenge themselves in natural, riskier environments.[5]

Although, of course there is a chance of injury, risky outdoor play is good for children overall. A systematic review published in 2015 by researchers in Canada, the United States, and Norway examined twenty-one different studies to learn the true benefits of this type of behavior. The first most obvious finding was that this type of risky outdoor play promoted physical activity and decreased sedentary behavior. Getting back to Chapter 1, in which we discussed the amount of physical activity toddlers engage in, giving them more freedom and hence making their activities riskier allows for more exercise. And aside from increased physical activity, the authors also found that this type of play promoted social interactions and creativity, getting back to our discussion in Chapter 5 on play.[6]

To tease out the lessons here for all of us and to summarize, there are three key points when it comes to toddler risk-taking. First, and most importantly, in order to learn a new skill or to achieve mastery in something we either don't know how to do or don't normally do, we need to take risks. Fear and setbacks are a normal, constructive part of the process. Second, sometimes others impose rules or guidelines that might not be in our best interest. It's okay to sometimes break those rules because more often than not, you are better at knowing your own limits than someone else. And third, risk-taking can be particularly helpful when it comes to physical activity. It allows you to potentially exercise more and, if done with others, build social connections.

Casino Ban

Although toddlers have a sense of when an activity may be too risky, "Better safe than sorry" is certainly not a toddler motto as it is for many adults. They are much more on the other end of the spectrum, favoring high risks and high rewards. And it's good that casinos have an age minimum, as these traits, combined with over-confidence, which we will discuss later in this chapter, would be a disaster at the blackjack table.

As we will see in the next section, comparing toddlers to adults in terms of risk-taking is not really fair. Toddlers win all the time. A fairer comparison would be with monkeys, as they have been shown to have a more flexible approach to risk.[7,8] In a study published in 2022, researchers from Normandy University in France compared two-year-olds with almost equally cute capuchin monkeys. In the first part of the experiment, twenty-four French two-year-olds were asked individually to come into a testing room. This was done just before lunch so that they would have some additional motivation toward food. In the room, they saw five upside-down bowls lined up. One was green, and the other four were blue. The toddlers were shown that the green bowl always had one chocolate chip while in the blue bowls, one had four chocolate chips and the rest had none. They could choose the safe, green bowl and always get a chocolate chip, or they could take a chance at more by selecting one of the blue bowls. They were each given two chances to choose a bowl. A similar experiment was then done with seven monkeys, this time swapping chocolate chips for grapes. The researchers found that toddlers showed a "strong preference for the risky option over the safe options" while the monkeys showed the opposite. In fact, twenty of the twenty-four toddlers chose the risky option both times.

To make the safe option even clearer, in the second part of the experiment the green bowl was replaced by a transparent bowl. Even with that chocolate chip right in front of them when they were hungry, a different group of toddlers overwhelmingly preferred the lottery ticket method with most ending up with nothing. The monkeys, however, chose the safe option every time that option was transparent.[9]

Toddlers have little grasp of statistics and probability, so unlike adults and capuchins, they make decisions differently. The authors of this study explain that a toddler's decisions are based on a model of the trade-offs between exploitation and exploration. Yes, the toddlers could get the outcome of gaining a chocolate chip, but for them, exploring other options and taking risks is better because of the possibility of higher rewards. They are okay with highly uncertain situations because they know that sticking with the safe option will not allow them to explore what might be available.[10]

The Safe Option Is Not Always the Best Option

As we get older, and we know more, we take fewer risks. The safe option often seems like the best option. Our desires for learning and exploration are never quite at the peak they were when we were toddlers, and so with that comes a fall in our willingness to take risks. This has even been shown in chimpanzees; younger chimps take more risks than older ones.[11] In humans, this was demonstrated in a study of 234 participants living in Albuquerque, New Mexico. What was unique about this study is that it included a vast age range of people, from five-year-olds to sixty-four-year-olds. The purpose of the study was to characterize how our risk tolerance changes over time using a series of age-appropriate experiments measuring how much risk people would take. Similar to the previous experiment we discussed, participants were able to choose either a guaranteed outcome or a gamble. For children, tokens were used that they could then redeem for toys at a store. For teenagers and adults, cash was used. What was most striking in this study was how differently young children behaved compared to adults and acted irrationally and opposite to what was predicted. Normally, as we have more certainty about a reward that we will receive, we are less likely to take a chance for a higher reward, and this is how the adults in the study behaved. The youngest children, however, did the exact opposite. Even as the certainty of getting tokens increased, they decided to choose to gamble more often. In one example, participants were given a scenario in which there was an 80 percent chance of certainty in the reward they would get. In this scenario, less than half of older adults took a gamble while nearly three quarters of the youngest children took the gamble.[12]

The pattern of decreased risk-taking as we age is not limited to economic risks. It extends beyond that to social situations as well. A study led by researchers at the University of Utah comparing younger adults to older adults found that older age was associated with a lower likelihood of taking risks in social situations. These were things such as "admitting that your tastes are different from those of a friend" and "defending an unpopular issue that you believe in at a social occasion." But as the authors point out, these types of social risks can be important where voicing your honest opinion is valuable for certain jobs, such as being a consultant.[13]

Age-related changes happen naturally for a number of reasons. First, as we discussed with toddlers who see the world as full of opportunity and want to explore, older adults may perceive there to be fewer opportunities in the future. This can decrease risk-taking.[14] Second, neuroanatomy research demonstrates that in the natural process of healthy aging, a specific part of our brain that is associated with taking risks shrinks. Decreasing gray matter in this region of our brain better accounts for decreased risk tolerance than age itself.[15] And third, life experience can have an enormous impact. As people progress through life, they may experience financial hardships, natural disasters, or health changes that all have an impact on their risk tolerance.[16]

Finally, aside from age in general, there are other important factors that affect our willingness and ability to take risks. First there are gender differences. This is most well documented when it comes to finances, with women being more conservative than men.[17] Hormones, specifically testosterone and cortisol, can also alter our appetite for risk.[18] There is a small contribution from our genes as well.[19] And, as we will discuss more later when we talk about confidence, the people around you can have a significant impact on your behavior, and this includes risk. In a study led by researchers at the California Institute of Technology, twenty-four adult participants participated in a gambling task. They were given the option of a safe ten dollars or gambling for a potentially higher payoff. Before they made their own gamble, they were given information on how another "person" behaved in this situation, but because this was a computer algorithm, it could be modified to demonstrate higher or lower risks. The participants then made their own gamble, and the researchers were able to show, like many other observed behaviors, that risk-taking or, conversely, risk-aversion was contagious.[20]

We can't stop the aging process, nor is hormonal therapy to increase our appetite for risk a good idea. But these are important things to keep in mind as we are presented with opportunities or have our own ideas of what might be possible. Part of this decision-making process, to be able to take that risk, will always come down to being comfortable with making decisions with less than perfect information.[21] Finally, those who we surround ourselves with make a significant impact in our lives. This is not only true for risk-taking but also for confidence, as we will see at the end of the chapter.

Be Bold

One of the best places to observe toddler risk-taking is at a toddler gym as they are constantly given new challenges. One of these challenges is a large inflatable runway called an Air Track. It's similar to a bouncy castle, but instead of jumping in one spot you have to run, hop, or roll from one end to the other, ideally without falling down. The first time I saw this in use, many of the little risk-takers, as expected, jumped right in to try it, but there were a few shy ones who observed for a few minutes. Despite seeing their friends unable to balance well and take many tumbles, the ones on the sidelines looked at them with awe. Not only were the toddlers off to the side encouraged to hop on and try it, but they also started following the more natural risk-takers in other activities. Those who were more willing to take risks logically became the leaders.

The way those toddlers looked at their peers who were willing to take bigger risks is similar to how we think of risk from a business leadership perspective. In this framework, risk is generally seen as something positive and necessary to move forward. Leaders are often rewarded for the risks they take. With this general attitude, it is important to note that failure, after taking a risk, is not seen with the same eye as it is in other domains. Not only is there an enormous positive side to taking a risk and succeeding, but there is also a diminished downside to taking a risk and failing.

These ideas were studied in detail by researchers at Kent State University. They conducted two studies using vignettes and asked participants how they felt about risk-taking in the workplace. In the first study they had 322 participants between the ages of eighteen and seventy-five. The participants read about two different employees at a company: One was a risk taker, and the other was a risk avoider. The work tasks that were given were offering a suggestion at a meeting, providing an innovation for a workplace procedure, or leading a new initiative. The risk-taker was successful in half the scenarios and unsuccessful in the other half. Participants were then asked to give the odds of five different outcomes for these hypothetical employees: being downsized, being promoted, being sent to a special management training program, receiving a pay increase, and receiving a bonus. First, it was clear that when the risk-taker succeeded, they were rated as more likely to have all the positive outcomes and less likely to have all the negative outcomes. What was more interesting, however, is how the employee who took risks and failed was rated compared to the employee who was risk averse. While it was true that the risk-taker was rated to have a higher likelihood of being downsized, there was no effect on pay differences, and most importantly, there was an advantage for being promoted and given a leadership opportunity.

In the second experiment with over five hundred participants, researchers started with the same methodology but then also asked participants to rate certain traits. They found that risk-takers, whether they were successful or not, were rated higher in likability, higher in agency, more competent, and lower in indecisiveness compared to risk avoiders. Because they are seen as more decisive and having more agency, risk-takers who failed were still perceived to be more likely to be hired and promoted. While this is a vignette study and does not measure actual workplace outcomes, it gives us good insight into how people think about risk in the workplace. As the authors write, "Risk-taking, even when resulting in failure, carries a cultural cachet that protects workers from punishment."[22]

Closely related to how we are perceived by taking risks at work is how we feel about our jobs. In 2023, researchers from Uppsala University in Sweden published a fantastic study showing a link between job satisfaction and risk-taking. They used data collected over four years at twenty-two assessment centers in the UK and included more than fifty thousand people ages thirty-seven to seventy-three. One of the questions that they were asked was "Would you describe yourself as someone who takes risks?" They were also asked to rate their job satisfaction. After analysis, researchers found that for both men and women, risk-taking was significantly associated with job satisfaction. While this correlation is difficult to tease out because there is so little research in this area, the authors hypothesize it could be due to several factors. First, as we discussed before, risk-taking is perceived positively by others in the workplace, and this could lead to increased satisfaction. Next, increased agency that risk-takers feel can heighten a worker's sense of involvement in their work. Third, risk-takers are more likely to work in positions with higher autonomy, such as leadership roles or being self-employed. And finally, they might be more likely to change jobs if they are unsatisfied.[23]

The workplace is unique when it comes to risk-taking. The rewards for taking risks are multiplied as they can both benefit the company, through innovation, for example, and improve how you are seen by others.[24] On the other hand, taking a risk and failing, while having some downside, also has potential benefits at work. On balance, we may find that the benefits outweigh the potential disadvantages. Taking more risks may take some time, practice, and perhaps most importantly, confidence, so let's talk more about what toddlers can teach us about confidence.

Self High Fives

Every morning after I pull my toddler out of her crib, she first looks at me with a smile and then at the mirror she has in her room, with a bigger smile. As we walk over to the mirror, she gets more excited until she can finally reach out her hand and give herself a big high five. She has been doing this even before she could speak, and so part of our weekly room cleanup has always included removing handprints from her mirror. This daily ritual signifies something that all toddlers feel: that they are great people and can do anything. When presented with familiar or unfamiliar tasks, toddlers never think, *I don't have the skills for that.* They are the opposite, overconfident in fact. And as we will see even in the face of evidence pointing to their overconfidence, they remain unfazed. This remarkable ability, something adults lack at critical times, is how toddlers are able to take risks and learn faster than most of us. Every day they look for opportunities to get out of their comfort zone because they know they will eventually figure it out.

The phenomenon of toddler and preschooler overconfidence is well documented across dozens of studies performed over several decades. In a classic experiment from 1975, researchers at the

University of Wisconsin–Madison performed a simple experiment in which they asked preschoolers, third-graders, and adults to predict how many pictures on cards they could recall. They were then tested on their recall to see how they would perform. In addition, they were also told how many pictures peers their own age could recall. The adults in this experiment were relatively accurate and were only 6 percent overconfident. The third-graders were much more overconfident, by 22 percent. And the preschoolers? They overestimated their abilities by 147 percent![25]

Since the 1970s many other studies have been done to see if giving young children more experience, information, or feedback would erode their confidence. In a more recent study, also from the University of Wisconsin–Madison published in 2020, sixty children ages four to six were tested using the Children's Gambling Task. This is a game with two decks of cards. One is called the safe deck, and over time, choosing cards from this deck is expected to have a positive payoff. The other deck is the risky deck, which has both higher gains and higher losses. Over time, it has a negative payoff if one were to continually select from it. To incentivize the children in both playing and choosing optimally, stickers were used as a payoff. As they progressed through the game, after picking ten cards, each child was asked to pause and predict how many stickers they would win in choosing the next ten cards. They could say "More," "About the same," "Less," or "Don't know." Each child chose a total of sixty cards, and halfway through the game, half the children were shown a video where a character lost all their stickers after choosing from the risky deck.

What the authors found was quite remarkable. Despite a large number of trials with consistent feedback, incentives, and the video demonstrating a total loss, one out of every three four-year-olds remained overconfident. The conclusion the authors draw is that "overconfidence is persistent and widespread during early childhood." Importantly, even in this experiment with a small span in age, already an age-related decline in confidence was noted, similar to risk-taking.[26]

Toddler confidence is so powerful that it even extends beyond themselves to others. In a similar memory experiment as discussed previously in which children were asked to predict how many cards they would remember, researchers at Kent State University asked preschoolers to do the same task but for other children. In this study, besides making predictions for themselves, they also watched a video of another child the same age play the same game. Out of ten, the child on the video got either three or four correct on each trial, but despite this, the children making the predictions remained overconfident for the other person, expecting they would get between five and seven correct. The authors point out that confidence is important for a number of reasons for young children. It can help maintain self-esteem and encourage trying new tasks. High levels of confidence can allow for persistence and, in turn, practice to achieve higher-level goals.[27]

Finally, it's important to note that toddler confidence is not restricted to memory tasks and gambling performance—it extends across every domain of their lives. Toddlers think they are stronger, faster, more skilled, and know more about things than they do.[28] But these characteristics, which can occasionally lead to injury and receiving fewer rewards, overall lead to improving their physical and cognitive skills.

The Importance of Being Gutsy

As we have seen, toddlers pretty well only have one mode in which they approach life: indestructible overconfidence. This is not dissimilar to our previous discussions in which we have seen how they are often extreme. And although we can learn a lot from them and get closer to their extreme to improve our own lives, it might be a bit harmful if we were to follow through in every case. Overconfidence, however, is something we might not want to completely avoid. True, there are scenarios in which overconfidence could be dangerous, such as driving, but there are other situations where toddler-like overconfidence can help. In this section we'll discuss some of the benefits of overconfidence, and in the next section we'll discuss scenarios in which we tend to be under-confident and need to act more like toddlers.

The most important place that overconfidence may play a vital role in our lives is in the workplace. This has been studied by numerous authors looking at business leaders. One of the most detailed studies to date examined a massive dataset of more than 1700 companies in 220 industries. CEO confidence was measured by how they managed their personal financial portfolios based on the company stock they held. After controlling for several important factors, both personally and at the company level, there was a strong positive effect between CEO overconfidence and firm performance.[29] In another study looking at fourteen years of data, CEOs who were overconfident and underestimated the chances of failing were more likely to pursue innovation and obtain patents. This finding was more pronounced in more competitive industries.[30]

In the workplace, overconfidence can help us take the risks needed to achieve our biggest goals. While there are drawbacks, such as potentially making more errors, overconfidence can also help outside work, with dating.[31] In Chapter 5 we discussed how playfulness is a characteristic that can help in all relationships, including romantic ones. Building on that, displaying yourself as highly confident may also help.

We know that in broad terms, both men and women across the age span prefer partners who are more confident than themselves.[32] To probe this idea in more detail, research led at the University of Queensland, Australia, looked at how people perceive online dating profiles and how they would react in hypothetical dating scenarios. The study included more than one thousand participants over five sub-studies and had adults over the age of twenty-five. They used a fascinating questionnaire to measure overconfidence, called the Overclaiming Questionnaire. It asks how familiar people are with certain items, and one out of every five is a nonexistent item such as "ultra lipids." In this way, they could measure who was more assured of themselves.

Through these experiments there were a few interesting findings. First, overconfident people naturally created more confident profiles as seen by others, and this predicted romantic desirability. There is, however, nuance to this as arrogance is seen as negative and less desirable, and there is a fine line between overconfidence and arrogance. The next fascinating finding was how overconfidence interacts with potential competitors for the same mate. To illustrate this, the researchers gave the participants the following hypothetical scenario. Imagine you are going to a singles' mixer. Ahead of the event, you have a chance to read the dating profiles of everyone who will be there and you have your heart set on one specific person. When you arrive, you are excited to see that person sitting at a table with a friend. Unfortunately, the person sitting across from them is clearly interested in them and flirting. This is your competitor. At another table you see two less-attractive singles sitting by themselves. Which table do you choose to go to? Interestingly, people were less likely to engage with competitors who were perceived as confident. And furthermore, the people who are overconfident themselves are more likely to choose to compete with another person when given the opportunity.[33]

In summary, while not broadly applicable, there are places where toddler-like overconfidence can come in handy in our adult lives. This is true in the workplace, especially in leadership positions as it allows us to underestimate failure and take the big risks needed to accelerate company performance. And outside work, it is helpful with dating. Overconfidence can give us the courage to approach people in more difficult and potentially awkward situations, and at the same time, it fends off the competition.

The Burden of Expertise

While toddler-like overconfidence can help in certain scenarios that we discussed, more often than not, we don't reach our full potential because of under-confidence. As we've seen throughout this book, toddlers can act in ways that sometimes defy logic, but it's important to note that adults also behave in ways that don't make sense. How much confidence they bring to a given task is a perfect example. For some tasks we are overconfident; some we are under-confident; and others, surprisingly, we get less confident with practice. Unlike toddlers, who can block out past performance and feedback and soldier on with their task while thinking they are awesome, adults take many other factors into account, often to their detriment. As we discussed in the previous chapter, imposter syndrome is problematic, as we devalue our skills and talents. Even in the face of objective evidence that demonstrates how good we are, we can still lack confidence to take the next steps. In this section we will talk about some of these issues so that we are aware of them and hopefully avoid under-confidence mode, a place unknown to toddlers.

The most important problem to be aware of was first introduced in 1999 by psychologists Justin Kruger and David Dunning, who were both at Cornell University at the time. In their now famous study with more than eight thousand citations, they asked undergraduates to assess their own abilities in three different domains: humor, logical reasoning, and English grammar. They then tested the participants in each of these domains to get objective scores. The graphs produced in the study are fascinating. Each one has a line for perceived ability and another for actual test score. At first, these lines are quite far apart and show that the people who are the least skilled grossly overestimate their abilities (the Dunning-Kruger Effect). Over time, however, something surprising happens: Skill increases, as expected, but confidence decreases. The lines intersect briefly when these two things match, but then diverge again to the point at which they end up in the opposite positions from where they started. In other words, highly skilled people underestimate their abilities. The authors refer to this as the "burden of expertise," and what is happening is that highly skilled people falsely assume that because they performed so well, so did others, and thus they undervalue their abilities in relation to others.[34]

The under-confidence we have extends beyond areas in which we are skilled, unfortunately. It also shows up in odd ways in our lives, depending on how difficult a task is. Like toddlers, we should continually tackle difficult goals and stay persistent. This is not, however, as easy for us because under-confidence paradoxically hits us when we need confidence the most. In another classic study by Kruger in 1999 and since replicated in 2022, there is an effect called the "below average-effect."[35,36] In these studies, adults were given a set of easy tasks, such as using a computer mouse and driving, and another set of difficult tasks, such as playing chess and computer programming. They were then asked a series of questions related to how difficult the tasks were and how they perceived their own abilities. In both the original study and the replication twenty-three years later, as well as multiple other studies in between, the results were the same.[37,38] In relation to others, we are under-confident in our abilities for difficult tasks and overconfident with easier tasks.

As if it wasn't enough that we are under-confident when we are highly skilled and with more difficult tasks, there is also a drop in confidence after we try certain learning and memory tasks. Research from multiple academic institutions over several decades has repeatedly demonstrated the phenomenon known as under-confidence with practice (UWP).[39,40] This is best understood as a drop from slight overconfidence before you start something to under-confidence after the first trial. And although the research has focused specifically on memory tasks, a wide variety of manipulations has shown that this finding is robust. For example, whether participants are given feedback or not given feedback, or given incentives or not, they still become under-confident after the first exposure. This is not true, however, for children. When similar types of experiments were done with third- and fifth-graders, they did not show the same UWP that adults do. When the researchers performing these experiments dug deeper, they found that the issue was that while children could remember their previous success well, they also "remember prior errors as successes."[41] They are optimistic and distort the past, making it more positive than it was. And while they are inaccurate, this is arguably better than the adult pathway, which overvalues failure and leads to under-confidence.

Dress for Success

When we look at a group of toddlers playing, we see pretend play that often involves dress-up clothes. One girl is wearing a black cape and jumping from ledges, another little boy has his hands up with his mouth wide open roaring, and a third friend, wearing a bright orange soccer jersey, is kicking a soccer ball against a wall. From the toddler perspective, however, what they see is Batman, a powerful lion, and Lionel Messi. They are those people (or animals), and with that comes all the confidence they will ever need. As we discussed in Chapter 7 on mentorship, the simple process of acting like someone else can help us become that person and possess their powers. Equally important are the people we surround ourselves with to both motivate and encourage us. In this final section, let's have a brief discussion on a couple of strategies that can help build confidence in our own lives.

Since it has been viewed more than 60 million times, you may have seen or heard of the YouTube video featuring social psychologist Amy Cuddy in which she describes her research on doing a power pose to boost your confidence.[42,43] While some of the results of the original work have been criticized, a meta-analysis published in 2022 that took into account seventy-three different studies can help illustrate the most important findings. The analysis went as far back as the 1980s and included more than seven thousand participants.

For context, the authors defined an expansive display (power pose) as a way that a person would make themselves appear taller and wider when compared to a neutral position. A contractive display is the opposite. The outcomes of importance here are how people felt after they did one of those poses and how they behaved. What the researchers found was fascinating, in that there was a strong connection between posture and how one feels and behaves, but the newer results suggested this was more driven by the absence of contractive poses. These types of poses include slouching, putting your head down, and folding your arms. Overall, not doing these things made people feel more powerful and confident and allowed for more risk-taking.[44]

And if you observe a toddler, you will notice contractive poses are unnatural for them. In a video posted online in 2020, little one-year-old Chloe marches into the living room to join her dad, who is watching TV. Her father, Logan, is sitting on the couch, arms folded. As Chloe walks in, sucking on her pacifier, she makes her way to her bright pink Minnie Mouse chair, sits down, and then crosses her arms. It's adorable because she clearly is copying her dad, and this is not a normal pose for her.[45] Toddlers can also avoid slouching because they are so active and choose not to sit for very long, like we often do.[46]

Avoiding contractive postures is a simple technique to boost confidence, and there are a few ways you might be able to minimize them in your daily routines. First, you want to try to notice yourself doing these so you can correct them. One idea is to examine your posture from pictures of yourself in which you did not notice the camera. These represent your natural posture in various scenarios and you might be able to identify activities where you should be more conscious about your posture. Another easy way to do this, especially with online meetings and a camera on you the whole time, is to periodically look at yourself and check your seating position. For presentations, I personally ask a trusted colleague to give me feedback afterward, not only on the content and delivery, but also my posture. This has now been made easier as so many presentations are recorded so I can review them myself. And finally, as toddlers do, it's important to get up, move around, and not sit for long periods. If sitting, experts recommend getting up at least once an hour.[47] And if possible, you could do some of your work standing up, with a standing desk or perhaps taking all your calls standing up.[48]

From our toddler example, pretending you are a lion can give you a healthy boost of confidence, but so can the group of people you are with. You intuitively know this already. Your mood is affected by people around you, and you naturally gravitate toward and away from certain people. This is true of happiness, which is linked to the individuals you are connected with.[49] The opposite is also true: Having a depressed roommate, for example, can bring down your mood.[50] Confidence is no different. In a study published in 2021 titled "The Social Transmission of Overconfidence," researchers conducted a series of six experiments in which they randomly assigned participants to work on joint tasks. They measured self-reported confidence both before and after working with a partner. Amazingly, not only did working with confident people give their partners a confidence boost, but it lasted days after the initial experiment, spread to people who were indirectly connected to the initial overconfident person, and happened without the participant's awareness. One caveat is that this effect was seen only if they were paired with someone they viewed as in their group. In this experiment, specifically, it meant attending the same university compared to a college football rival university. The researchers describe this transmission of confidence as a type of social learning to "rapidly and efficiently acquire local confidence norms."[51,52]

Another method to build confidence is writing. So far, we have discussed how powerful and useful writing can be if we want to be more playful, kind, plan a more interesting day off, or increase the chances a work-related project gets finished on time. Writing can also be used as a method to document our accomplishments and protect against imposter syndrome. Kevin Cokley, educational psychologist at the University of Texas at Austin, recommends keeping a work diary. He suggests writing down every instance of positive feedback, accomplishment, and progress.[53] This can be reviewed weekly or monthly to remind yourself of all the things you can be objectively confident about.

Finally, another toddler favorite can also boost your confidence: playing dress-up. We know from multiple studies that other people perceive us differently based on how we dress.[54] But more importantly is how we feel about ourselves when we dress differently. Clothing can be symbolic, and when we wear certain clothes, we can take on certain qualities. The term "enclothed cognition" describes the influence of clothes on our own psychological processes and was first introduced by two researchers at Northwestern University. In a series of experiments with undergraduate students, they showed that wearing a white lab coat increased selective attention. In addition, they also showed that simply changing the description of the coat that was worn from a painter's coat to a doctor's coat increased performance on sustained attention tasks.[55] More practically, wearing formal clothes such as a suit has been shown to make us feel more powerful and better able to process information in an abstract way allowing for more broad thinking, and it can make us better negotiators.[56,57] So go ahead and experiment with the clothing that works best for you. It may be a blazer or a cape, but dress-up is another easy way to feel more confident.

While there is nothing wrong with playing it safe, our lives could be quite different—and potentially much better—if we learned from toddlers about how to take risks more easily and be more confident. This would be particularly helpful in the workplace but also in our personal lives. Unfortunately, as we get older and more skilled, the forces of age-related risk aversion and under-confidence continue to work against us. But there are decisions we can make to change this trajectory and focus on exploration as toddlers do. This is the only way to discover what we are truly capable of.

Toddler Teachings

To reach your maximal potential physically and cognitively, it is important that you take risks.
It's okay not to follow the rules sometimes and push yourself to see how high you can climb.
You might end up with fewer stickers in the short term, but choosing the risky option helps you learn.
You are awesome at everything you do, and thinking this way can help you remain persistent and improve your performance.
Your friends are also awesome at everything they try and do. Believe in them.
It doesn't matter how you performed yesterday or last year; you are still awesome.
Playing dress-up, spending time around confident people, and avoiding slouching can give you a daily confidence boost.

Conclusion

In the introduction, we started our discussion with a hypothetical scenario of what it would be like for your toddler self to go through part of an adult day. I had described the world of a toddler as a "different type of world," and truly, it is. As idealistic as it may have seemed compared to our lives as adults, it was not romanticized. The wonderful toddler world is real, and it is an incredible place.

Throughout this book we have reviewed a mountain of evidence demonstrating how amazing toddlers are and many of the important lessons we can learn from them. Without a doubt, there is nobody kinder, more curious, or more playful than a toddler. No one else cares as much about teamwork, is willing to take risks, or enjoys laughter as much as they do. The evidence is irrefutable. Toddlers are among the best people in our society.

As we learn more about different groups of people and society progresses over time, some labels become obsolete as they are offensive. For toddlers, terms like *terrible twos, threenager,* and *eff-you fours* clearly do not describe them and are now outdated. They should be replaced with labels such as "thoughtful twos," "threeangel," and "friendly fours." By observing toddlers and studying them, not only can we learn about the fascinating ways they spend their time, but we can also learn many valuable lessons. Much of their natural behavior is inspirational for us, and instead of focusing on the idea that we need to be teaching them, hopefully what you have taken away from this book is that they have a lot to teach us. As a reminder, have a look at the toddler teachings at the end of each chapter for a summary of the most important lessons. In the appendix, "A Gold Star Day," there is a sample schedule highlighting some of the most important toddler takeaways that you can incorporate into your day.

One of the common threads in this book is how we can both be inspired and alter our behavior with reminders of childhood. In Chapter 2 we saw how recalling childhood memories, both positive and negative, allowed adults to act in a kinder way. In Chapter 5, thinking like a child helped adults plan a more fun, playful day off. Thinking this way also helped adults to be more present minded. In Chapter 7, even with an indirect reminder of childhood, we saw how a simple superhero poster on the wall altered adult behavior, allowing them to do more work and stay persistent.

So my final recommendation is this. Go find a photo of yourself as a toddler, somewhere in that magical age between one and five. You might have to go look through a pile of old photos or ask a family member, but trust me, it will be worth it. Once you have that photo, frame it and put it somewhere where you are going to see it every day. It could be your desk, your kitchen table, or perhaps a wall you pass by. This photo will then serve as a reminder—a reminder of a time that is quite fuzzy in your memory but a time when you were driven to learn, laughed constantly, looked for people to help, and had the confidence to do anything. Overall, you simply enjoyed your life more. Those qualities still exist, and that special person still exists. They're just in a taller and older body now. But that kindhearted toddler, and all the wonderful qualities they have, is not lost. Go find them.

Acknowledgments

First, I would like to thank the thousands of toddlers who I have had the privilege of caring for over the years. You are all inspirational, and this book would not have happened without these interactions. Thank you for continuing to be kind, thoughtful, and generous. The world is a better place because of all of you, and I hope this book shines some light on the wonderful people you are.

This book also would not have been possible without the help of my incredibly supportive and encouraging agent, Laurie Abkemeier. Thank you for always believing in me and this book. A special thank-you to my editor, Darcie Abbene, for making the book come alive with more toddler stories. I would also like to thank Lindsey Triebel, my publicist, and the entire team at HCI for all your hard work on this book. I am grateful to have had such a talented publishing group.

I have been fortunate to have had some incredible clinical mentors who helped me learn how to care for toddlers and all children: Greg Hagan, Jill Kasper, and Shannon Scott-Vernaglia at Harvard Medical School, and Susan Niermeyer at the University of Colorado.

Thank you for everything you do to improve the lives of children and for the education you provide to the doctors who care for them.

I also want to acknowledge my past and present research mentors who continue to improve the lives of children and adults on a global scale: Nancy Lightfoot at Laurentian University; Jonathan Spector and Atul Gawande at Harvard Medical School; Abdul Bachani and Adnan Hyder at Johns Hopkins University; Zulfiqar Bhutta, Shaun Morris; and Mark Tessaro at the Hospital for Sick Children; and Anthony Chan and Mohit Bhandari at McMaster University. A special thank-you also to Sabrina Latorre, my academic administrative assistant for helping to ensure all our research projects continued smoothly while I was writing and for managing my calendar to the highest level of efficiency to allow me to write more.

Thank you to my brother, Rehman, for your enthusiasm and continually sending me new pieces of data to use in this book, as well as reviewing every piece of writing I sent. It was important to have someone challenge me, in a kind way, to improve the messages I was conveying. Thank you to my parents, Shamsh and Salma, for allowing me to have every opportunity in life. I am forever grateful. The stories you relayed to me about my own toddlerhood, such as the ten-minute morning self-talk routine I had, helped reinforce many ideas in this book. These stories also helped me rediscover how I can get some of my own toddler qualities back.

Finally, and most importantly, thank you to my wife, Zuleikha. Our evening talks and shared excitement about what Arya did during the day led me to many more research questions. I would not have been able to complete this book if it weren't for your love and support along the way. Thank you.

Appendix:

A Gold Star Day

Throughout this book, we discussed many strategies to improve your well-being. Most of them are simple and relatively easy to implement, and others will take some time and practice. This is a sample schedule to help get you started on the most important toddler lessons.

TIME	ACTIVITIES
Wake-up period	• Give yourself a high five confidence booster. • Have breakfast and stop eating as soon as you are full. • Whether you commute to work or not, make sure to include some form of exercise, even if it's only a longer walk from the end of the parking lot or around your home.
Morning work period	• Greet coworkers with a big smile and engage in small talk. • Try some jokes, but if they don't stick, switch to simulated laughter. • Focus on good communication and respect when working with your team. • Hold a walking meeting. • Decline a request, politely. • Put on a cape or look at photos of your favorite superhero to stay on task at the end of the morning.
Lunch period	• Include your favorite vegetables. • Eat with the funniest person in the office. • Have a bit of playtime. If you can't think of what to do, think of your childhood self.

TIME	ACTIVITIES
Afternoon work period	• Engage in third-person self-talk as you prepare for the afternoon. • Take a risk on a new idea you have. • Have a good laugh before learning anything new. • Think about your toddler self, which will help you act more prosocially. • Meet with your mentor and ask many questions. • Give a colleague a loud "hooray!" or other encouragement. • Ask for help whenever you need it. • Take a power nap if possible.
Evening	• If you are on a date, ask follow-up questions and be confident. • Rather than watch television, spend some time playing, exercising, or reading. • Turn screens off one hour before bedtime. • Reflect on how you played during the day to help you do more tomorrow. • Complete your standard bedtime routine of a warm shower or bath, apply lotion, and then read for twenty to forty minutes.

Notes

Introduction

1. A. Gopnik, A. N. Meltzoff, P. K. Kuhl, *The Scientist in the Crib: Minds, Brains, and How Children Learn* (New York, NY: William Morrow, 1999).

2. P. R. Huttenlocher, "Morphometric Study of Human Cerebral Cortex Development," *Neuropsychologia* 28, no. 6 (1990), doi:10.1016/0028-3932(90)90031-1

3. S. Siddiqui, U. Chatterjee, D. Kumar, et al., "Neuropsychology of Prefrontal Cortex," *Indian Journal of Psychiatry* 50, no. 3 (2008), doi:10.4103/0019-5545.43634.

4. N. J. Blanco and V. M. Sloutsky, "Adaptive Flexibility in Category Learning? Young Children Exhibit Smaller Costs of Selective Attention Than Adults," *Developmental Psychology* 55, no. 10 (2019): 2060–2076, doi:10.1037/dev0000777.

5. S. L. Thompson-Schill, M. Ramscar, and E. G. Chrysikou, "Cognition Without Control: When a Little Frontal Lobe Goes a Long Way," *Current Directions in Psychological Science* 18, no. 5 (2009), doi:10.1111/j.1467-8721.2009.01648.x.

6. T. Wujec, *Build a Tower, Build a Team* [Video], TED, February 2020, https://www.ted.com/talks/tom_wujec_build_a_tower_build_a _team/transcript.

7. Thompson-Schill et al., "Cognition Without Control."

8. D. J. Siegel and T. P. Bryson, *The Whole-Brain Child: 12 Revolutionary Strategies to Nurture Your Child's Developing Mind* (New York, NY: Bantam, 2012).

9. A. Gopnik, S. O'Grady, C. G. Lucas, et al., "Changes in Cognitive Flexibility and Hypothesis Search Across Human Life History from Childhood to Adolescence to Adulthood," *Proceedings of the National Academy of Sciences of the United States of America* 114, no. 30 (2017): 7892–7899, doi:10.1073/pnas.1700811114.

10. F. H. Gage, "Structural Plasticity of the Adult Brain," *Dialogues in Clinical Neuroscience* 6, no. 2 (2004): 135–141, doi:10.31887/ DCNS.2004.6.2/fgage.

11. B. Laditan, *Toddlers Are A**holes: It's Not Your Fault* (New York, NY: Workman Publishing Company, 2015).

12. M. M. Chouinard, "Children's Questions: A Mechanism for Cognitive Development," *Monographs of the Society for Research in Child Development* 72, no. 1 (2007): 1–126, doi:10.1111/j.1540-5834.2007. 00412.x.

13. S. J. Bober, R. Humphry, H. W. Carswell, et al., "Toddlers' Persistence in the Emerging Occupations of Functional Play and Self-Feeding," *American Journal of Occupational Therapy* 55, no. 4 (2001): 369–376, doi:10.5014/ajot.55.4.369.

Chapter 1

1. NowThis Kids, *Adorable Toddler Goes Viral on TikTok for Healthy Eating* [Video], YouTube, August 7, 2021, https://www.youtube.com /watch?v=2lMT9fBqGqM.

2. L. Maxwell, "Anchorage Boy Becomes TikTok Sensation by Eating Vegetables," *Alaska's News Source,* August 23, 2021, https://www .alaskasnewssource.com/2021/08/24/anchorage-boy-becomes-tiktok -sensation-by-eating-vegetables/.

3. Organization for Economic Co-operation and Development (OECD), "Obesity Update 2017," https://www.oecd.org/els/health-systems /Obesity-Update-2017.pdf.

4. A. Malhotra, T. Noakes, and S. Phinney, "It Is Time to Bust the Myth of Physical Inactivity and Obesity: You Cannot Outrun a Bad Diet," *British Journal of Sports Medicine* 49 (2015): 967–968, doi:10.1136 /bjsports-2015-094911.

5. M. Reiner, C. Niermann, D. Jekauc, et al., "Long-Term Health Benefits of Physical Activity—a Systematic Review of Longitudinal Studies," *BMC Public Health* 13, no. 1 (2013), doi:10.1186/1471-2458-13-813.

6. J. S. Savage, J. O. Fisher, and L. L. Birch, "Parental Influence on Eating Behavior: Conception to Adolescence," *Journal of Law, Medicine and Ethics* 351, no. 1 (2007): 22–34, doi:10.1111/j.1748-720X.2007.00111.x.

7. J. O. Fisher and L. L. Birch, "Restricting Access to Palatable Foods Affects Children's Behavioral Response, Food Selection, and Intake," *American Journal of Clinical Nutrition* 69, no. 6 (1999): 1264–1272, doi:10.1093/ajcn/69.6.1264.

8. C. F. Emery, K. L. Olson, V. S. Lee, et al., "Home Environment and Psychosocial Predictors of Obesity Status Among Community-Residing Men and Women," *International Journal of Obesity* 39, no. 9 (2015): 1401–1407, https://doi.org/10.1038 /ijo.2015.70.

9. M. K. Fox, B. Devaney, K. Reidy, et al., "Relationship Between Portion Size and Energy Intake Among Infants and Toddlers: Evidence

of Self-Regulation," *Journal of the American Dietetic Association* 106 (2006, 1 Suppl.): 77–83, doi:10.1016/j.jada.2005.09.039.

10. A. D. Smethers, L. S. Roe, C. E. Sanchez, et al., "Portion Size Has Sustained Effects over 5 Days in Preschool Children: A Randomized Trial," *American Journal of Clinical Nutrition* 109, no. 5 (2019): 1361–1372, doi:10.1093/ajcn/nqy383.

11. I. Steenhuis and M. Poelman, "Portion Size: Latest Developments and Interventions," *Current Obesity Reports* 6, no. 1 (2017): 10–17, doi:10.1007/s13679-017-0239-x.

12. S. L. Johnson, S. O. Hughes, X. Cui, et al., "Portion Sizes for Children Are Predicted by Parental Characteristics and the Amounts Parents Serve Themselves," *American Journal of Clinical Nutrition* 99, no. 4 (2014): 763–770, doi:10.3945/ajcn.113.078311.

13. Fox et al., "Relation Between Portion Size and Energy Intake."

14. J. Harvey, R. Krukowski, J. Priest, et al., "Log Often, Lose More: Electronic Dietary Self-Monitoring for Weight Loss," *Obesity* 27, no. 3 (2019): 380–384, doi:10.1002/oby.22382.

15. D. Buettner, "Enjoy Food and Lose Weight with One Simple Phrase," *Psychology Today,* January 10, 2011, https://www.psychologytoday.com/intl/blog/thrive/201101/enjoy-food-and-lose-weight-one-simple-phrase.

16. J. K. Orrell-Valente, L. G. Hill, W. A. Brechwald, et al., "'Just Three More Bites': An Observational Analysis of Parents' Socialization of Children's Eating at Mealtime," *Appetite* 48, no. 1 (2007): 37–45, doi:10.1016/j.appet.2006.06.006.

17. Savage, Fisher, and Birch, "Parental Influence on Eating Behavior."

18. Consensus Conference Panel, Nathaniel F. Watson, M. Safwan Badr, Gregory Belenky, et al., "Recommended Amount of Sleep for a Healthy Adult: A Joint Consensus Statement of the American

Academy of Sleep Medicine and Sleep Research Society," *Journal of Clinical Sleep Medicine* 11, no. 6 (2015): 591–592, and *Journal of Clinical Sleep Medicine* 38, no. 6 (2015): 843–844, doi:10.5665/sleep.4716.

19. C. M. Depner, E. L. Melanson, R. H. Eckel, et al., "Ad Libitum Weekend Recovery Sleep Fails to Prevent Metabolic Dysregulation During a Repeating Pattern of Insufficient Sleep and Weekend Recovery Sleep," *Current Biology* 29, no. 6 (2019): 957–967, doi:10.1016/j.cub.2019.01.069.

20. J. Willumsen and F. Bull, "Development of WHO Guidelines on Physical Activity, Sedentary Behavior, and Sleep for Children Less Than 5 Years of Age," *Journal of Physical Activity and Health* 17, no. 1 (2020): 96–100, doi:10.1123/jpah.2019-0457.

21. L. Matricciani, T. Olds, and J. Petkov, "In Search of Lost Sleep: Secular Trends in the Sleep Time of School-Aged Children and Adolescents," *Sleep Medicine Reviews* 16, no. 3 (2012): 203–211, doi:10.1016/j.smrv.2011.03.005.

22. J. A. Mindell, E. S. Leichman, C. Lee, et al., "Implementation of a Nightly Bedtime Routine: How Quickly Do Things Improve?," *Infant Behavior & Development* 49 (2017): 220–227, doi:10.1016/j.infbeh.2017.09.013.

23. H. Merali, "For Better Sleep, Borrow the Bedtime Routine of a Toddler," *Popular Science*, December 5, 2021, https://www.popsci.com/diy/how-to-sleep-better/.

24. J. A. Mindell and A. A. Williamson, "Benefits of a Bedtime Routine in Young Children: Sleep, Development, and Beyond," *Sleep Medicine Reviews* 40 (2018): 93–108, doi:10.1016/j.smrv.2017.10.007.

25. J. A. Mindell, L. S. Telofski, B. Wiegand, et al., "A Nightly Bedtime Routine: Impact on Sleep in Young Children and Maternal Mood," *Sleep* 32, no. 5 (2009): 599–606, doi:10.1093/sleep/32.5.599.

26. Mindell et al., "Implementation of a Nightly Bedtime Routine."

27. Merali, "For Better Sleep."

28. L. Hale, L. M. Berger, M. K. LeBourgeois, et al., "A Longitudinal Study of Preschoolers' Language-Based Bedtime Routines, Sleep Duration, and Well-Being," *Journal of Family Psychology* 25, no. 3 (2011): 423–433, doi:10.1037/a0023564.

29. A. Huffington, *The Sleep Revolution: Transforming Your Life, One Night at a Time* (Harmony, 2017).

30. R. Umoh, "Why Arianna Huffington Literally Tucks Her Phone into Bed Every Night—and Why You Should Too," *CNBC*, November 28, 2017, https://www.cnbc.com/2017/11/28/why-arianna-huffington-literally-tucks-her-phone-into-bed-every-night.html.

31. A. D. Staples, C. Hoyniak, M. E. McQuillan, et al.,"Screen Use Before Bedtime: Consequences for Nighttime Sleep in Young Children," *Infant Behavior & Development* 62 (2021): 101522, doi:10.1016/j.infbeh.2020.101522.

32. Z. Xie, F. Chen, W. A. Li, et al., "A Review of Sleep Disorders and Melatonin," *Neurological Research* 39, no. 6 (2017): 559–565, doi:10.1080/01616412.2017.1315864.

33. S. M. W. Rajaratnam, B. Middleton, B. M. Stone, et al., "Melatonin Advances the Circadian Timing of EEG Sleep and Directly Facilitates Sleep Without Altering Its Duration in Extended Sleep Opportunities in Humans," *The Journal of Physiology* 561, no. 1 (2004): 339–351, doi:10.1113/jphysiol.2004.073742.

34. K. E. West, M. R. Jablonski, B. Warfield, et al., "Blue Light from Light-Emitting Diodes Elicits a Dose-Dependent Suppression of Melatonin in Humans," *Journal of Applied Physiology* 110, no. 3 (2011): 619–626, doi:10.1152/japplphysiol.01413.2009.

35. C. Cajochen, "Alerting Effects of Light," *Sleep Medicine Reviews* 11, no. 6 (2007): 453–464, doi:10.1016/j.smrv.2007.07.009.

36. L. Hale and S. Guan, "Screen Time and Sleep Among School-Aged Children and Adolescents: A Systematic Literature Review," *Sleep Medicine Reviews* 21 (2015): 50–58, doi:10.1016/j.smrv.2014.07.007.

37. L. Exelmans and J. van den Bulck, "Bedtime Mobile Phone Use and Sleep in Adults," *Social Science & Medicine* 148 (2016): 93–101, doi:10.1016/j.socscimed.2015.11.037.

38. N. Hughes and J. Burke, "Sleeping with the Frenemy: How Restricting 'Bedroom Use' of Smartphones Impacts Happiness and Wellbeing," *Computers in Human Behavior* 85 (2018): 236–244, doi:10.1016/j.chb.2018.03.047.

39. M. Weissbluth, "Naps in Children: 6 Months–7 Years," *Sleep* 18, no. 2 (1995): 82–87, doi:10.1093/sleep/18.2.82.

40. T. M. Ward, C. Gay, T. F. Anders, et al.,"Sleep and Napping Patterns in 3-to-5-Year-Old Children Attending Full-Day Childcare Centers," *Journal of Pediatric Psychology* 33, no. 6 (2007): 666–672, doi:10.1093/jpepsy/jsm102.

41. S. E. Williams and J. S. Horst, "Goodnight Book: Sleep Consolidation Improves Word Learning via Storybooks," *Frontiers in Psychology* 5 (2014): 1–12, doi:10.3389/fpsyg.2014.00184.

42. A. L. Miller, R. Seifer, R. Crossin, et al., "Toddler's Self-Regulation Strategies in a Challenge Context Are Nap-Dependent," *Journal of Sleep Research* 24, no. 3 (2015): 279–287, doi:10.1111/jsr.12260.

43. R. Dhand and H. Sohal, "Good Sleep, Bad Sleep! The Role of Daytime Naps in Healthy Adults," *Current Opinion in Internal Medicine* 6, no. 1 (2007): 91–94, doi:10.1097/01.mcp.0000245703.92311.d0.

44. A. Birat, P. Bourdier, E. Piponnier, et al., "Metabolic and Fatigue Profiles Are Comparable Between Prepubertal Children and

Well-Trained Adult Endurance Athletes," *Frontiers in Physiology* 9 (2018), doi:10.3389/fphys.2018.00387.

45. M. Gavin, "Fitness and Your 2- to 3-Year-Old," *Nemours KidsHealth,* 2019, https://kidshealth.org/en/parents/fitness-2-3.html.

46. M. S. Tremblay, J. P. Chaput, K. B. Adamo, et al., "Canadian 24-Hour Movement Guidelines for the Early Years (0–4 years): An Integration of Physical Activity, Sedentary Behaviour, and Sleep," *BMC Public Health* 17 (2017, Suppl 5), https://doi.org/10.1186/s12889-017-4859-6.

47. R. W. Taylor, J. J. Haszard, K. A. Meredith-Jones, et al. "24-h Movement Behaviors from Infancy to Preschool: Cross-Sectional and Longitudinal Relationships with Body Composition and Bone Health," *International Journal of Behavioral Nutrition and Physical Activity* 15, no. 1 (2018):118, doi:10.1186/s12966-018-0753-6.

48. A. M. Gibson, D. J. Muggeridge, A. R. Hughes, et al., "An Examination of Objectively Measured Sedentary Behavior and Mental Well-Being in Adults across Week Days and Weekends," *PLOS One* 12, no. 9 (2017): e0185143, doi:10.1371/journal.pone.0185143.

Chapter 2

1. L. B. Aknin, C. P. Barrington-Leigh, E. W. Dunn, et al., "Prosocial Spending and Well-Being: Cross-Cultural Evidence for a Psychological Universal," *Journal of Personality and Social Psychology* 104, no. 4 (2013): 635–652, doi:10.1037/a0031578

2. A. V. Whillans, E. W. Dunn, G. M. Sandstrom, et al., "Is Spending Money on Others Good for Your Heart?," *Health Psychology* 35, no. 6 (2016): 574–583, doi:10.1037/hea0000332.

3. K. E. Buchanan and A. Bardi, "Acts of Kindness and Acts of Novelty Affect Life Satisfaction," *Journal of Social Psychology* 150, no. 3 (2010): 235–237, doi:10.1080/00224540903365554.

4. N. P. Podsakoff, S. W. Whiting, P. M. Podsakoff, et al., "Individual- and Organizational-Level Consequences of Organizational Citizenship Behaviors: A Meta-Analysis," *Journal of Applied Psychology* 94, no. 1 (2009): 122–141, doi:10.1037/a0013079.

5. Charities Aid Foundation, "World Giving Index 2022: A Global View of Giving Trends," 2023, https://www.cafonline.org/about-us/publications/2022-publications/caf-world-giving-index-2022.

6. M. Kay, *Kids Decide Between Helping the Homeless or Ice Cream* [Video], May 27, 2015, YouTube, https://www.youtube.com/watch?v=rksBNj1CsxA.

7. J. Ulber, K. Hamann, and M. Tomasello, "Extrinsic Rewards Diminish Costly Sharing in 3-Year-Olds," *Child Development* 87, no. 4 (2016): 1192–1203, doi:10.1111/cdev.12534.

8. A. Grant, *Give and Take: A Revolutionary Approach to Success* (New York, NY: Viking, 2013).

9. R. C. Barragan, R. Brooks, and A. N. Meltzoff, "Altruistic Food Sharing Behavior by Human Infants After a Hunger Manipulation," *Scientific Reports* 10, no. 1 (2020), doi:10.1038/s41598-020-58645-9.

10. D. U. Martin, M. I. MacIntyre, C. Perry, et al., "Young Children's Indiscriminate Helping Behavior toward a Humanoid Robot," *Frontiers in Psychology* 11 (2020): 239, doi:10.3389/fpsyg.2020.00239.

11. A. M. Rosenthal-von der Pütten, F. P. Schulte, S. C. Eimler, et al., "Investigations on Empathy Towards Humans and Robots Using fMRI," *Computers in Human Behavior* 33 (2014): 201–212, https://doi.org/10.1016/j.chb.2014.01.004.

12. C. Berridge, Y. Zhou, J. M. Robillard, et al., "Companion Robots to Mitigate Loneliness Among Older Adults: Perceptions of Benefit and Possible Deception," *Frontiers in Psychology* 14 (2023), https://doi.org/10.3389/fpsyg.2023.1106633.

13. A. Dahl, R. K. Schuck, and J. J. Campos, "Do Young Toddlers Act on Their Social Preferences?," *Developmental Psychology* 49, no. 10 (2013): 1964–1970, doi:10.1037/a0031460.

14. C. Sebastián-Enesco, M. V. Hernández-Lloreda, and F. Colmenares, "Two and a Half-Year-Old Children Are Prosocial Even When Their Partners Are Not," *Journal of Experimental Child Psychology* 116, no. 2 (2013): 186–198, doi:10.1016/j.jecp.2013.05.007.

15. F. Warneken and M. Tomasello, "The Emergence of Contingent Reciprocity in Young Children," *Journal of Experimental Child Psychology* 116, no. 2 (2013): 338–350, doi:10.1016/j.jecp.2013.06.002.

16. J. M. Horowitz, A. Brown, and K. Cox, "Views on Race in America 2019," *Pew Research Center,* 2019, https://www.pewresearch.org/social-trends/2019/04/09/race-in-america-2019/.

17. K. Shutts, "Young Children's Preferences: Gender, Race, and Social Status," *Child Development Perspectives* 9, no. 4 (2015): 262–266, doi:10.1111/cdep.12154.

18. K. D. Kinzler and E. S. Spelke, "Do Infants Show Social Preferences for People Differing in Race?," *Cognition* 119, no. 1 (2011): 1–9, doi:10.1016/j.cognition.2010.10.019.

19. A. Hofmeyer, K. Kennedy, and R. Taylor, "Contesting the Term 'Compassion Fatigue': Integrating Findings from Social Neuroscience and Self-Care Research," *Collegian* 27, no. 2 (2020): 232–237, doi:10.1016/j.colegn.2019.07.001.

20. D. Laible, E. Karahuta, W. Stout, et al., "Toddlers' Helping, Sharing, and Empathic Distress: Does the Race of the Target Matter?," *Developmental Psychology* 57, no. 9 (2021): 1452–1462, doi:10.1037/dev0001233.

21. F. Warneken, C. Sebastián-Enesco, N. E. Benjamin, et al., "Pay to Play: Children's Emerging Ability to Use Acts of Generosity for Selfish Ends," *Journal of Experimental Child Psychology* 188 (2019): 104675, doi:10.1016/j.jecp.2019.104675.

22. Y. Song, M. L. Broekhuizen, and J. S. Dubas, "Happy Little Bene-
factor: Prosocial Behaviors Promote Happiness in Young Children
from Two Cultures," *Frontiers in Psychology* 11 (2020), doi:10.3389/
fpsyg.2020.01398.

23. Ulber, Hamann, and Tomasello, "Extrinsic Rewards Diminish Costly
Sharing in 3-Year-Olds."

24. L. B. Aknin, J. K. Hamlin, and E. W. Dunn, "Giving Leads to Happiness in Young Children," *PLOS One* 7, no. 6 (2012): e39211,
doi:10.1371/journal.pone.0039211.

25. J. Andreoni, "Impure Altruism and Donations to Public Goods:
A Theory of Warm-Glow Giving," *Economic Journal* 100, no. 401
(1990): 464–477, doi:10.2307/2234133.

26. J. Moll, F. Krueger, R. Zahn, et al., "Human Fronto-Mesolimbic Networks Guide Decisions about Charitable Donation," *Proceedings of
the National Academy of Sciences of the United States of America* 103,
no. 42 (2006): 15623–15628, doi: 10.1073/pnas.0604475103.

27. L. Dossey, "The Helper's High," *Explore* 14, no. 6 (2018): 393–399,
doi:10.1016/j.explore.2018.10.003.

28. E. O'Brien and S. Kassirer, "People Are Slow to Adapt to the Warm
Glow of Giving," *Psychological Science* 30, no. 2 (2019): 193–204,
doi:10.1177/0956797618814145.

29. C. Vinney, "What's the Difference Between Eudaimonic and Hedonic Happiness?," *ThoughtCo.*, 2020, https://www.thoughtco
.com/eudaimonic-and-hedonic-happiness-4783750.

30. B. P. H. Hui, J. C. K. Ng, E. Berzaghi, et al., "Rewards of Kindness?
A Meta-Analysis of the Link Between Prosociality and Well-Being,"
Psychological Bulletin 146, no. 12 (2020): 1084–1116, doi:10.1037
/bul0000298.

31. Hui et al., "Rewards of Kindness?"

32. F. Borgonovi, "Doing Well by Doing Good. The Relationship Between
Formal Volunteering and Self-Reported Health and Happiness,"

Social Science & Medicine 66, no. 11 (2008): 2321–2334, https://doi.org/10.1016/j.socscimed.2008.01.011.

33. I. Lok and E. W. Dunn, "Are the Benefits of Prosocial Spending and Buying Time Moderated by Age, Gender, or Income?," *PLOS One* 17, no. 6 (2022): e0269636, https://doi.org/10.1371/journal.pone.0269636.

34. Charities Aid Foundation, "World Giving Index 2022."

35. A. M. Sparks, D. M. T. Fessler, and C. Holbrook, "Elevation, an Emotion for Prosocial Contagion, Is Experienced More Strongly by Those with Greater Expectations of the Cooperativeness of Others," *PLOS One* 14, no. 12 (2019): e0226071, doi:10.1371/journal.pone.0226071.

36. K. Ko, S. Margolis, J. Revord, et al., "Comparing the Effects of Performing and Recalling Acts of Kindness," *Journal of Positive Psychology* 16, no. 1 (2021): 73–81, doi:10.1080/17439760.2019.1663252.

37. F. Gino and S. D. Desai, "Memory Lane and Morality: How Childhood Memories Promote Prosocial Behavior," *Journal of Personality and Social Psychology* 102, no. 4 (2012): 743–758, doi:10.1037/a0026565.

38. S. Grueneisen and F. Warneken, "The Development of Prosocial Behavior—from Sympathy to Strategy," *Current Opinion in Psychology* 43 (2022): 323–328, doi:10.1016/j.copsyc.2021.08.005.

39. F. Warneken, *Need Help? Ask a 2-Year-Old* [Video], TEDx, April 22, 2014, https://www.youtube.com/watch?v=-qul57hcu4I.

Chapter 3

1. B. M. Waller and R. I. M. Dunbar, "Differential Behavioural Effects of Silent Bared Teeth Display and Relaxed Open Mouth Display in Chimpanzees (Pan troglodytes)," *Ethology* 111, no. 2 (2005): 129–142, doi:10.1111/j.1439-0310.2004.01045.x.

2. C. Addyman and I. Addyman, "The Science of Baby Laughter," *Comedy Studies* 4, no. 2 (2013): 143–153, doi:10.1386/cost.4.2.143_1.

3. E. Hoicka, B. Soy Telli, E. Prouten, et al., "The Early Humor Survey (EHS): A Reliable Parent-Report Measure of Humor Development for 1-to47-Month-Olds," *Behavior Research Methods* 54, no. 4 (2022): 1928 –1953, doi:10.3758s13428-021-01704-4.

4. A. Moore, "You've Got to Laugh: Why a Sense of Humour Helps in Dark Times," *The Guardian,* October 11, 2020, https://www .theguardian.com/lifeandstyle/2020/oct/11/you-have-got-to -laugh-why-a-sense-of-humour-helps-in-dark-times.

5. J. Aaker and N. Bagdonas, *Why Great Leaders Take Humor Seriously* [Video]. TED, August 2021, https://www.ted.com/talks/jennifer_ aaker_and_naomi_bagdonas_why_great_leaders_take_humor _seriously/c.

6. R. Holden, *Living Wonderfully* (New York, NY: HarperCollins Publishers, 1994).

7. A. Cekaite and M. Andrén, "Children's Laughter and Emotion Sharing with Peers and Adults in the Preschool," *Frontiers in Psychology* 10 (2019): 852, doi:10.3389/fpsyg.2019.00852.

8. C. Haviva and K. B. Starzyk, "Zero to 60 Laughs per Hour: Observed Laughter, Physical Health, Personality, and Well-Being in People Aged 67 to 95, an Exploratory Study," *Journal of Nonverbal Behavior* 46, no. 4 (2022): 363–381, doi:10.1007/s10919-022-00407-4.

9. Cekaite and Andrén, "Children's Laughter and Emotion," 852.

10. Math and Reading Help Blog, "Sesame Street Strives to Combine Humor and Science," October 2011, http://mathandreadinghelp .org/articles/Sesame_Street_Strives_to_Combine_Humor_and _Science.html.

11. Sesame Street, *James Marsden: Engineer* [Video], YouTube January 6, 2012, https://www.youtube.com/watch?v=3bPAGchXF4I.

12. R. Esseily, L. Rat-Fischer, E. Somogyi, et al.,"Humour Production May Enhance Observational Learning of a New Tool-Use Action

in 18-Month-Old Infants," *Cognition & Emotion* 30, no. 4 (2016): 817–825, doi:10.1080/02699931.2015.1036840.

13. R. A. Wise, "Dopamine, Learning and Motivation," *Nature Reviews Neuroscience* 5, no. 6 (2004): 483–494, doi:10.1038/nrn1406.

14. R. L. Garner, "Humor in Pedagogy: How Ha-Ha Can Lead to Aha!," *College Teaching* 54, no. 1 (2006): 177–180, doi:10.3200/CTCH.54.1.177-180.

15. J. C. Coronel, M. B. O'Donnell, P. Pandey, et al., "Political Humor, Sharing, and Remembering: Insights from Neuroimaging," *Journal of Communication* 71, no. 1 (2021): 129–161, doi:10.1093/joc/jqaa041.

16. G. S. Bains, L. S. Berk, N. Daher, et al., "The Effect of Humor on Short-Term Memory in Older Adults: A New Component for Whole-Person Wellness," *Advances in Mind-Body Medicine* 28, no. 2 (2014): 16–24.

17. G. S. Bains, L. S. Berk, E. Lohman, et al., "Humors Effect on Short-Term Memory in Healthy and Diabetic Older Adults," *Alternative Therapies in Health and Medicine* 21, no. 3 (2015): 16–25.

18. B. M. Savage, H. L. Lujan, R. R. Thipparthi, et al., "Staying Current: Humor, Laughter, Learning, and Health! A Brief Review," *Advances in Physiology Education* 41 (2017): 341–347, doi:10.1152/advan.00030.2017.-Human.

19. J. A. Banas, N. Dunbar, D. Rodriguez, et al., "A Review of Humor in Educational Settings: Four Decades of Research," *Communication Education* 60, no. 1 (2011): 115–144, doi:10.1080/03634523.2010.496867.

20. M. B Wanzer, A. B. Frymier, and J. Irwin, "An Explanation of the Relationship Between Instructor Humor and Student Learning: Instructional Humor Processing Theory," *Communication Education* 59, no. 1 (2010): 1–18, doi:10.1080/03634520903367238.

21. J. A. Banas, R. S. Bisel, M. W. Kramer, et al., "The Serious Business of Instructional Humor Outside the Classroom: A Study of Elite Gymnastic Coaches' Uses of Humor During Training," *Journal of Applied Communication Research* 47, no. 6 (2019): 628–647, doi:10.1080/00 909882.2019.1693052.

22. T. S. Z. T. Badli and M. A. Dzulkifli, "The Effect of Humour and Mood on Memory Recall," *Procedia—Social and Behavioral Sciences* 97 (2013): 252–257, doi:10.1016/j.sbspro.2013.10.230.

23. F. F. Y. Chan, "The Use of Humor in Television Advertising in Hong Kong," *Humor—International Journal of Humor Research* 24, no. 1 (2011): 43–61, doi:10.1515/humr.2011.003.

24. Coronel et al., "Political Humor, Sharing, and Remembering."

25. M. J. Baldassari and M. Kelley, "Make 'em Laugh? The Mnemonic Effect of Humor in a Speech," *Psi Chi Journal of Psychological Research* 17, no. 1 (2012): 2–9.

26. L. Mineo, "Good Genes Are Nice, but Joy Is Better, *Harvard Gazette*, April 11, 2017, https://news.harvard.edu/gazette/story/2017/04/over -nearly-80-years-harvard-study-has-been-showing-how-to-live-a -healthy-and-happy-life/.

27. L. C. Giles, "Effect of Social Networks on 10 Year Survival in Very Old Australians: The Australian Longitudinal Study of Aging," *Journal of Epidemiology and Community Health* 59, no. 7 (2005): 574–579, doi:10.1136/jech.2004.025429

28. J. Pryce-Jones, *Happiness at Work: Maximizing Your Psychological Capital for Success* (Wiley, 2010).

29. Olivet Nazarene University, "Research on Friends at Work," 2018, https://online.olivet.edu/news/research-friends-work.

30. A. W. Gray, B. Parkinson, and R. I. Dunbar, "Laughter's Influence on the Intimacy of Self-Disclosure," *Human Nature* 26, no. 1 (2015): 28–43, doi:10.1007/s12110-015-9225-8.

31. L. E. Kurtz and S. B. Algoe, "When Sharing a Laugh Means Sharing More: Testing the Role of Shared Laughter on Short-Term Interpersonal Consequences," *Journal of Nonverbal Behavior* 41, no. 1 (2017): 45–65, doi:10.1007/s10919-016-0245-9.

32. A. Jones, "Don't Panic: There Are Actually Some Huge Benefits to Your Toddler's Lovey Attachment," *Romper,* July 8, 2019, https://www.romper.com/p/your-toddlers-lovey-attachment-is-about-more-than-just-a-soft-toy-according-to-experts-18169778.

33. Mayo Clinic, "Chronic Stress Puts Your Health at Risk," August 1, 2023, https://www.mayoclinic.org/healthy-lifestyle/stress-management/in-depth/stress/art-20046037.

34. J. Yim, "Therapeutic Benefits of Laughter in Mental Health: A Theoretical Review," *Tohoku Journal of Experimental Medicine* 239, no. 3 (2016): 243–249, doi:10.1620/tjem.239.243.

35. J. Zhao, H. Yin, G. Zhang, et al., "A Meta-Analysis of Randomized Controlled Trials of Laughter and Humour Interventions on Depression, Anxiety and Sleep Quality in Adults," *Journal of Advanced Nursing* 75, no. 11 (2019): 2435–2448, doi:10.1111/jan.14000.

36. D. Louie and E. Frates, "The Laughter Prescription: A Tool for Lifestyle Medicine," *American Journal of Lifestyle Medicine* 10, no. 4 (2016): 262–267, doi:10.1177/1559827614550279.

37. Y. Yoshikawa, E. Ohmaki, H. Kawahata, et al., "Beneficial Effect of Laughter Therapy on Physiological and Psychological Function in Elders," *Nursing Open* 6, no. 1 (2019): 93–99, doi:10.1002/nop2.190.

38. S. Romundstad, S. Svebak, A. Holen, et al., "A 15-Year Follow-Up Study of Sense of Humor and Causes of Mortality," *Psychosomatic Medicine* 78, no. 3 (2016): 345–353.

39. K. Hayashi, I. Kawachi, T. Ohira, et al., "Laughter Is the Best Medicine? A Cross-Sectional Study of Cardiovascular Disease among

Older Japanese Adults," *Journal of Epidemiology* 26, no. 10 (2016): 546–552, doi:10.2188/jea.JE20150196.

40. C. Addyman, C. Fogelquist, L. Levakova, et al., "Social Facilitation of Laughter and Smiles in Preschool Children," *Frontiers in Psychology* 9 (2018), doi:10.3389/fpsyg.2018.01048.

41. R. R. Provine, "Laughter as a Scientific Problem: An Adventure in Sidewalk Neuroscience," *Journal of Comparative Neurology* 524, no. 8 (2016): 1532–1539, doi:10.1002/cne.23845.

42. E. Hoicka and N. Akhtar, "Early Humour Production," *British Journal of Developmental Psychology* 30, no. 4 (2012): 586–603, doi:10.1111/j.2044-835X.2011.02075.x.

43. Animalkind, "'Hi, I'm Maisie!' Watch This Adorable Toddler Greeting Some Household Ants," *USA Today*, August 3, 2023, https://www.usatoday.com/videos/life/animalkind/2023/08/03/nature-loving-toddler-introduces-herself-ants/12313763002/.

44. H. Merali, "How to Make Yourself Laugh," *Popular Science*, July 25, 2022, https://www.popsci.com/diy/how-to-make-yourself-laugh/.

45. C. N. van der Wal and R. N. Kok, "Laughter-Inducing Therapies: Systematic Review and Meta-Analysis," *Social Science & Medicine* 232 (2019): 473–488, doi:10.1016/j.socscimed.2019.02.018.

46. R. M. Ripoll, "Simulated Laughter Techniques for Therapeutic Use in Mental Health," *Journal of Psychology & Clinical Psychiatry* 8, no. 2 (2017), doi:10.15406/jpcpy.2017.08.00479.

47. K. Stiwi and J. Rosendahl, "Efficacy of Laughter-Inducing Interventions in Patients with Somatic or Mental Health Problems: A Systematic Review and Meta-Analysis of Randomized-Controlled Trials," *Complementary Therapies in Clinical Practice* 47 (2022), doi:10.1016/j.ctcp.2022.101552.

48. D. Bressington, J. Mui, C. Yu, et al., "Feasibility of a Group-Based Laughter Yoga Intervention as an Adjunctive Treatment for Residual Symptoms of Depression, Anxiety and Stress in People

with Depression," *Journal of Affective Disorders* 248 (2019): 42–51, doi:10.1016/j.jad.2019.01.030.

49. M. Stewart and M. Johnson, "What Happened When We Introduced Four-Year-Olds to an Old People's Home," *The Conversation*, August 7, 2017, https://theconversation.com/what-happened-when -we-introduced-four-year-olds-to-an-old-peoples-home-82164.

50. ABC TV, *Celebrating the Last Day Together | Old People's Home for 4 Year Olds* [Video], YouTube, May 3, 2021, https://www .youtube.com/watch?v=Znep0lJoOqw.

Chapter 4

1. C. Clark and A. Teravainen-Goff, "Children and Young People's Reading in 2019," *National Literacy Trust*, 2020, http://cdn -literacytrust-production.s3.amazonaws.com/media/documents /Reading_trends_in_2019_-_Final.pdf.

2. US Bureau of Labor Statistics, "People Age 65 and Older More Likely Than Younger People to Read for Personal Interest," 2018, https://www.bls.gov/opub/ted/2018/people-age-65-and-older -more-likely-than-younger-people-to-read-for-personal-interest .htm.

3. B. Martin and E. Carle, *Brown Bear, Brown Bear, What Do You See?* (New York, NY: Henry Holt and Company, LLC, 1996).

4. R. Gelles-Watnick and A. Perrin, "Who Doesn't Read Books in America?," *Pew Research Center*, 2021, https://www.pewresearch.org/ short-reads/2021/09/21/who-doesnt-read-books-in-america/.

5. C. M. Zettler-Greeley, "Reading Milestones," *Nemours KidsHealth*, May 2022, https://kidshealth.org/en/parents/milestones.html.

6. M. L. Greif, D. G. K. Nelson, F. C. Keil, et al., "What Do Children Want to Know About Animals and Artifacts? Domain-Specific Requests for Information," *Psychological Science* 17, no. 6 (2006): 455–459, doi:10.1111/j.1467-9280.2006.01727.x.

7. D. M. Sobel and K. H. Corriveau, "Children Monitor Individuals' Expertise for Word Learning," *Child Development* 81, no. 2 (2010): 669–679, https://doi.org/10.1111/j.1467-8624.2009.01422.x.

8. J. Piaget, *The Origins of Intelligence in Children* (Madison, CT: International Universities Press, 1952).

9. S. Jenkins, *What Do You Do When Something Wants to Eat You?* (New York, NY: Clarion Books, 2001).

10. S. Jenkins, *Biggest, Strongest, Fastest* (New York, NY: Clarion Books, 1997).

11. M. Shavlik, J. R. Bauer, and A. E. Booth, "Children's Preference for Causal Information in Storybooks," *Frontiers in Psychology* 11 (2020), doi:10.3389/fpsyg.2020.00666.

12. S. Dehaene and L. Cohen, "Cultural Recycling of Cortical Maps," *Neuron* 56, no. 2 (2007): 384–398, doi:10.1016/j.neuron.2007.10.004.

13. W. Piper, *The Little Engine That Could* (New York, NY: Grosset & Dunlap, 2001).

14. J. S. Hutton, K. Phelan, T. Horowitz-Kraus, et al., "Shared Reading Quality and Brain Activation During Story Listening in Preschool-Age Children," *Journal of Pediatrics* 191 (2017): 204–211, doi:10.1016/j.jpeds.2017.08.037.

15. S. Dehaene, F. Pegado, L. W. Braga, et al., "How Learning to Read Changes the Cortical Networks for Vision and Language," *Science* 330, no. 6009 (2010): 1359–1364, doi:10.1126/science.1194140.

16. T. E. Moffitt, L. Arseneault, D. Belsky, et al., "A Gradient of Childhood Self-Control Predicts Health, Wealth, and Public Safety," *Proceedings of the National Academy of Sciences of the United States of America* 108, no. 7 (2011): 2693–2698, doi:10.1073/pnas.1010076108.

17. K. Haimovitz, C. S. Dweck, and G. M. Walton, "Preschoolers Find Ways to Resist Temptation After Learning That Willpower Can Be Energizing," *Developmental Science* 23, no. 3 (2020): e12905, doi:10.1111/desc.12905.

18. L. H. Owen, O. B. Kennedy, C. Hill, et al., "Peas, Please! Food Familiarization Through Picture Books Helps Parents Introduce Vegetables into Preschoolers' Diets," *Appetite* 128 (2018): 32–43, doi:10.1016/j.appet.2018.05.140.

19. G. S. Berns, K. Blaine, M. J. Prietula, et al., "Short- and Long-Term Effects of a Novel on Connectivity in the Brain," *Brain Connect* 3, no. 6 (2013): 590–600, doi:10.1089/brain.2013.0166.

20. K. Oatley, "Fiction: Simulation of Social Worlds," *Trends in Cognitive Sciences* 20, no. 8 (2016): 618–628, doi:10.1016/j.tics.2016.06.002.

21. R. A. Mar, K. Oatley, J. Hirsh, et al., "Bookworms Versus Nerds: Exposure to Fiction Versus Non-Fiction, Divergent Associations with Social Ability, and the Simulation of Fictional Social Worlds," *Journal of Research in Personality* 40, no. 5 (2006): 694–712, doi:10.1016/j.jrp.2005.08.002.

22. D. I. Tamir, A. B. Bricker, D. Dodell-Feder, et al.,"Reading Fiction and Reading Minds: The Role of Simulation in the Default Network," *Social Cognitive and Affective Neuroscience* 11, no. 2 (2015): 215–224, doi:10.1093/scan/nsv114.

23. C. Hammond, "Does Reading Fiction Make Us Better People?," *BBC Future*, June 2, 2019, https://www.bbc.com/future/article/20190523-does-reading-fiction-make-us-better-people.

24. R. Munsch and S. McGraw, *Love You Forever* (Richmond Hill, ON, Canada: Firefly Books, 1995).

25. Weill Institute for Neurosciences UCSF, "Healthy Aging vs. Diagnosis," 2023, https://memory.ucsf.edu/symptoms/healthy-aging.

26. R. C. Petersen, O. Lopez, M. J. Armstrong, et al., "Practice Guideline Update: Mild Cognitive Impairment," *Neurology* 90, no. 3 (2018): 126–135, doi:10.1212/WNL.0000000000004826.

27. Y. H. Chang, I. C. Wu, and C. A. Hsiung, "Reading Activity Prevents

Long-Term Decline in Cognitive Function in Older People: Evidence from a 14-Year Longitudinal Study," *International Psychogeriatrics* 33, no. 1 (2021): 63–74, doi:10.1017/S1041610220000812.

28. Directorate-General of Budget, Accounting and Statistics, Executive Yuan, "Survey on Social Development Trends, 2004," 2005, https://doi.org/10.6141/TW-SRDA-AA200007-1.

29. E. A. L. Stine-Morrow, G. S. McCall, I. Manavbasi, et al., "The Effects of Sustained Literacy Engagement on Cognition and Sentence Processing Among Older Adults," *Frontiers in Psychology* 13 (2022), doi:10.3389/fpsyg.2022.923795.

30. University of Michigan Institute for Social Research, "2019 Consumption and Activities Mail Survey (CAMS)," 2021, https://hrsdata.isr.umich.edu/data-products/2019-consumption-and-activities-mail-survey-cams.

31. A. Bavishi, M. D. Slade, and B. R. Levy, "A Chapter a Day: Association of Book Reading with Longevity," *Social Science & Medicine* 164 (2016): 44–48, doi:10.1016/j.socscimed.2016.07.014.

32. M. Wolf, "Skim Reading Is the New Normal. The Effect on Society Is Profound," *The Guardian,* August 25, 2018, https:/www.theguardian.com/commentisfree/2018/aug/25/skim-reading-new-normal-maryanne-wolf.

33. M. Wolf and M. Barzillai, "The Importance of Deep Reading," *Educational Leadership* 66 (2009): 32–37.

34. Z. Liu, "Digital Reading: An Overview," *Chinese Journal of Library and Informational Science* 5, no. 1 (2012): 85–94.

35. Maastricht University, "Project Deep Learning," 2022, https://www.maastrichtuniversity.nl/meta/437653/project-deep-reading.

36. R. Turner, "Deep Reading Has Become a Lost Art as Digital Screens Take Over, but You Can Retrain Your Brain," *ABC News,* December 20, 2019, https://www.abc.net.au/news/2019-12-21/how-to-engage-your-deep-reading-brain-to-combat-digital-screens/11819682.

37. Turner, "Deep Reading Has Become a Lost Art."

38. V. Clinton-Lisell, "Listening Ears or Reading Eyes: A Meta-Analysis of Reading and Listening Comprehension Comparisons," *Review of Educational Research* 92, no. 4 (2022): 543–582, doi:10.3102/00346543211060871.

39. N. Kucirkova and K. Littleton, "The Digital Reading Habits of Children: A National Survey of Parents' Perceptions of and Practices in Relation to Children's Reading for Pleasure with Print and Digital Books," *Book Trust*, 2016, https://www.booktrust .org.uk/globalassets/resources/research/digital_reading_survey -final-report-8.2.16.pdf.

40. T. G. Munzer, A. L. Miller, H. M. Weeks, et al., "Differences in Parent-Toddler Interactions with Electronic Versus Print Books," *Pediatrics* 143, no. 4 (2019): e20182012, doi:10.1542/peds.2018-2012.

41. P. Delgado, C. Vargas, R. Ackerman, et al., "Don't Throw Away Your Printed Books: A Meta-Analysis on the Effects of Reading Media on Reading Comprehension," *Educational Research Review* 25 (2018): 23–38, doi:10.1016/j.edurev.2018.09.003.

42. L. G. Duncan, S. P. Mcgeown, Y. M. Griffiths, et al., "Adolescent Reading Skill and Engagement with Digital and Traditional Literacies as Predictors of Reading Comprehension," *British Journal of Psychology* 107, no. 2 (2016): 209–238, doi:10.1111/bjop.12134.

43. T. Lauterman and R. Ackerman, "Overcoming Screen Inferiority in Learning and Calibration," *Computers in Human Behavior* 35 (2014): 455–463, doi:10.1016/j.chb.2014.02.046.

Chapter 5

1. M. Yogman, A. Garner, J. Hutchinson, et al., "The Power of Play: A Pediatric Role in Enhancing Development in Young Children," *Pediatrics* 142, no. 3 (2018): e20182058, doi:10.1542/peds.2018-2058.

2. Yogman et al., "The Power of Play."

3. S. Shaheen, "How Child's Play Impacts Executive Function-Related Behaviors," *Applied Neuropsychology: Child* 3, no. 3 (2014): 182–187, doi:10.1080/21622965.2013.839612.

4. T. Rice, "Commentary: How Child's Play Impacts Executive Function-Related Behaviors," *Frontiers in Psychology* 7 (2016), doi:10.3389/fpsyg.2016.00968.

5. Yogman et al., "The Power of Play."

6. K. Wong, "How to Add More Play to Your Grown-Up Life, Even Now," *New York Times*, August 14, 2020, https://www.nytimes.com/2020/08/14/smarter-living/adults-play-work-life-balance.html.

7. US Bureau of Labor Statistics, "Average Hours per Day Spent in Selected Leisure and Sports Activities by Age," 2021, https://www.bls.gov/charts/american-time-use/activity-leisure.htm.

8. K. Brauer, R. T. Proyer, and G. Chick, "Adult Playfulness: An Update on an Understudied Individual Differences Variable and Its Role in Romantic Life," *Social and Personality Psychology Compass* 15, no. 4 (2021): e12589, doi:10.1111/spc3.12589.

9. Brauer, Proyer, and Chick, "Adult Playfulness."

10. R. T. Proyer, F. Gander, E. J. Bertenshaw, et al., "The Positive Relationships of Playfulness with Indicators of Health, Activity, and Physical Fitness," *Frontiers in Psychology* 9 (2018), doi:10.3389/fpsyg.2018.01440.

11. B. Nabavizadeh, N. Hakam, J. T. Holler, et al., "Epidemiology of Child Playground Equipment-Related Injuries in the USA: Emergency Department Visits, 1995–2019," *Journal of Paediatrics and Child Health* 58, no. 1 (2022): 69–76, doi:10.1111/jpc.15644.

12. D. Koller, "Therapeutic Play in Pediatric Health Care: The Essence of Child Life Practice," *Child Life Council*, 2008, https://www.childlife.org/docs/default-source/research-ebp/therapeutic-play-in-pediatric-health-care-the-essence-of-child-life-practice.pdf?sfvrsn=8902b14d_2.

13. R. T. Proyer, F. Gander, K. Brauer, et al., "Can Playfulness Be Stimulated? A Randomised Placebo-Controlled Online Playfulness Intervention Study on Effects on Trait Playfulness, Well-Being, and Depression," *Applied Psychology: Health and Well-Being* 13, no. 1 (2021): 129–151, doi:10.1111/aphw.12220.

14. R. T. Proyer, "Examining Playfulness in Adults: Testing Its Correlates with Personality, Positive Psychological Functioning, Goal Aspirations, and Multi-Methodically Assessed Ingenuity," *Psychological Test and Assessment Modeling* 54, no. 2 (2012): 103–127.

15. R. T. Proyer, "Playfulness over the Lifespan and Its Relation to Happiness," *Zeitschrift Für Gerontologie Und Geriatrie* 47, no. 6 (2014): 508–512, doi:10.1007/s00391-013-0539-z.

16. L. A. Barnett, "How Do Playful People Play? Gendered and Racial Leisure Perspectives, Motives, and Preferences of College Students," *Leisure Sciences* 33, no. 5 (2011): 382–401, doi:10.1080/01490400.2011.606777.

17. R. T. Proyer, "The Well-Being of Playful Adults: Adult Playfulness, Subjective Well-Being, Physical Well-Being, and the Pursuit of Enjoyable Activities," *European Journal of Humour Research* 1, no. 1 (2013): 84–98, doi:10.7592/EJHR2013.1.1.proyer.

18. C. Clifford, E. Paulk, Q. Lin, et al.,"Relationships Among Adult Playfulness, Stress, and Coping During the COVID-19 Pandemic," *Current Psychology* 21 (2022): 1–10, doi:10.1007/s12144-022-02870-0.

19. Proyer et al., "The Positive Relationships of Playfulness."

20. R. T. Proyer, N. Tandler, and K. Brauer, "Playfulness and Creativity: A Selective Review," in *Creativity and Humor,* eds. Sarah R. Luria, John Baer, and James C. Kaufman (Philadelphia, PA: Elsevier, 2019), 43–60, doi:10.1016/B978-0-12-813802-1.00002-8.

21. S. West, E. Hoff, and I. Carlsson, "Enhancing Team Creativity with Playful Improvisation Theater: A Controlled Intervention Field

Study," *International Journal of Play* 6, no. 3 (2017): 283–293, doi:10.1080/21594937.2017.1383000.

22. S. E. West, E. Hoff, and I. Carlsson, "Play and Productivity Enhancing the Creative Climate at Workplace Meetings with Play Cues," *American Journal of Play* 9, no. 1 (2016): 71–86.

23. N. Althuizen, B. Wierenga, and J. Rossiter, "The Validity of Two Brief Measures of Creative Ability," *Creativity Research Journal* 22, no. 1 (2010): 53–61, doi:10.1080/10400410903579577.

24. D. L. Zabelina and M. D. Robinson, "Child's Play: Facilitating the Originality of Creative Output by a Priming Manipulation," *Psychology of Aesthetics, Creativity, and the Arts* 4, no. 1 (2010): 57–65, doi:10.1037/a0015644.

25. Brauer, Proyer, and Chick, "Adult Playfulness: An Update."

26. G. Chick, C. Yarnal, and A. Purrington, "Play and Mate Preference: Testing the Signal Theory of Adult Playfulness," *American Journal of Play* 4, no. 4 (2012): 407–440.

27. R. T. Proyer, K. Brauer, A. Wolf, et al., "Adult Playfulness and Relationship Satisfaction: An APIM Analysis of Romantic Couples," *Journal of Research in Personality* 79 (2019): 40–48, doi:10.1016/j.jrp.2019.02.001.

28. Y. L. de Moraes, M. A. C. Varella, C. Santos Alves da Silva, et al., "Adult Playful Individuals Have More Long- and Short-Term Relationships," *Evolutionary Human Sciences* 3 (2021): e24, https://doi.org/10.1017/ehs.2021.19.

29. K. Brauer, S. F. Friedemann, G. Chick, et al., "Play with Me, Darling!" Testing the Associations Between Adult Playfulness and Indicators of Sexuality," *Journal of Sex Research* 60, no. 4 (2023): 522–534, doi:10.1080/00224499.2022.2077289.

30. D. Babis, O. Korin, U. Ben-Shalom, et al., "Medical Clowning's Contribution to the Well-Being of Older Adults in a Residential Home,"

Educational Gerontology 48, no. 9 (2022): 404–414, doi:10.1080/036 01277.2022.2043663.

31. H. Suszek, M. Kofta, and M. Kopera, "Returning to the Present Moment: Thinking About One's Childhood Increases Focus on the Hedonistic Present," *Journal of General Psychology* 146, no. 2 (2019): 170–199, doi:10.1080/00221309.2018.1543646.

32. R. T. Proyer, F. Gander, K. Brauer, et al., "Can Playfulness Be Stimulated? A Randomised Placebo-Controlled Online Playfulness Intervention Study on Effects on Trait Playfulness, Well-Being, and Depression," *Applied Psychology: Health & Wellbeing* 13, no. 1 (2021): 129–151, doi:10.1111/aphw.12220.

Chapter 6

1. M. Tomasello and K. Hamann, "The 37th Sir Frederick Bartlett Lecture: Collaboration in Young Children," *Quarterly Journal of Experimental Psychology* 65, no. 1 (2012): 1–12, doi:10.1080/17470218.201 1.608853.

2. Global News, *Tiny BC Toddler Becomes Viral TikTok Sensation Working in his Parents' Store* [Video], YouTube, February 16, 2023, https://www.youtube.com/watch?v=m7phULYVknw.

3. R. Cross, R. Rebele, and A. Grant, "Collaborative Overload," *Harvard Business Review,* January-February 2016, https://hbr .org/2016/01/collaborative-overload.

4. F. Delice, M. Rousseau, and J. Feitosa, "Advancing Teams Research: What, When, and How to Measure Team Dynamics over Time," *Frontiers in Psychology* 10 (2019), doi:10.3389/fpsyg.2019.01324.

5. F. Warneken, F. Chen, and M. Tomasello, "Cooperative Activities in Young Children and Chimpanzees," *Child Development* 77, no. 3 (2006): 640–663, doi:10.1111/j.1467-8624.2006.00895.x.

6. M. Tomasello, *Becoming Human: A Theory of Ontogeny* [Video],

Association for Psychological Science Annual Convention, May 28, 2019, https://www.youtube.com/watch?v=BNbeleWvXyQ.

7. Warneken, Chen, and Tomasello, "Cooperative Activities in Young Children."

8. "Communication Barriers in the Modern Workplace," *Economist*, 2018, https://www.lucidchart.com/pages/research/economist-report.

9. Warneken, Chen, and Tomasello, "Cooperative Activities in Young Children."

10. U. Kachel, M. Svetlova, and M. Tomasello, "Three-Year-Olds' Reactions to a Partner's Failure to Perform Her Role in a Joint Commitment," *Child Development* 89, no. 5 (2018): 1691–1703, doi:10.1111/cdev.12816.

11. "The Psychology of Computer Rage," *Psychology in Action*, 2015, https://www.psychologyinaction.org/2015-12-27-the-psychology-of-computer-rage/.

12. "Survey: Over a Third of Americans Confess to Verbal or Physical Abuse of Their Computers," *Business Wire*, 2013, https://www.businesswire.com/news/home/20130730005132/en/Survey-Americans-Confess-Verbal-Physical-Abuse-Computers.

13. Kachel, Svetlova, and Tomasello, "Three-Year-Olds' Reactions."

14. M. Timms, "Blame Culture Is Toxic. Here's How to Stop It," *Harvard Business Review*, February 9, 2022, https://hbr.org/2022/02/blame-culture-is-toxic-heres-how-to-stop-it.

15. B. M. Lloyd-Walker, A. J. Mills, and D. H. T. Walker, "Enabling Construction Innovation: The Role of a No-Blame Culture as a Collaboration Behavioural Driver in Project Alliances," *Construction Management and Economics* 32, no. 3 (2014): 229–245, doi:10.1080/01446193.2014.892629.

16. M. Kew, "Mercedes FE Employing Same 'No Blame' Culture as F1 Team," Motorsport.com, February 5, 2021, https://www.motorsport.com/formula-e/news/mercedes-no-blame-culture-f1/5282171/.

17. B. Dattner, "An Overview of the Blame Game," *Psychology Today,* February 9, 2011, https://www.psychologytoday.com/ca/blog/credit -and-blame-at-work/201102/an-overview-of-the-blame-game.

18. U. Kachel, M. Svetlova, and M. Tomasello, "Three- and 5-Year-Old Children's Understanding of How to Dissolve a Joint Commitment," *Journal of Experimental Child Psychology* 184 (2019): 34–47, doi:10.1016/j.jecp.2019.03.008.

19. R. Knight, "How to Quit Your Job Without Burning Bridges," *Harvard Business Review,* December 4, 2014, https://hbr.org/2014/12/ how-to-quit-your-job-without-burning-bridges.

20. B. Nogrady, "Exiting Gracefully: How to Leave a Job Behind," *Nature* 601 (2022): 151–153.

21. P. Grocke, F. Rossano, and M. Tomasello, "Young Children Are More Willing to Accept Group Decisions in Which They Have Had a Voice," *Journal of Experimental Child Psychology* 166 (2018): 67–78, doi:10.1016/j.jecp.2017.08.003.

22. Q. Ong, Y. E. Riyanto, and S. M. Sheffrin, "How Does Voice Matter? Evidence from the Ultimatum Game," *Experimental Economics* 15, no. 4 (2012): 604–621, doi:10.1007/s10683-012-9316-x.

23. A. Adhvaryu, T. Molina, and A. Nyshadham, "Expectations, Wage Hikes, and Worker Voice," *Economic Journal* 132, no. 645 (2022): 1978–1993, doi.org/10.1093/ej/ueac001.

24. A. W. Woolley, C. F. Chabris, A. Pentland, et al., "Evidence for a Collective Intelligence Factor in the Performance of Human Groups," *Science* 330, no. 6004 (2010): 686–688, doi:10.1126/science.1193147.

25. A. C. Edmondson and M. Mortensen, "What Psychological Safety Looks Like in a Hybrid Workplace," *Harvard Business Review,* April 19, 2021, https://hbr.org/2021/04/what-psychological -safety-looks-like-in-a-hybrid-workplace.

26. J. Rozovsky, "The Five Keys to a Successful Google Team," *re:Work,* November 17, 2015, https://rework.withgoogle.com/blog/five-keys -to-a-successful-google-team/.

27. C. Duhigg, "What Google Learned from Its Quest to Build the Perfect Team," *New York Times Magazine,* February 25, 2016, https://www.nytimes.com/2016/02/28/magazine/what-google-learned-from-its-quest-to-build-the-perfect-team.html.

28. J. M. Engelmann and M. Tomasello, "Children's Sense of Fairness as Equal Respect," *Trends in Cognitive Sciences* 23, no. 6 (2019): 454–463, doi:10.1016/j.tics.2019.03.001.

29. V. Masterson, "6 Surprising Facts About the Global Gender Pay Gap," *World Economic Forum,* March 8, 2022, https://www.weforum.org/agenda/2022/03/6-surprising-facts-gender-pay-gap/.

30. P. Kanngiesser and F. Warneken, "Young Children Consider Merit When Sharing Resources with Others," *PLOS One* 7, no. 8 (2012): e43979, doi:10.1371/journal.pone.0043979.

31. K. Hamann, J. Bender, and M. Tomasello, "Meritocratic Sharing Is Based on Collaboration in 3-Year-Olds, *Developmental Psychology* 50, no. 1 (2014): 121–128, doi:10.1037/a0032965.

32. N. Baumard, O. Mascaro, and C. Chevallier, "Preschoolers Are Able to Take Merit into Account when Distributing Goods," *Developmental Psychology* 48, no. 2 (2012): 492–498, doi:10.1037/a0026598.

33. F. Yang, Y.J. Choi, A. Misch, et al., "In Defense of the Commons: Young Children Negatively Evaluate and Sanction Free Riders," *Psychological Science* 29, no. 10 (2018): 1598–1611, doi:10.1177/0956797618779061.

34. A. P. Melis, K. Altrichter, and M. Tomasello, "Allocation of Resources to Collaborators and Free-Riders in 3-Year-Olds," *Journal of Experimental Child Psychology* 114, no. 2 (2013): 364–370, doi:10.1016/j.jecp.2012.08.006.

35. F. Warneken, K. Lohse, A. P. Melis, et al., "Young Children Share the Spoils After Collaboration," *Psychological Science* 22, no. 2 (2011): 267–273, doi: 10.1177/0956797610395392.

36. Engelmann and Tomasello, "Children's Sense of Fairness as Equal Respect."

37. Engelmann and Tomasello.

38. H. Rakoczy, M. Kaufmann, and K. Lohse, "Young Children Understand the Normative Force of Standards of Equal Resource Distribution," *Journal of Experimental Child Psychology* 150 (2016): 396–403, doi:10.1016/j.jecp.2016.05.015.

39. "Sociometric Badges," *MIT Media Laboratory*, 2011, https://hd .media.mit.edu/badges/.

40. A. S. Pentland, "The New Science of Building Great Teams," *Harvard Business Review*, April 2012, https://hbr.org/2012/04 /the-new-science-of-building-great-teams.

41. A. Pentland, "Defend Your Research: We Can Measure the Power of Charisma," *Harvard Business Review*, January 2010, https://hbr.org/2010/01/defend-your-research-we-can-measure -the-power-of-charisma.

Chapter 7

1. M. Oxenden, "'Now, Let's Be a Starfish!': Learning with Ms. Rachel, Song by Song," *New York Times*, July 2, 2023, https://www .nytimes.com/2023/06/30/style/ms-rachel-youtube-videos.html.

2. *Ms. Rachel–Toddler Learning Videos*, "Blippi & Ms. Rachel Learn Vehicles—Wheels on the Bus—Videos for Kids—Tractor, Car, Truck +More [Video]," YouTube, July 29, 2023, https://www.youtube.com /watch?v=gFuEoxh5hd4.

3. L. T. Eby, T. D. Allen, S. C. Evans, et al., "Does Mentoring Matter? A Multidisciplinary Meta-Analysis Comparing Mentored and Non-Mentored Individuals," *Journal of Vocational Behavior* 72, no. 2 (2008): 254–267, doi:10.1016/j.jvb.2007.04.005.

4. C. Morselli, P. Tremblay, and B. McCarthy, "Mentors and Criminal Achievement," *Criminology* 44, no. 1 (2006): 17–43, doi:10.1111/j .1745-9125.2006.00041.x.

5. L. T. Eby and M. M. Robertson, "The Psychology of Workplace Mentoring Relationships," *Annual Review of Organizational Psychology*

and Organizational Behavior 7 (2020): 75–100, doi:10.1146/annurev-orgpsych-012119.

6. K. Klein and P. Cappelli, "Workplace Loyalties Change, but the Value of Mentoring Doesn't," *Knowledge at Wharton,* May 16, 2007, https://knowledge.wharton.upenn.edu/podcast/knowledge-at-wharton-podcastworkplace-loyalties-change-but-the-value-of-mentoring-doesnt/.

7. A. J. Duvall, "Calculating a Mentor's Effect on Salary and Retention," *Financial Management,* December 1, 2016, https://www.fm-magazine.com/issues/2016/dec/mentors-effect-on-salary-and-retention.html.

8. L. Tan and J. B. Main, "Faculty Mentorship and Research Productivity, Salary, and Job Satisfaction," in American Society for Engineering Education Annual Conference Proceedings, 2021.

9. T. D. Allen, E. Lentz, and R. Day, "Career Success Outcomes Associated with Mentoring Others: A Comparison of Mentors and Non-mentors," *Journal of Career Development* 32, no. 3 (2006): 272–285, doi:10.1177/0894845305282942.

10. Olivet Nazarene University, "New Research Examines How Mentors Factor in the Workplace," 2019, https://online.olivet.edu/research-statistics-on-professional-mentors.

11. J. C. Leary, E. G. Schainker, and J. A. K. Leyenaar, "The Unwritten Rules of Mentorship: Facilitators of and Barriers to Effective Mentorship in Pediatric Hospital Medicine," *Hospital Pediatrics* 6, no. 4 (2016): 219–225, doi:10.1542/hpeds.2015-0108.

12. S. E. Straus, M. O. Johnson, C. Marquez, et al., "Characteristics of Successful and Failed Mentoring Relationships: A Qualitative Study across Two Academic Health Centers," *Academic Medicine* 88, no. 1 (2013): 82–89, doi:10.1097/ACM.0b013e31827647a0.

13. J. A. Leonard, S. R. Cordrey, H. Z. Liu, et al., "Young Children Calibrate Effort Based on the Trajectory of Their Performance,"

Developmental Psychology 59, no. 3 (2023): 609–619, doi:10.1037/dev0001467.

14. A. Ten, P. Kaushik, P. Y. Oudeyer, et al., "Humans Monitor Learning Progress in Curiosity-Driven Exploration," *Nature Communications* 12, no. 1 (2021), doi:10.1038/s41467-021-26196-w.

15. X. Zhang, S. D. McDougle, and J. A. Leonard, "Thinking About Doing: Representations of Skill Learning," in *Proceedings of the 44th Annual Conference of the Cognitive Science Society* 44, no. 44 (2022).

16. J. A. Leonard, Y. Lee, and L. E. Schulz, "Infants Make More Attempts to Achieve a Goal When They See Adults Persist," *Science* 357 (2017): 1290–1294, https://osf.io/j4935/.

17. J. A. Leonard, A. Garcia, and L. E. Schulz, "How Adults' Actions, Outcomes, and Testimony Affect Preschoolers' Persistence," *Child Development* 91, no. 4 (2020): 1254–1271, doi:10.1111/cdev.13305.

18. D. Hu, J. N. Ahn, M. Vega, et al., "Not All Scientists Are Equal: Role Aspirants Influence Role Modeling Outcomes in STEM," *Basic and Applied Social Psychology* 42, no. 3 (2020): 192–208, doi:10.1080/01973533.2020.1734006.

19. C. Cotroneo, "Forget Geniuses. Hard Workers Make the Best Role Models," *Treehugger,* March 13, 2020, https://www.treehugger.com/genius-role-model-einstein-edison-4859419.

20. Leonard, Garcia, and Schulz, "How Adults' Actions, Outcomes, and Testimony."

21. Leonard, Garcia, and Schulz.

22. M. Mayfield and J. Mayfield, "The Effects of Leader Motivating Language Use on Employee Decision Making," *International Journal of Business Communication* 53, no. 4 (2016): 465–484, doi:10.1177/2329488415572787.

23. D. McGinn, "The Science of Pep Talks," *Harvard Business Review,* July 2017, https://hbr.org/2017/07/the-science-of-pep-talks26, 2023.

24. Mayfield and Mayfield, "The Effects of Leader Motivating Language Use."

25. T. Van Bommel, "The Power of Empathy in Times of Crisis and Beyond," *Catalyst,* 2021, https://www.catalyst.org/reports/empathy -work-strategy-crisis/.

26. A. L. Duckworth, C. Peterson, M. D. Matthews, et al.,"Grit: Perseverance and Passion for Long-Term Goals," *Journal of Personality and Social Psychology* 92, no. 6 (2007): 1087–1101, doi:10.1037/0022-3514.92.6.1087.

27. J. A. Leonard, D. M. Lydon-Staley, S. D. S. Sharp, et al., "Daily Fluctuations in Young Children's Persistence," *Child Development* 93, no. 2 (2022): e222–e236, doi:10.1111/cdev.13717.

28. B. J. Morris and S. R. Zentall, "High Fives Motivate: The Effects of Gestural and Ambiguous Verbal Praise on Motivation," *Frontiers in Psychology* 5 (2014), doi:10.3389/fpsyg.2014.00928.

29. J. A. Leonard, D. N. Martinez, S. C. Dashineau, et al., "Children Persist Less When Adults Take Over," *Child Development* 92, no. 4 (2021): 1325–1336, doi:10.1111/cdev.13492.

30. J. Verrey, "Here, Let Me Do It: Task Takeover Hurts Team Performance," Bachelor's thesis, Harvard College, 2019, http://nrs .harvard.edu/urn-3:HUL.InstRepos:41971553.

31. Y. Kim, *What Kids Can Teach Adults About Asking for Help* [Video], TED, October 28, 2020, https://www.youtube.com/watch ?v=EG6QA47rMNgc.

32. X. Zhao and N. Epley, "Surprisingly Happy to Have Helped: Underestimating Prosociality Creates a Misplaced Barrier to Asking for Help," *Psychological Science* 33, no. 10 (2022): 1708–1731, doi:10.1177/09567976221097615.

33. K. Lucca, R. Horton, and J. A. Sommerville, "Infants Rationally Decide When and How to Deploy Effort," *Nature Human Behaviour* 4, no. 4 (2020): 372–379, doi:10.1038/s41562-019-0814-0.

34. Make-A-Wish Foundation of America, "Our History," https://wish .org/about-us.

35. A. D. Patel, P. Glynn, A. M. Falke, et al., "Impact of a Make-A-Wish Experience on Healthcare Utilization," *Pediatric Research* 85, no. 5 (2019): 634–638, doi:10.1038/s41390-018-0207-5.

36. B. Chappell, "Holy Empathy! Batkid Lives Superhero Dream in San Francisco," *National Public Radio*, November 15, 2013, https://www.npr.org/sections/thetwo-way/2013/11/15/245480296/ holy-empathy-batkid-lives-superhero-dream-in-san-francisco.

37. D. Nachman, (Director), *Batkid Begins* [Film], 2015, Warner Bros.

38. A. Duckworth, *Grit: The Power of Passion and Perseverance* (New York, NY: Scribner, 2016).

39. R. E. White, E. O. Prager, C. Schaefer, et al., "The 'Batman Effect': Improving Perseverance in Young Children," *Child Development* 88, no. 5 (2017): 1563–1571, doi:10.1111/cdev.12695.

40. R. Karniol, L. Galili, D. Shtilerman, et al., "Why Superman Can Wait: Cognitive Self-Transformation in the Delay of Gratification Paradigm," *Journal of Clinical Child and Adolescent Psychology* 40, no. 2 (2011): 307–317, doi:10.1080/15374416.2011.546040.

41. D. M. Marx, S. J. Ko, and R. A. Friedman, "The 'Obama Effect': How a Salient Role Model Reduces Race-Based Performance Differences," *Journal of Experimental Social Psychology* 45, no. 4 (2009): 953–956, doi:10.1016/j.jesp.2009.03.012.

42. D. R. van Tongeren, R. Hibbard, M. Edwards, et al., "Heroic Helping: The Effects of Priming Superhero Images on Prosociality," *Frontiers in Psychology* 9 (2018), doi:10.3389/fpsyg.2018.02243.

43. Karniol et al., "Why Superman Can Wait."

Chapter 8

1. *The Ellen DeGeneres Show*, "Ellen Meets Adorable Viral Hugging Toddlers" [Video], September 18, 2019, YouTube, https://www.youtube.com/watch?v=6TyBCufF3RM.

2. Y. J. Yu, "This 4-Year-Old Narrating While Snowboarding Is Melting

Our Hearts," *Good Morning America,* February 11, 2022, https://
www.goodmorningamerica.com/family/story/year-narrating
-snowboarding-melting-hearts-82823802.

3. A. Winsler, R. M. Diaz, D. J. Atencio, et al.,"Verbal Self-Regulation
over Time in Preschool Children at Risk for Attention and Behavior
Problems," *Journal of Child Psychology and Psychiatry, and Allied Disciplines* 41, no. 7 (2000): 875–886.

4. R. M. Duncan and J. A. Cheyne, "Private Speech in Young Adults:
Task Difficulty, Self-Regulation, and Psychological Predication,"
Cognitive Development 16, no. 4 (2001): 889–906, https://doi
.org/10.1016/S0885-2014(01)00069-7.

5. A. Orvell, B. D. Vickers, B. Drake, et al., "Does Distanced Self-Talk
Facilitate Emotion Regulation Across a Range of Emotionally Intense
Experiences?," *Clinical Psychological Science* 9, no. 1 (2021): 68–78,
doi:10.1177/2167702620951539.

6. Y. Theodorakis, S. Chroni, K. Laparidis, et al., "Self-Talk in a Basket-
ball-Shooting Task," *Perceptual and Motor Skills* 92 (2001): 309–315.

7. N. A. Kompa and J. L. Mueller, "Inner Speech as a Cognitive Tool—
or What Is the Point of Talking to Oneself? *Philosophical Psychology*
(2022): 1–24, doi:10.1080/09515089.2022.2112164.

8. C. S. White and M. Daugherty, "Creativity and Private Speech in
Young Children," in *Private Speech, Executive Functioning, and the
Development of Verbal Self-Regulation,* eds. Adam Winsler, Charles
Fernyhough, and Ignacio Montero (Cambridge, UK: Cambridge Uni-
versity Press, 2009).

9. Kompa and Mueller, "Inner Speech as a Cognitive Tool."

10. Kompa and Mueller.

11. B. N. Jack, M. E. Le Pelley, N. Han, et al., "Inner Speech Is Ac-
companied by a Temporally Precise and Content-Specific Corol-
lary Discharge," *Neuroimage* 198 (2019): 170–180, doi:10.1016/j.
neuroimage.2019.04.038.

12. X. Tian, J. M. Zarate, and D. Poeppel, "Mental Imagery of Speech Implicates Two Mechanisms of Perceptual Reactivation," *Cortex* 77 (2016): 1–12, doi:10.1016/j.cortex.2016.01.002.

13. A. Fishbach, "Society for the Science of Motivation Presidential Address: Can We Harness Motivation Science to Motivate Ourselves?," *Motivation Science* 7, no. 4 (2021): 363–374, doi:10.1037/mot0000243.

14. A. Mulvihill, N. Matthews, P. E. Dux, et al., "Preschool Children's Private Speech Content and Performance on Executive Functioning and Problem-Solving Tasks," *Cognitive Development* 60, no. 2 (2021), doi:10.1016/j.cogdev.2021.101116.

15. J. Sawyer, "I Think I Can: Preschoolers' Private Speech and Motivation in Playful Versus Non-Playful Contexts," *Early Childhood Research Quarterly* 38 (2017): 84–96, doi:10.1016/j.ecresq.2016.09.004.

16. Duncan and Cheyne, "Private Speech in Young Adults."

17. D. Alarcón-Rubio, J. A. Sánchez-Medina, and A. Winsler, "Private Speech in Illiterate Adults: Cognitive Functions, Task Difficulty, and Literacy," *Journal of Adult Development* 20, no. 2 (2013): 100–111, doi:10.1007/s10804-013-9161-y.

18. G. Lupyan and D. Swingley, "Self-Directed Speech Affects Visual Search Performance," *Quarterly Journal of Experimental Psychology* 65, no. 6 (2012): 1068–1085, doi:10.1080/17470218.2011.647039.

19. M. Whedon, N. B. Perry, E. B. Curtis, et al., "Private Speech and the Development of Self-Regulation: The Importance of Temperamental Anger," *Early Childhood Research Quarterly* 56 (2021): 213–224, doi:10.1016/j.ecresq.2021.03.013.

20. E. Kross, *Chatter: The Voice in Our Head, Why It Matters, and How to Harness It* (New York, NY: Crown Publishing, 2021).

21. M. Horvat, D. Kukolja, and D. Ivanec, "Comparing Affective Responses to Standardized Pictures and Videos: A Study Report," in *Proceedings of the 38th International Convention on Information*

and *Communication Technology, Electronics and Microelectronics* (MIPRO), IEEE, 1394–1398.

22. J. S. Moser, A. Dougherty, W. I. Mattson, et al., "Third-Person Self-Talk Facilitates Emotion Regulation Without Engaging Cognitive Control: Converging Evidence from ERP and fMRI," *Scientific Reports* 7, no. 1 (2017), doi:10.1038/s41598-017-04047-3.

23. J. B. Leitner, O. Ayduk, R. Mendoza-Denton, et al., "Self-Distancing Improves Interpersonal Perceptions and Behavior by Decreasing Medial Prefrontal Cortex Activity During the Provision of Criticism," *Social Cognitive and Affective Neuroscience* 12, no. 4 (2017): 534–543, doi:10.1093/scan/nsw168.

24. E. Kross, E. Bruehlman-Senecal, J. Park, et al., "Self-Talk as a Regulatory Mechanism: How You Do It Matters," *Journal of Personality and Social Psychology* 106, no. 2 (2014): 304–324, doi:10.1037/a0035173.

25. C. R. Furman, E. Kross, and A. N. Gearhardt, "Distanced Self-Talk Enhances Goal Pursuit to Eat Healthier," *Clinical Psychological Science* 8, no. 2 (2020): 366–373, doi:10.1177/2167702619896366.

26. D. M. Cutton and D. Landin, "The Effects of Self-Talk and Augmented Feedback on Learning the Tennis Forehand," *Journal of Applied Sport Psychology* 19, no. 3 (2007): 288–303, doi:10.1080/10413200701328664.

27. C. Edwards, D. Tod, and M. McGuigan, "Self-Talk Influences Vertical Jump Performance and Kinematics in Male Rugby Union Players," *Journal of Sports Sciences* 26, no. 13 (2008): 1459–1465, doi:10.1080/02640410802287071.

28. A. Hatzigeorgiadis, N. Zourbanos, E. Galanis, et al., "Self-Talk and Sports Performance: A Meta-Analysis," *Perspectives on Psychological Science* 6, no. 4 (2011): 348–356, doi:10.1177/1745691611413136.

29. A. Papaioannou, F. Ballon, Y. Theodorakis, et al., "Combined Effect of Goal Setting and Self-Talk in Performance of a Soccer-Shooting Task," *Perceptual and Motor Skills* 98, no. 1 (2004): 89–99, doi:10.2466/pms.98.1.89-99.

30. J. Tutek, H. E. Gunn, and K. L. Lichstein, "Worry and Rumination Have Distinct Associations with Nighttime Versus Daytime Sleep Symptomology," *Behavioral Sleep Medicine* 19, no. 2 (2021): 192–207, doi:10.1080/15402002.2020.1725012.

31. Kross, *Chatter: The Voice in Our Head.*

32. M. McGonigle-Chalmers, H. Slater, and A. Smith, "Rethinking Private Speech in Preschoolers: The Effects of Social Presence," *Developmental Psychology* 50, no. 3 (2014): 829–836, doi:10.1037/a0033909.

33. L. Manfra and A. Winsler, "Preschool Children's Awareness of Private Speech," *International Journal of Behavioral Development* 30, no. 6 (2006): 537–549, doi:10.1177/0165025406072902.

34. A. Winsler and R. M. Diaz, "Private Speech in the Classroom: The Effects of Activity Type, Presence of Others, Classroom Context, and Mixed-Age Grouping," *International Journal of Behavioral Development* 18, no. 3 (1995): 463–487, doi:10.1177/016502549501800305.

35. S. Breyel and S. Pauen, "Private Speech During Problem-Solving: Tool Innovation Challenges Both Preschoolers' Cognitive and Emotion Regulation," *Journal of Cognition and Development* 24, no. 3 (2023): 354–374, doi:10.1080/15248372.2022.2144319.

36. White and Daugherty, "Creativity and Private Speech in Young Children."

37. B. Borzykowski, "Why Talking to Yourself Is the First Sign of . . . Success," *BBC Worklife,* April 27, 2017, https://www.bbc.com/worklife/article/20170428-why-talking-to-yourself-is-the-first-sign-of-success.

38. K. Wong, "The Benefits of Talking to Yourself," *New York Times,* June 8, 2017, https://www.nytimes.com/2017/06/08/smarter-living/benefits-of-talking-to-yourself-self-talk.html.

Chapter 9

1. T. Kushnir and M. A. Koenig, "What I Don't Know Won't Hurt You: The Relation between Professed Ignorance and Later Knowledge Claims,"

Developmental Psychology 53, no. 5 (2017): 826–835, doi:10.1037/dev0000294.

2. J. Sully, *Studies of Childhood* (New York, NY: D. Appleton and Company, 1896).

3. B. MacWhinney, "CHILDES: Child Language Data Exchange System," Carnegie Mellon University, (n.d.), retrieved August 5, 2023, https://www.lti.cs.cmu.edu/projects/spoken-interfaces-and-dialogue-processingchildes-child-language-data-exchange-system.

4. M. M. Chouinard, P. L. Harris, and M. P. Maratsos, "Children's Questions: A Mechanism for Cognitive Development," *Monographs of the Society for Research in Child Development* 72, no. 1 (2007): 1–129, doi:10.1111/j.1540-5834.2007.00412.x.

5. R. L. Koegel, J. L. Bradshaw, K. Ashbaugh, et al., "Improving Question-Asking Initiations in Young Children with Autism Using Pivotal Response Treatment," *Journal of Autism and Developmental Disorders* 44, no. 4 (2014): 816–827, doi:10.1007/s10803-013-1932-6.

6. D. M. Bravata, S. A. Watts, A. L. Keefer, et al., "Prevalence, Predictors, and Treatment of Impostor Syndrome: A Systematic Review." *Journal of Autism and Developmental Disorders* 35, no. 4 (2020): 1252–1275, doi:10.1007/s11606-019-05364-1.

7. I. Cojuharenco and N. Karelaia, "When Leaders Ask Questions: Can Humility Premiums Buffer the Effects of Competence Penalties?," *Organizational Behavior and Human Decision Processes* 156 (2020): 113–134, doi:10.1016/j.obhdp.2019.12.001.

8. Cojuharenco and Karelaia, "When Leaders Ask Questions."

9. M. T. McDermott, "Mistaken for Pregnant? Readers Respond," *New York Times,* September 21, 2016, https://www.nytimes.com/2016/09/20/well/family/mistaken-for-pregnant-readers-respond.html.

10. E. Hart, E. M. VanEpps, and M. E. Schweitzer, "The (Better than Expected) Consequences of Asking Sensitive Questions," *Organizational Behavior and Human Decision Processes* 162 (2021): 136–154, doi:10.1016/j.obhdp.2020.10.014.

11. J. M. Bugg and M. A. McDaniel, "Selective Benefits of Question Self-Generation and Answering for Remembering Expository Text," *Journal of Educational Psychology* 104, no. 4 (2012): 922–931, doi:10.1037/a0028661.

12. S. C. Pan, I. Zung, M. N. Imundo, et al., "User-Generated Digital Flashcards Yield Better Learning Than Premade Flashcards," *Journal of Applied Research in Memory and Cognition,* published online 2022, doi:10.1037/mac0000083.

13. M. Yeomans, A. Kantor, and D. Tingley, "The Politeness Package: Detecting Politeness in Natural Language," *The R Journal* 10, no. 2 (2018): 489–502.

14. N. Vitukevich, "Water Cooler Talk: Weather, 'Game of Thrones,' Football Dominate Office Chatter," *Office Pulse,* September 15, 2016, https://officepulse.captivate.com/watercooler-talk-what -professionals-are-discussing-at-the-office.

15. J. R. Methot, E. H. Rosado-Solomon, P. E. Downes, et al.,"Office Chitchat as a Social Ritual: The Uplifting Yet Distracting Effects of Daily Small Talk at Work," *Academy of Management Journal* 64, no. 5 (2021): 1445–1471, doi:10.5465/AMJ.2018.1474.

16. K. Huang, M. Yeomans, A. W. Brooks, et al., "It Doesn't Hurt to Ask: Question-Asking Increases Liking," *Journal of Personality and Social Psychology* 113, no. 3 (2017): 430–452, doi:10.1037/pspi0000097.

17. Huang et al., "It Doesn't Hurt to Ask."

18. Raising Children Network (Australia), "Language Development: Children 0–8 Years," February 17, 2021, https://raising -children.net.au/babies/development/language-development/ language-development-0-8.

19. J. Hayes, I. Stewart, and J. McElwee, "Children's Answering of Yes-No Questions: A Review of Research Including Particular Consideration of the Relational Evaluation Procedure," *The Behavioral Development*

Bulletin 22, no. 1 (2017): 173–182, doi:10.1037/bdb0000027.

20. M. Okanda and S. Itakura, "Do Young and Old Preschoolers Exhibit Response Bias Due to Different Mechanisms? Investigating Children's Response Time," *Journal of Experimental Child Psychology* 110, no. 3 (2011): 453–460, doi:10.1016/j.jecp.2011.04.012.

21. D. Laible, T. Panfile, and D. Makariev, "The Quality and Frequency of Mother-Toddler Conflict: Links with Attachment and Temperament," *Child Development* 79, no. 2 (2008): 426–443.

22. N. Martyn, "Infancy and Early Childhood Matter So Much Because of Attachment," *The Conversation*, May 29, 2019, https://theconversation.com/infancy-and-early-childhood-matter-so-much-because-of-attachment-117733.

23. R. A. Spitz, *No and Yes. On the Genesis of Human Communication* (Madison, CT: International Universities Press, 1957).

24. N. Alia-Klein, R. Z. Goldstein, D. Tomasi, et al., "What Is in a Word? No Versus Yes Differentially Engage the Lateral Orbitofrontal Cortex," *Emotion* 7, no. 3 (2007): 649–659.

25. X. Zhao and N. Epley, "Surprisingly Happy to Have Helped: Underestimating Prosociality Creates a Misplaced Barrier to Asking for Help," *Psychological Science* 33, no. 10 (2022): 1708–1731, doi:10.1177/09567976221097615.

26. C. Carter, "Five Research-Based Ways to Say No," *Greater Good Magazine*, November 25, 2015, https://greatergood.berkeley.edu/article/item/5_research_based_ways_to_say_no.

27. V. K. Bohns, M. M. Roghanizad, and A. Z. Xu, "Underestimating Our Influence over Others' Unethical Behavior and Decisions," *Personality and Social Psychology Bulletin* 40, no. 3 (2014): 348–362, doi:10.1177/0146167213511825.

28. D. Kahneman and A. Tversky, "Intuitive Prediction: Biases and Corrective Procedures," *TIMS Studies in Management Science* 12 (1977): 313–327.

29. R. Buehler, D. Griffin, and M. Ross, "Exploring the 'Planning Fallacy': Why People Underestimate Their Task Completion Times," *Journal of Personality and Social Psychology* 67, no. 3 (1994): 366–381, https://doi.org/10.1037/0022-3514.67.3.366.

30. B. M. Katt, A. Tawfik, V. Lau, et al., "The Planning Fallacy in the Orthopedic Operating Room," *Cureus* 13, no. 1 (2021): e12433, doi:10.7759/cureus.12433.

31. S. A. Spiller and J. G. Lynch, "Consumers Commit the Planning Fallacy for Time but Not for Money," *ACR North American Advances* 36 (2009): 1040–1041.

32. Sydney Opera House, "Interesting Facts about the Sydney Opera House," https://www.sydneyoperahouse.com/building/interesting -facts-about-sydney-opera-house.

33. K. Pyke, "Faculty Gender Inequity and the 'Just Say No to Service' Fairytale," in *Disrupting the Culture of Silence: Confronting Gender Inequality and Making Change in Higher Education* (Stylus Publishing, 2014).

34. J. Moss, "Burnout Is About Your Workplace, Not Your People," *Harvard Business Review,* December 11, 2019, https://hbr.org/2019/12 /burnout-is-about-your-workplace-not-your-people.

35. K. Dickinson, "The Planning Fallacy: Why Your Plans Go Awry and 5 Steps to Get Back on Track," *Big Think,* January 18, 2023, https://bigthink.com/the-learning-curve/the-planning-fallacy-and -how-to-get-back-on-track/.

36. D. K. Forsyth and C. D. B. Burt, "Allocating Time to Future Tasks: The Effect of Task Segmentation on Planning Fallacy Bias," *Memory & Cognition* 36, no. 4 (2008): 791–798, doi:10.3758/MC.36.4.791.

37. J. Kruger and M. Evans, "If You Don't Want to Be Late, Enumerate: Unpacking Reduces the Planning Fallacy," *Journal of Experimental Social Psychology* 40, no. 5 (2004): 586–598, doi:10.1016/j.jesp .2003.11.001.

38. Krueger and Evans, "If You Don't Want to Be Late, Enumerate."

39. S. Koole and M. van't Spijker, "Overcoming the Planning Fallacy Through Willpower: Effects of Implementation Intentions on Actual and Predicted Task-Completion Times," *European Journal of Social Psychology* 30, no. 6 (2000): 873–888, doi:10.1002/1099 -0992(200011/12)30:6<873::AID-EJSP22>3.0.CO;2-U.

40. Y. Huang, Z. Yang, and V. G. Morwitz, "How Using a Paper Versus Mobile Calendar Influences Everyday Planning and Plan Fulfillment, *Journal of Consumer Psychology* 33, no. 1 (2023): 115–122, doi:10.1002/jcpy.1297.

41. Z. J. Ayres, *Managing Your Mental Health during Your PhD* (New York, NY: Springer International Publishing, 2022), doi:10.1007/978-3-031-14194-2.

42. L. M. Giurge and V. K. Bohns, "You Don't Need to Answer Right Away! Receivers Overestimate How Quickly Senders Expect Responses to Non-Urgent Work E-mails," *Organizational Behavior and Human Decision Processes* 167 (2021): 114–128, doi:10.1016/j. obhdp.2021.08.002.

43. V. M. Patrick and H. Hagtvedt, "'I Don't' Versus 'I Can't': When Empowered Refusal Motivates Goal-Directed Behavior," *Journal of Consumer Research* 39, no. 2 (2012): 371–381, doi:10.1086/663212.

44. A. Connor, "Why You Need to Say 'I Don't,' Versus 'I Can't,'" Medium, November 14, 2018, https://medium.com/writing-cooperative /why-you-need-to-say-i-dont-versus-i-can-t-4112028ea6f2.

Chapter 10

1. E. B. Hansen Sandseter, "Categorising Risky Play—How Can We Identify Risk-Taking in Children's Play?," *European Early Childhood Education Research Journal* 15, no. 2 (2007): 237–252, doi:10.1080/13502930701321733.

2. E. B. H. Sandseter, "Children's Expressions of Exhilaration and Fear in Risky Play," *Contemporary Issues in Early Childhood* 10, no. 2 (2009): 92–106, doi:10.2304/ciec.2009.10.2.92.

3. Ø. Kvalnes, E. B. Hansen Sandseter, "Experiences, Mastery, and Development Through Risk," in *Risky Play* (New York, NY: Springer International Publishing, 2023), doi:10.1007/978-3-031-25552-6.

4. S. Wyver, P. Tranter, G. Naughton, et al., "Ten Ways to Restrict Children's Freedom to Play: The Problem of Surplus Safety," *Contemporary Issues in Early Childhood* 11, no. 3 (2010): 263–277, doi:10.2304/ciec.2010.11.3.263.

5. Wyver et al., "Ten Ways to Restrict."

6. M. Brussoni, R. Gibbons, C. Gray, et al., "What Is the Relationship between Risky Outdoor Play and Health in Children? A Systematic Review," *International Journal of Environmental Research and Public Health* 12, no. 6 (2015): 6423–6454, doi:10.3390/ijerph120606423.

7. A. Roig, H. Meunier, E. Poulingue, et al., "Is Economic Risk Proneness in Young Children (Homo sapiens) Driven by Exploratory Behavior? A Comparison with Capuchin Monkeys (Sapajus apella)," *Journal of Comparative Psychology* 136, no. 2 (2022): 140–150, doi:10.1037/com0000314.supp.

8. J. Rivière, M. Stomp, E. Augustin, et al., "Decision-Making Under Risk of Gain in Young Children and Mangabey Monkeys," *Developmental Psychobiology* 60, no. 2 (2018): 176–186, doi:10.1002/dev.21592.

9. Roig et al., "Is Economic Risk Proneness in Young Children."

10. Roig et al.

11. A. G. Rosati, M. E. Thompson, R. Atencia, et al., "Distinct Developmental Trajectories for Risky and Impulsive Decision-Making in Chimpanzees," *Journal of Experimental Psychology: General* 152, no. 6 (2023): 1551–1564, doi:10.1037/xge0001347.

12. W. T. Harbaugh, K. Krause, and L. Vesterlund, "Risk Attitudes of Children and Adults: Choices over Small and Large Probability

Gains and Losses," *Experimental Economics* 5 (2002): 53–84, https://doi.org/10.1023/A:1016316725855.

13. R. K. Delaney, J. N. Strough, N. J. Shook, et al., "Don't Risk It. Older Adults Perceive Fewer Future Opportunities and Avoid Social Risk Taking," *International Journal of Aging & Human Development* 92, no. 2 (2021): 139–157, doi:10.1177/0091415019900564.

14. Delaney et al., "Don't Risk It."

15. M. A. Grubb, A. Tymula, S. Gilaie-Dotan, Pet al., "Neuroanatomy Accounts for Age-Related Changes in Risk Preferences," *Nature Communications* 7 (2016), doi:10.1038/ncomms13822.

16. P. Ayton, G. Bernile, A. Bucciol, et al., "The Impact of Life Experiences on Risk Taking," *Journal of Economic Psychology* 79 (2020), doi:10.1016/j.joep.2020.102274.

17. R. Faff, T. Hallahan, and M. McKenzie, "Women and Risk Tolerance in an Aging World," *International Journal of Accounting & Information Management* 19, no. 2 (2011): 100–117, doi:10.1108/18347641111136427.

18. C. Cueva, R. E. Roberts, T. Spencer, et al., "Cortisol and Testosterone Increase Financial Risk Taking and May Destabilize Markets," *Scientific Reports* 5 (2015), doi:10.1038/srep11206.

19. G. Aydogan, R. Daviet, R. Karlsson Linnér, et al., "Genetic Underpinnings of Risky Behaviour Relate to Altered Neuroanatomy," *Nature Human Behavior* 5. no. 6 (2021): 787–794, doi:10.1038/s41562-020-01027-y.

20. S. Suzuki, E. L. S. Jensen, P. Bossaerts, et al., "Behavioral Contagion During Learning About Another Agent's Risk-Preferences Acts on the Neural Representation of Decision-Risk," *Proceedings of the National Academy of Sciences of the United States of America* 113, no. 14 (2016): 3755–3760, doi:10.1073/pnas.1600092113.

21. S. Pillay, "3 Reasons You Underestimate Risk," *Harvard Business Review,* July 17, 2014, https://hbr.org/2014/07/3-reasons-you-underestimate-risk.

22. S. R. Fisk and J. Overton, "Bold or Reckless? The Impact of Workplace Risk-Taking on Attributions and Expected Outcomes," *PLOS One* 15, no. 3 (2020), doi:10.1371/journal.pone.0228672.

23. M. J. T. de Ruijter, A. D. Dahlén, G. Rukh, et al., "Job Satisfaction Has Differential Associations with Delay Discounting and Risk-Taking," *Scientific Reports* 13, no. 1 (2023), doi:10.1038/s41598-023-27601-8.

24. N. K. Mai, T. T. Do, N. A. Phan, "The Impact of Leadership Traits and Organizational Learning on Business Innovation," *Journal of Innovation and Knowledge* 7, no. 3 (2022), doi:10.1016/j.jik.2022.100204.

25. S. R. Yussen and V. M. Levy, "Developmental Changes in Predicting One's Own Span of Short-Term Memory," *Journal of Experimental Child Psychology* 19, no. 3 (1975): 502–508, doi:10.1016/0022-0965(75)90079-X.

26. D. M. Piehlmaier, "Overconfidence Among Young Decision-Makers: Assessing the Effectiveness of a Video Intervention and the Role of Gender, Age, Feedback, and Repetition," *Scientific Reports* 10, no. 1 (2020), doi:10.1038/s41598-020-61078-z.

27. A. R. Lipko, J. Dunlosky, W. E. Merriman, "Persistent Overconfidence Despite Practice: The Role of Task Experience in Preschoolers' Recall Predictions," *Journal of Experimental Child Psychology* 103, no. 2 (2009): 152–166, doi:10.1016/j.jecp.2008.10.002.

28. H. E. Shin, D. F. Bjorklund, and E. F. Beck, "The Adaptive Nature of Children's Overestimation in a Strategic Memory Task," *Cognitive Development* 22, no. 2 (2007): 197–212, doi:10.1016/j.cogdev.2006.10.001.

29. T. Reyes, R. S. Vassolo, E. E. Kausel, et al., "Does Overconfidence Pay Off When Things Go Well? CEO Overconfidence, Firm

Performance, and the Business Cycle," *Strategic Organization* 20, no. 3 (2022): 510–540, doi:10.1177/1476127020930659.

30. A. Galasso and T. S. Simcoe, "CEO Overconfidence and Innovation," *Management Science* 57, no. 8 (2011): 1469–1484, doi:10.1287/mnsc.1110.1374.

31. S. C. Murphy, W. von Hippel, S. L. Dubbs, et al., "The Role of Overconfidence in Romantic Desirability and Competition," *Personality and Social Psychology Bulletin* 41, no. 8 (2015): 1036–1052, doi:10.1177/0146167215588754.

32. B. P. Buunk, P. Dijkstra, D. Fetchenhauer, et al., "Age and Gender Differences in Mate Selection Criteria for Various Involvement Levels," *Personal Relationships* 9, no. 3 (2002): 271–278, doi:10.1111/1475-6811.00018.

33. Murphy et al., "The Role of Overconfidence in Romantic Desirability."

34. J. Kruger and D. Dunning, "Unskilled and Unaware of It: How Difficulties in Recognizing One's Own Incompetence Lead to Inflated Self-Assessments," *Journal of Personality and Social Psychology* 77, no. 6 (1999): 1121–1134, doi:10.1037//0022-3514.77.6.1121.

35. M. Korbmacher, C. Kwan, and G. Feldman, "Both Better and Worse Than Others Depending on Difficulty: Replication and Extensions of Kruger's (1999) Above and Below Average Effects," *Judgment and Decision Making* 17, no. 2 (2022): 449–486, doi:10.1017/s1930297500009189.

36. J. Kruger, "Lake Wobegon Be Gone! The 'Below-Average Effect' and the Egocentric Nature of Comparative Ability Judgments," *Journal of Personality and Social Psychology* 77, no. 2 (1999): 221–232.

37. D. A. Moore and P. J. Healy, "The Trouble with Overconfidence," *Psychological Review* 115, no. 2 (2008): 502–517, doi:10.1037/0033-295X.115.2.502.

38. D. A. Moore, "Not So Above Average After All: When People Believe They Are Worse Than Average and Its Implications for Theories of

Bias in Social Comparison," *Organizational Behavior and Human Decision Processes* 102, no. 1 (2007): 42–58, doi:10.1016/j.obhdp.2006.09.005.

39. B. Finn and J. Metcalfe, "The Role of Memory for Past Test in the Underconfidence with Practice Effect," *Journal of Experimental Psychology: Learning, Memory and Cognition* 33, no. 1 (2007): 238–244, doi:10.1037/0278-7393.33.1.238.

40. A. Koriat, L. Sheffer, and H. Ma'ayan, "Comparing Objective and Subjective Learning Curves: Judgments of Learning Exhibit Increased Underconfidence with Practice," *Journal of Experimental Psychology: General* 131, no. 2 (2002): 147–162, doi:10.1037/0096-3445.131.2.147.

41. B. Finn and J. Metcalfe, "Overconfidence in Children's Multi-Trial Judgments of Learning," *Learning and Instruction* 32 (2014): 1–9, doi:10.1016/j.learninstruc.2014.01.001.

42. D. R. Carney, A. J. C. Cuddy, and A. J. Yap, "Power Posing: Brief Nonverbal Displays Affect Neuroendocrine Levels and Risk Tolerance," *Psychological Science* 21, no. 10 (2010): 1363–1368, doi:10.1177/0956797610383437.

43. A. Cuddy, *Your Body Language May Shape Who You Are* [Video], TED, June 2012, https://www.ted.com/talks/amy_cuddy_your_body_language_may_shape_who_you_are/comments.

44. E. Elkjær, M. B. Mikkelsen, J. Michalak, et al., "Expansive and Contractive Postures and Movement: A Systematic Review and Meta-Analysis of the Effect of Motor Displays on Affective and Behavioral Responses," *Perspectives on Psychological Science* 17, no. 1 (2022): 276–304, doi:10.1177/1745691620919358.

45. *Good Morning America*, "Toddler Adorably Mimics Dad's Crossed Arm Pose [Video]," YouTube, November 30, 2022, https://www.you-tube.com/watch?v=5JwIuZS_8js.

46. T. Bulmash, "To Fix Your Posture, Sit Like a Kid," *Medium,* January 13, 2021, https://elemental.medium.com/the-key-to-balance-may -come-from-your-past-490579fc23f5.

47. Mayo Clinic Health System, "Do You Have Good Posture?" September 22, 2019, https://www.mayoclinichealthsystem.org/ hometown-health/speaking-of-health/do-you-have-good-posture.

48. Mayo Clinic Health System, "Office Ergonomics: Your How-to Guide," May 25, 2023, https://www.mayoclinic.org/healthy-lifestyle/ adult-health/in-depth/office-ergonomics/art-20046169.

49. J. H. Fowler and N. A. Christakis, "Dynamic Spread of Happiness in a Large Social Network: Longitudinal Analysis over 20 Years in the Framingham Heart Study," *The BMJ* (Online) 338, no. 7685 (2009): 23–26, doi:10.1136/bmj.a2338.

50. M. J. Howes, J. E. Hokanson, and D. A. Loewenstein, "Induction of Depressive Affect After Prolonged Exposure to a Mildly Depressed Individual," *Journal of Personality and Social Psychology* 49, no. 4 (1985): 1110–1113, doi:10.1037/0022-3514.49.4.1110.

51. J. T. Cheng, C. Anderson, E. R. Tenney, et al., "The Social Transmission of Overconfidence," *Journal of Experimental Psychology: General* 150, no. 1 (2021): 157–186, doi:10.1037/xge0000787.

52. J. T. Cheng, E. R. Tenney, D. A. Moore, et al., "Overconfidence Is Contagious," *Harvard Business Review,* November 17, 2020, https:/ /hbr.org/2020/11/overconfidence-is-contagious.

53. K. Wong, "Dealing with Impostor Syndrome When You're Treated as an Imposter," *New York Times,* June 12, 2018, https://www.nytimes .com/2018/06/12/smarter-living/dealing-with-impostor-syndrome -when-youre-treated-as-an-impostor.html.

54. N. Howlett, K. Pine, I. Orakçıoğlu, et al., "The Influence of Clothing on First Impressions," *Journal of Fashion Marketing and Management: An International Journal* 17, no. 1 (2013): 38–48, doi .org/10.1108/13612021311305128.

55. H. Adam and A. D. Galinsky, "Enclothed Cognition," *Journal of Experimental Social Psychology* 48, no. 4 (2012): 918–925, doi .org/10.1016/j.jesp.2012.02.008.

56. M. L. Slepian, S. N. Ferber, J. M. Gold, et al., "The Cognitive Consequences of Formal Clothing," *Social Psychological and Personality Science* 6, no. 6 (2015): 661–668, doi.org/10.1177/1948550615579462.

57. M. W. Kraus and W. B. Mendes, "Sartorial Symbols of Social Class Elicit Class-Consistent Behavioral and Physiological Responses: A Dyadic Approach," *Journal of Experimental Psychology: General* 143, no. 6 (2014): 2330–2340, doi.org/10.1037/xge0000023.

Index

About the Author

Hasan Merali, MD, MPH, is an associate professor in the Department of Pediatrics, Division of Pediatric Emergency Medicine at McMaster's Children's Hospital in Hamilton, Ontario. He received his medical degree from Harvard Medical School and Master of Public Health degree from Johns Hopkins University. His research focuses on child injury prevention in low- and middle-income countries. He has published more than twenty-five peer-reviewed journal articles, and his writing has been featured in *Science,* the *Boston Globe,* NBC, CBC, and *Popular Science.* Dr. Merali lives in Oakville, Ontario, with his wife and their toddler daughter.

X: @Hasan_Merali
Website: HasanMerali.com